CAMBRIDGE STUDIES IN
AMERICAN LITERATURE AND CULTURE

Poet's prose

Cambridge Studies in American Literature and Culture

For a complete listing of books available in the series, see the pages following the Index.

Poet's prose

The crisis in American verse

SECOND EDITION

STEPHEN FREDMAN

Department of English
University of Notre Dame

CAMBRIDGE UNIVERSITY PRESS

Cambridge

New York   Port Chester   Melbourne   Sydney

Published by the Press Syndicate of the University of Cambridge
The Pitt Building, Trumpington Street, Cambridge CB2 1RP
40 West 20th Street, New York, NY 10011, USA
10 Stamford Road, Oakleigh, Melbourne 3166, Australia

First published 1983
Second edition 1990

Printed in Canada

Library of Congress Cataloging-in-Publication Data
Fredman, Stephen, 1948–
Poet's prose: the crisis in American verse / Stephen Fredman. –
2nd ed.
p.   cm. – (Cambridge studies in American literature and
culture)
Includes bibliographical references and index.
ISBN 0-521-39098-2. – ISBN 0-521-39994-7 (pbk.)
1. American poetry – 20th century – History and criticism. 2. Prose
poetry, American – History and criticism. 3. Williams, William
Carlos, 1883–1963. Kora in hell. 4. Creeley, Robert, 1926–
Presences. 5. Ashbery, John. Three poems. I. Title. II. Series.
PS323.5.F7   1990
811'.509 – dc20   90-36663
                                                   CIP

British Library Cataloguing in Publication Data
Fredman, Stephen, 1948–
Poet's prose: the crisis in American verse. – 2nd ed. –
(Cambridge studies in American literature and culture).
1. Prose poetry in English. American writers, 1900– –
Critical studies
I. Title
811.5209

ISBN 0-521-39098-2 hardback
ISBN 0-521-39994-7 paperback

The following publishers have generously given permission to use quotations from copyrighted works: From *Tight Corners & What's Around Them* (p. 23) by David Bromige, © 1974 by David Bromige, by permission of the publisher, Black Sparrow Press. "The Letter" (pp. 65–6) *For Love: Poems 1950–1960* by Robert Creeley, © 1962 by Robert Creeley, by permission of the publisher, Charles Scribner's Sons. "Sunshine Today" (pp. 148–9) *The Mutabilities* by Michael Davidson, © 1976 by Michael Davidson, by permission of the publisher, Sand Dollar Books. "A Defect" (p. 44) in *My Poetry* by David Bromige, © 1980 by David Bromige, by permission of the publisher, The Figures. "The Dead Seal near McClure's Beach" (pp. 54–5) in *The Morning Glory* by Robert Bly, © 1975 by Robert Bly, by permission of the publisher, Harper & Row. From "Song of the Year" (p. 43) by William Carlos Williams, © 1983 by William Eric Williams and Paul H. Williams; "The Late Singer" (p. 50) and "The Great Figure" (p. 53) by William Carlos Williams, from *Collected Earlier Poems of William Carlos Williams,* © 1938 by New Directions Publishing Corporation; "3 improvisations" (pp. 15, 25, 45) by William Carlos Williams from *Imaginations,* © 1970 by Florence Williams; "When the Ceiling Cries" (p. 133) by Russell Edson, from *The Very Thing that Happens,* © 1964 by Russell Edson; "The Structure of Rime I" (pp. 97–8) by Robert Duncan, from *The Opening of the Field,* © 1960 by Robert Duncan, by permission of New Directions Publishing Corporation. 'The Recluse" (p. 83) in *Poems of Federico Garcia Lorca,* © 1979 by Joan Blackburn and the Estate of Federico Garcia Lorca, by permission of the publisher, New Directions.

CONTENTS

PREFACE TO
THE SECOND EDITION

The issues explored in this book first arose for me in the context of the poetry scene in San Francisco in the seventies. As I thought about a second edition, I felt it was important to make this context more explicit by giving a glimpse of the dynamic poetry scene in which I found posed in compelling ways questions that guided the inquiry in this book: questions about modern poetry, about American poetry, and about the place of prose within poetry. My investigation of these issues has, I now recognize, a necessarily circular quality: The contemporary poetry scene posed its questions; I conducted an inquiry into a number of modern, postmodern, and even transcendentalist poets who have conceived of prose as central to their writing of poetry; this inquiry led me to return to the contemporary scene with a clearer appreciation of its aims, antecedents, crises, and accomplishments. What follows in this preface is a brief attempt at historical placement, presenting the inception of this book mostly through the words of poets participating in an informal, cranky, but nonetheless highly provocative debate. Through reading the heated and sometimes partially obscure conversation held among the members of this poetic community, we can sense the urgency and glimpse the issues at stake for the poets who were actively engaged in writing the new poet's prose.

In San Francisco, in the spring of 1977, the poet Bob Perelman began hosting a series of talks by other poets. In a time that saw the recent prominence of Conceptual Art and the rising fashion of Performance Art, it seemed appropriate that these talks occur in lofts, galleries, and museums. The work of the poets who gave and listened to these talks has, for the most part, been gathered under the rubric "Language poetry," one of whose distinguishing features – a fierce devotion to critical theorizing and polemic – was highlighted by these occasions.

On July 20, 1978, Michael Davidson delivered a talk entitled "The Prose of Fact" at the 80 Langton Street Gallery, which I attended. In this talk (a transcription of which was published alongside other talks in *Hills* 6–7, Spring 1980), Davidson sought to provide a genealogy and a justification for the poetry in prose that he and a rapidly increasing number of other poets were writing. At the outset, Davidson defined the territory of his investigation as follows:

> I thought I'd begin with an epigram from Francis Ponge: "Taking the side of things equals taking account of words." I want to take account of the problem of things and the way they are infected by language. And I want to do it in terms of a history of prose, a very personal history of prose. Because I'm talking here about a kind of prose I write myself, and many people in this room. . . . I'd like the "prose of fact" to be a point of conjecture around which I am constantly writing and thinking about things.
>
> I have a kind of naive idea of what a fact is. To paraphrase Wittgenstein, it's a point of departure for further investigation. (p. 166)

By means of a genealogy of the term "prose," traced briefly through philosophy and literature, Davidson contended that "prose," like the term "fact," has always been defined through opposition to other terms. In other words, "prose" refers not to any particular qualities of language or of writing but rather to a counter or placeholder within historical debates about truth; "fact," too, is a counter in these same debates when the focus turns to objectivity or certainty. By uniting "prose" with "fact," Davidson hoped to evoke an area for active investigation of the mediatory function of language – the ways its materiality impedes and diverts the realization of univocal signification. Invoking Derrida, Davidson claimed:

> This moves into the question of whether a prose of fact is possible, or has it always been a rhetoric of fact and a problem of mediation. Its history has been a history of infection, corruption ["I use this word to mean its inability to remain objective" (p. 171)], a desire on the part of the writer to come as close as he can to an event, an object, and instantly realizing the forms of mediation and seeing himself translating. And meanwhile the fact disappears into the play of signification. (p. 176)

At this point in the talk, other poets in the audience began to object. The question in the air was something like the following: Given that we can recognize the artfulness of applying such critical insights to the reading of literature, of what use are these insights to us as writers? Aren't these insights rather debilitating? Bob Perelman initiated the attack in a friendly way:

Perelman: As a writer, what are your ways of avoiding the certainties of rhetoric you were born into?

Davidson: I don't think you can. I don't mean to imply that I can get away from the scandal of acquired gestures.

Perelman: Do you see that as a problem? How do you attack it?

Davidson: I don't think I can attack it by avoiding it. I have to attack it by going into it. The solution has been to try to provide something new and strange, some alternative. I want to see if those terms will work for me, even in the most despised prose, even in the most rhetorical and so-called artificial prose.

Perelman: So you end up finding yourself waltzing in the masquerade ball, quite often. Which is asking a lot of your readers. You're asking them to recognize that there's various degrees of quotes around certain words.

Davidson: I'm interested in persuading the reader to read. To read language as an activity and not a solution to the problem of meaning – not a solution to the problem of meaning, but as the problem of meaning itself. (p. 177)

Perelman's objections seemed to center on the issue of evasion, implying that Davidson willfully relinquished a responsibility to the reader by not taking himself seriously. At this point Barrett Watten leapt in dramatically, accusing Davidson of writing and speaking in bad faith: "It seems to me a practical problem is to start from a fact. It seems like in your method you're excluding facts entirely. There's not one fact yet in the entire talk. You're not allowing yourself to be vulnerable to any decision that anyone in this room might make as to what you stand for in terms of fact" (p. 178). As the argument between Watten and Davidson proceeded, it became clear that while Watten, too, was intensely concerned with the materiality of language, he chose to regard that materiality as a fact, following upon his dedication to the objectivist poetics of Louis Zukofsky. Arguing that one Zukofsky poem is "a fact of words" and that another invests "significance in the world of facts" through representing the details of "a specific cultural experience," Watten claimed, "But the thing that Zukofsky did, that is totally courageous and heroic and makes him the greatest poet of the century {laughter} is to write those things down. He chose. And the act of his mind choosing those facts and that representation gives you the access to this way of thinking [i.e., about language as mediation]. And that's why I just throw out all this French stuff {laughter}" (p. 179).

Other poets entered the fray at this point. Ron Silliman sought to clarify Watten's objections by applying them to specific points in Davidson's work, and Michael Palmer reinforced Davidson's position. Bob

Perelman attempted to restate the issue, in order to keep the two sides engaged with each other:

> *Perelman:* In this last exchange I get the sense that Barry was saying that a fact was an act, but your act, Michael, is always a recognition of the dual or tripartite – the nebulousness of trying to tack a fact onto the outside world.
> *Watten:* No, I was saying that a fact is inescapable.
> *Perelman:* Choice, though; you said Zukofsky was courageous, he *chose.*
> *Watten:* Choice in Zukofsky is a fact. You can't get past it.
> *Perelman:* I.e., an act.
> *Palmer:* So Zukofsky is directly responsible to what qualifies fact in a way that Derrida isn't?
> *Watten:* It's obvious that it's much more useful to think about a writer's representations of fact as he's managed to be able to make them than it is to consider somebody's meditations on the possibility of representing a fact as he hasn't done. The sense that Zukofsky made works that both were facts and included the world in a very interesting way.
> *Palmer:* Well, what if that meditation on possibility is a fact in itself? It is a fact; beyond a mere fact, an activity. (p. 181)

To illustrate why he refused to consider it justifiable for a poet to ruminate over the mere possibility of writing a fact, Watten cited the example of John Ashbery's *Three Poems,* "which is a meditation in writing about what a fact is, and the avoidance of that, constant delay, I would find myself rejecting that, and saying, Out, forget it, enough, had it" (p. 181). From here, the argument (largely untranscribed in *Hills*) moved into a contention over whether the prose of Ashbery's *Three Poems* was as authentic in its investigation of fact as was the more objectivist prose of Robert Creeley's *Day Book.* Everyone agreed that the fabulations of contemporary prose poets like W. S. Merwin were completely unconcerned with issues of fact or of language's mediatory function and so were outside the realm of crucial investigation, but the hard-line objectivists argued intensely for a canon of factive prose poetry that would exclude the endless deferrals of Ashbery's meditations.

Ashbery's prose or Creeley's prose? I found myself contemplating this debate incessantly over the next few months, certain that there must be a way to construct a theory in which both poets, whose prose constituted signal examples for me as a writer of prose poetry, would find a place. I also thought long about the genealogy of prose that Michael Davidson had offered, which was a striking attempt to distance himself from the genre of the French prose poem while affiliating himself with a long tradition of debate about truth and representation in writing and with current trends in critical theory. These poets, this particular occasion in San Francisco, and Michael Davidson's proposal of a prose of fact were all instrumental in the inception of this book; without them it would not have been written. In one sense, this book is merely an investigation of the issues set forth in that one lively debate. Along the way, too, I received invaluable aid from another talk in the series, Ron Silliman's "New Sentence," which I did not hear but read as it circulated in manuscript, before it was revised and published in the *Hills* "Talks" issue and then in a book of Silliman's critical writings called *The New Sentence*. This watershed essay draws attention to the sentence as a neglected unit of writing, showing how much poetic energy lies available within it for unleashing by poets who want to interrogate the relationship between writing and truth.

Since *Poet's Prose* was first published, the volume of poet's prose has increased dramatically, and American poet's prose has begun to receive serious critical treatment. I have revised the Introduction and the notes to reflect some of these developments. To the final chapter, I have added an epilogue that discusses the latest poet's prose as a form of "theoretical poetry" and tries to place it within the unsettled terrain of contemporary poetry and critical thinking.

PREFACE TO
THE FIRST EDITION

This book is an attempt to elucidate a type of writing, poet's prose, that, for various reasons, has thus far escaped attention in English. In speaking of a relatively nongeneric form, one cannot rely upon accumulated critical assumptions; thus I take a variety of vantage points in discussing the subject. The term "poet's prose" is a response to the terminological nightmare surrounding nonversified poetry. The more common "prose poem" is unsatisfactory for two reasons: It is an oxymoron aimed at defamiliarizing lyric poetry, and it remains redolent with the atmospheric sentiment of French Symbolism. "Poet's prose" escapes the oxymoron and is proposed as a more encompassing term to cover all (not only lyric) poetry written in sentences and without versification. The term is descriptive instead of normative; it applies to works that are conceived of and read as extensions of poetry rather than as contributions to one of the existing prose genres.

This book considers poet's prose of a single nationality in order to show the relationship of such a problematic form to the poetry around it. I will argue that American poet's prose, rightly understood, has occupied an especially crucial place in American poetry from Emerson's day to the present. To make this argument I engage in close readings of exemplary texts and piece together, during these readings, a critical vocabulary for speaking about poet's prose in general and American poet's prose in particular. The greater portion of the book consists of detailed examinations of three texts: William Carlos Williams's *Kora in Hell*, Robert Creeley's *Presences*, and John Ashbery's *Three Poems*. Discussion of these works is meant to demonstrate not only how to read and enjoy three worthy but heretofore recalcitrant texts; it also attempts to shed light upon the entire oeuvre of each poet and to place poet's prose squarely within the battleground of modern poetry.

Retaining its imagination and playfulness, the poetry of our time seems increasingly philosophical and critical. In the most ambitious poet's prose, the poetic faculty is turned back upon its own medium, language, resulting in an investigative, exploratory poetry rather than a poetry of striking images encapsulated in tightly crafted lines. Conventional poetry presents things; poet's prose often chooses to investigate how things arise from the matrix of language. Presumably the ultimate goal of poet's prose would be an interchange with language so highly charged that one would apprehend the absolutely constitutive role language plays in the world.

I would like to express my gratitude to a number of people who have made my work easier, clearer, and more apt. Albert Gelpi has had a light though decisive hand in the work from its inception to its present form. I marvel at my fortune in finding such an able, authoritative, and encouraging advisor. At Stanford I also profited from the early advice and attentive criticism of John Felstiner and Herbert Lindenberger. Two critics who have an interest in the same territory, Marjorie Perloff and Donald Wesling, have given substantially of their wisdom and expertise in reading and commenting upon drafts of this book; at the same time, I would like to thank an unrevealed reader for Cambridge University Press, whose fair-minded queries helped me strengthen the focus and enlarge the scope of the book. The reader most sensitive to tone, whose unflagging dedication to the book has been invaluable, is Katherine Shikes. In the early stages I profited from discussions with Robert Duncan and Michael Palmer; in the later stages, David Bromige and Robert Creeley were extremely helpful in reviewing and discussing portions of the book devoted to their work. At Notre Dame, John Matthias and Joseph Buttigieg each gave expert readings to the book as a whole and discussed many particulars with me. I am thankful to other colleagues and students at Notre Dame for listening with an open mind to my ideas and for responding with candor and interest. Several librarians have been assiduous in securing materials for this study: William Allen at Stanford's Green Library, and Eric Carpenter and Robert Bertholf, successive directors of the Poetry Collection at the State University of New York at Buffalo. James Laughlin and New Directions Press have been generous in granting me access to unpublished materials. Summer grants from the Graduate Division of Stanford University and the College of Arts and Letters of the University of Notre Dame provided me with assistance to complete the work.

I dedicate this book to Faiya and Milton Fredman.

LIST OF ABBREVIATIONS

The following abbreviations for works frequently cited are used in the notes and in short-form citations in the text.

APR   Terry R. Bacon, "How He Knows When to Stop: Creeley on Closure: A Conversation with the Poet," *American Poetry Review*, 5, no. 6 (November/December 1976):5–7.

b2   William Spanos, ed., "Robert Creeley: A Gathering," *boundary 2*, 6–7 (Spring–Fall 1978):1–570.

CON   Louis A. Osti, interviewer, "The Craft of John Ashbery," *Confrontation*, 9 (Fall 1974):84–96.

COP   William Packard, ed., *The Craft of Poetry: Interviews from "The New York Quarterly."* New York: Doubleday, 1974.

GS   Friedrich Nietzsche, *The Gay Science*, trans. Walter Kaufmann. New York: Random House, 1974.

ILL   Walter Benjamin, *Illuminations*, ed. Hannah Arendt, trans. Harry Zohn. New York: Harcourt, Brace & World, 1968.

Imaginations   William Carlos Williams, *Imaginations*, ed. Webster Schott. New York: New Directions, 1970.

Mabel   Robert Creeley, *Mabel: A Story and Other Prose*. London: Marion Boyars, 1976.

OWL   Martin Heidegger, *On the Way to Language*, trans. Peter D. Hertz. New York: Harper & Row, 1971.

QG   Robert Creeley, *A Quick Graph: Collected Notes & Essays*, ed. Donald Allen. San Francisco: Four Seasons Foundation, 1970.

Three Poems   John Ashbery, *Three Poems*. New York: Viking, 1975.

WTRP   Robert Creeley, *Was That a Real Poem & Other Essays,*
                     ed. Donald Allen. Bolinas, Calif.: Four Seasons Foun-
                     dation, 1979.

INTRODUCTION: PROSE AND THE AMERICAN CRISIS OF VERSE

We are trying with mortal hands to paint a landscape which would be a
faithful reproduction of the exquisite and terrible scene that stretches around us.
                                        John Ashbery, Three Poems

In 1972 John Ashbery published a 118-page book of prose, divided into
three sections, that he called *Three Poems*. What is meant by such a
gesture? How are we to read a prose text that an American poet conceives
of as poetry? The present study is an attempt to pursue that question
along two avenues: first, by a detailed reading of Ashbery's text and of
two other long works of prose by American poets, William Carlos Williams's *Kora in Hell: Improvisations* (1920) and Robert Creeley's *Presences:
A Text for Marisol* (1976); and second, by a theoretical and historical
consideration of the place of prose works in the canon of American
poetry, which includes the latest developments in poet's prose.

I was initially led to undertake this study through my engagement –
both as writer and reader – with contemporary prose by poets. I have
felt for a number of years that the most talented poets of my own postwar
generation and an increasing number from previous generations have
turned to prose as a form that, in its pliancy and its linguistic density,
seems to promise "a faithful reproduction of the exquisite and terrible
scene that stretches around us." It would be difficult to mistake these
prose works for fiction or for purely discursive prose; they evidence a
fascination with language (through puns, rhyme, repetition, elision, disjunction, excessive troping, and subtle foregrounding of diction) that
interferes with the progression of story or idea, while at the same time
inviting and examining the "prose" realms of fact and anecdote and
reclaiming for poetry the right to investigate the domain of truth.
Through a tracing of historical and theoretical lineages, as well as through
explications of individual poems, I would like to offer a means of entry
into work of signal importance. Although critics are just beginning to
sense the centrality of poet's prose, the poets themselves have consistently

1

spoken of these works as among their most ground-breaking and progenitive.

During the writing of this book I have come to understand how deeply the impulse toward prose is embedded in the larger issues of the character of American poetry and the crisis of modernity. From this vantage point, poet's prose is both an important element in and a key indicator of the overall direction of American poetry. In the nineteenth century we have a central body of prose texts that carry our poetry beyond the lyric mode, works such as Poe's "Eureka" (subtitled "A Prose Poem"), Emerson's essays (which he and others referred to as "prose-poetry"), Thoreau's *Walden*, Whitman's 1855 preface to *Leaves of Grass*, and Dickinson's letters. In the twentieth century one could compile a suggestive list of poets who have written poetry in prose, whether as a central preoccupation or as an occasional gesture: William Carlos Williams, T. S. Eliot, H.D., e. e. cummings; Laura Riding, Louis Zukofsky, Kenneth Patchen, Karl Shapiro, John Hollander; Harry Crosby, Charles Henri Ford, Parker Tyler, Philip Lamantia; Gilbert Sorrentino, Guy Davenport, Robert Creeley, Robert Duncan, Jack Spicer, John Ashbery, James Schuyler; and Russell Edson, David Ignatow, Robert Bly, James Wright, W. S. Merwin, Anne Sexton, William Matthews, James Tate, and Michael Benedikt. And presently a new generation of poets has arisen for whom verse has given way almost wholly to new forms of prose or to non-versified performance texts; a selective list of these poets might include David Bromige, Ron Silliman, and Michael Davidson; Bernadette Mayer, Clark Coolidge, Michael Palmer, Barbara Einzig, Kathleen Fraser, Barrett Watten, Lyn Hejinian, Rosemarie Waldrop, Charles Bernstein, Bruce Andrews, Kit Robinson, Carla Harryman, Steve Benson, Hannah Weiner, Susan Howe, Maureen Owen, and Bob Perelman; David Antin, Jerome Rothenberg, Jackson MacLow, Steve McCaffery, and Kathy Acker.

What does a poet try to accomplish by the paradoxical act of writing poetry in prose? The terms "poetry" and "prose" usually take their definitions from the ideal opposition of one to the other: We think of poetry as succinct, essential, transcendent; we think of prose as prolix, descriptive, mundane. Jeffrey Kittay and Wlad Godzich, in their provocative book *The Emergence of Prose: An Essay in Prosaics*, show the derivations of such distinctions by giving a historical and semiotic account of the emergence of modern prose in medieval France. Arguing that the dominant "signifying practice" (culturally sanctioned mode for transmitting specified kinds of messages) of an era presents itself as a "natural" means of expression, Kittay and Godzich demonstrate in great detail the battle waged by a new signifying practice – prose – in its successful attempt to naturalize itself by wresting the domain of truth away from the central vernacular signifying practice of the age, the jongleur's verse performance. When medieval society began to split and stratify into new estates and classes, the jongleur could no longer retain his centrality as the guardian and performer of the cultural patrimony, and so the momentous shift from an oral to a written culture ensued as a new means of storing and verifying important social messages. The first step taken into writing was, of course, to transcribe the verse of the jongleur's performance; however, this written verse still depended for its *deixis* (its pointing to or grounding in something outside itself) on the now-discredited jongleur, whose performance is still implied by the text. The next step made in attempting to escape this contamination of the written record by the jongleur was to "de-rhyme" the poems. But this proved a highly unstable procedure, because it began to strip the deixis from the signifying practice, without supplying a new grounding. By taking advantage of the free-floating situation created by de-rhyming, prose gradually emerged in France as a new signifying practice. It achieved hegemony as a new guarantor of truth when writers learned how to create deixis internally, to ground one discourse within another inside the written text.

One of the major ways in which the mutual grounding of discourses takes place in prose, Kittay and Godzich argue, is through hypotactic syntax. In the written verse of the oral epics, the verbs graph a linear movement through time and space, referring back to the step-by-step, paratactic presentation of the jongleur's performance. In any particular scene of the epic, this paratactic syntax "gives each element its equal due, endowing cognition with the same space and time as action." Prose, on the other hand, "operates in a space of its own making, a purely textual space, rather than one of performance." Through the use of hypotaxis, prose evolves a powerful way to create a deixis, an outside, folded within the text itself: "Syntactic subordination in prose effects an articulation and a hierarchization that is of a logical nature (not according to some sort of universal logic but according to the logic of a given text); it constructs space and time according to its needs."' The uses of hypotaxis and parataxis in poet's prose will be investigated in detail during the course of this study.

If prose has become the "natural" signifying practice of the modern age, having succeeded so well in displacing other practices, such as verse and oratory, that we now think of prose as somehow prior to other practices (e.g., we define poetry as "artful" prose, and thus testify to our acceptance of prose as natural), then poets have had to contend with this fact. One way poetry has chosen to rebel against the hegemony of prose is, as Kittay and Godzich explain, to privilege

the lyric (Petrarch), which allows verse to attempt to recapture the ground of its own deixis, anchoring it in the *subject* who produces

the verse and for whom there is no other discourse. . . . In performance, voice was but one element among many others; its transcription is taken to be the inscription of a deixis and thus a trace
of presence. In other words, in writing, all that is left of presence
is "voice." . . . Thus the lyric covers a segment staked out by the
terms trace and presence and oscillates in a dilemma so delimited.
Verse can function within this segment and successfully resist the
encroachment of prose, for it will either ground its deixis in presence or thematize its inability to do so. In any case, it does not
ground its deixis in prose. (p. 203)

Beginning in the nineteenth century, poets tentatively set out in another direction, attempting to outflank what they must have felt was the
accelerating dominance of prose, as evidenced for them by the overwhelming popularity and legitimation of prose fiction and prose history.
While still accepting the defensive definition of verse as primarily lyric,
French poets such as Baudelaire, Rimbaud, and Mallarmé began a new
relation between poetry and prose that continues to expand in importance
during the late twentieth century. In their first attempts at a poet's prose,
the French symbolists hoped that by preemptively "surrendering to the
enemy," they could marshal prose's overwhelming power as support for
their disruptive skirmishes within the tidy, enclosed world of poetic
genres. In one sense, this was the ultimate lyric gesture, for it allowed
the poets to assert the deictic claim that the prose poem represented the
momentary impulses of the soul, without generic mediation, and thus
that it liberated the individual from all social manipulations. As Baudelaire exclaimed ecstatically, "Which one of us, in his moments of
ambition, has not dreamed of the miracle of a poetic prose, musical,
without rhythm and without rhyme, supple enough and rugged enough
to adapt itself to the lyrical impulses of the soul, the undulations of
reverie, the jibes of conscience?"[2]
   On the other hand, though, this new poetic prose opened up the
possibility of poetry's going beyond the lyric and appropriating qualities
of prose, as a signifying practice, that were only dimly apprehended in
the nineteenth century. Twentieth-century poets have begun to construct
a poetics of prose that foregrounds the devices, the discourses, and the
deictic procedures (particularly the syntax) of prose. Submitting the qualities of prose to a poetics uproots prose from its position as a "natural"
signifying practice, enabling poets to dedicate its energies to the fundamental project of modern poetry: the investigation of language.
   Although Mallarmé too initially sought the individual poet's escape
from the enclosure of restrictive genres into an apotheosis of the lyric,
he understood that the ultimate purpose of such a liberation of poetry

by prose was to shift the focus of the poet's attention and practice to language:

> What is remarkable is that, for the first time in the literary history of a people, in rivalry to the great general organs of past centuries where orthodoxy is exalted in accordance with a concealed keyboard, an individual possessing a talent for individual execution and hearing can make of himself an instrument as soon as he touches, strikes or blows into it with skill; can play that instrument and dedicate it, as with other methods, to Language.[3]

Mallarmé's proclamation occurs in his famous essay "Crise de vers." There is likely to be little disagreement that the choice by major poets to write in prose, rather than in the venerable forms of verse, which in French enforce a particularly rigid orthodoxy, constitutes a "crisis of verse" – although, as we have seen, prose has already played a major part in precipitating that crisis. Moreover, from a political perspective the abdication by poetry of generic underpinnings parallels attempts to destroy social boundaries, which genres, of course, reinforce.[4] From a formal perspective, the prose poem is a leading agent in the nineteenth-century breakdown and amalgamation of genres that foreshadows the massive hybrids of the twentieth century, such as *The Cantos*, *Paterson*, and *Finnegans Wake*. In itself the prose poem can be thought of as a kind of "last genre," proposing to unite two of the basic categories of literature that have remained as distinct sparring partners since ancient Greece and, in so doing, to effect what Octavio Paz calls "the mixture and ultimate abolition of genres."[5] The prose poem hovers at the edge of this precipice, however, caught in a paradoxical situation: It has survived for a century, now, as the codification of a moment of generic dissolution, and, especially in France, has become another genre within the purview of the lyric poem. The expanding history of the prose poem gives testimony that the urge to stand inside the socially and literarily sanctioned sphere of a genre survives, even within a form of writing dedicated to the destruction of genre.[6]

There are, however, modern European poets who have taken their prose beyond the confines of the genre we call the prose poem: Francis Ponge, Edmond Jabès, Helmut Heissenbüttel, Samuel Beckett, Geoffrey Hill, and Charles Tomlinson, to name a bare few. This is not to deny that their texts often confront the issue of genre in the form of echoes, allusions, parodies, or other investigative devices but to allege that the writers do not situate themselves wholly within the sphere of a genre: From the standpoint of genre, they write into the open. Since that statement begins – properly, I think – to sound philosophical, it may be useful to cite here the parallel situation in modern philosophy. One can find a

rough analogy to the "last genre" of the prose poem in the "last philosophy" of Nietzsche, a philosophy that unites poetry and thought in
an attempt to dismantle the traditional categories of Western philosophy,
such as ethics, epistemology, and metaphysics. When the theoretical bases
for both literature and philosophy are shaken, poets such as the Europeans
just mentioned and many of the American writers of poet's prose, as
well as philosophers who followed Nietzsche, such as Ludwig Wittgenstein, Martin Heidegger, Hans-Georg Gadamer, Jacques Derrida, Gilles
Deleuze, and Michel Foucault, find themselves deconstructing or aban-
doning the suspect genres of their respective fields. Once the self-
sufficiency of the generic or discursive medium, with its powerful social,
historical, and metaphysical supports, collapses, one turns of necessity
to the medium that remains, a medium simultaneously more accessible
and more fundamental: language. Language, then, free to disregard or
transgress generic restrictions, becomes the medium, and language likewise becomes the object of investigation or creation; in Mallarmé's terms,
language is both the instrument and that to which its music is dedicated.

We think of a "crisis" as a time of great danger, and we have come to
accept ourselves as living in an "age of crisis." We are so used to thinking
of our time as an age of crisis, though, that the term has begun to lose
its meaning of a turning point, or moment of decisive change; now we
attempt to adapt to accelerating danger as though it were a steady state.
The root meaning of "crisis" – discrimination or decision, a necessary
decision – describes the situation of American poetry, which, in a strict
sense, has always been in crisis, always called upon to make necessary
existential decisions. Will there be an American poetry? How will it differ
from, or develop from, European poetry? What is the place of self and
of society in this poetry? American poets characteristically feel themselves
called upon to make these decisions, to affirm anew the very vocation
of poetry – an act unthinkable (because unnecessary) in Europe. William
Carlos Williams, for instance, arrived at a climactic moment of despair
and triumph near the end of his career: "I am a poet. I / am. I am. I am
a poet, I reaffirmed, ashamed."[7] The decision to write an American
poetry is always crucial, always existential, never merely a case of deciding upon a subject matter and a verse form. When the primary issue
in writing poetry shifts from the choice of matter and meter to the
decision as to whether poetry, under present conditions, is possible, then
that poetry can truly be spoken of as in crisis. Modern European poetry
is hardly immune to this crisis of verse, which our present discussion
has taken beyond Mallarmé's terms, but nonetheless there is a legitimate
sense in which America can be called the homeland of verse in crisis.
This, in turn, accounts for a characteristic feature of American poetry:

Out of this drastic situation arises an often drastic poetry – contentious, overwrought, over- or understated, at war with decorum. The most drastic, and therefore the most representative, forms that this extreme poetry assumes are the long poem (such as *Song of Myself*, *The Cantos*, *"A,"* and *The Maximus Poems*) and the poetry of prose.

Like so many other issues in American poetry, the crisis of verse comes to full articulation in Emerson; moreover, both of the prominent responses to the crisis of verse, the long poem and poet's prose, can be seen emerging from the ground Emerson prepares. At the practical level, Emerson's entire career manifests an extreme crisis of verse: He is a poet who agonizes over the difficulty he has writing in verse and the uncertain results he achieves; what issues from this crisis is a prose stretched to carry the burden of his metaphorical, gnomic imagination. As a conscious promoter of the idea of the American crisis of verse, Emerson begins early, in *Nature*, to enjoin writers to represent experience and not tradition, to discover a world rather than inherit one. Discovery is a complex metaphor, though, with both active and passive connotations in American usage, as can be seen in the two Emersonian stances it authorizes: Call them willfulness and receptivity, or appropriation and accommodation.

These two tendencies not only account for a significant dichotomy in the American character; they also give rise to the two drastic forms, the long poem and poet's prose, that continue to clamor for recognition as definitive American poetic gestures in the late twentieth century. Each form represents one of the sides of this dichotomy, with respective opportunities for heroism and temptations to excess. We shall speak of heroism and excess momentarily, but first, how different are these two forms? The long poem tends toward what Michael Bernstein calls the "verse epic" or (borrowing Pound's words) "the tale of the tribe," an attempt to integrate the poet and the people with their past and present – a very ambitious, didactic, public act.[8] The poetry of prose, particularly the meditative works investigated in depth in this study, would seem to be an intensely private art. Much of this work, however, is an equally ambitious hermeneutic attempt to render experience visible in the language of our time; the prose is not as private or as ahistorical as it seems.

In their temptations toward heroism and excess, however, poet's prose and the long poem stand poles apart. Pound's quest in *The Cantos* for coherence – for a vision large enough to order history, his own time, and himself – offers a paradigm of the heroic imposition, the willful appropriation, that the American poet perpetrates in the verse epic; it is an imperial – potentially a tragic – gesture, one that would have excited Emerson and Whitman. Putting it this way makes evident immediately the excess that beckons to poets like Pound, Williams, and Zukofsky:

The poet's hubristic exertion of personal control over collective events can place him in an awkward and ungracious position.[9] As Charles Olson cautions, "Ez's epic solves [the] problem [of history] by his ego: his single emotion breaks all down to his equals or inferiors . . . he has driven through it so sharply by the beak of his ego."[10]

A poet like Creeley or Ashbery, who chooses to write in prose, courts a wholly different, though equally Emersonian, sort of heroism – a heroism of negation and receptivity. Rather than endeavoring to master reality, the American poet who writes in prose more properly confronts the times by a heroic accommodation – a scrupulous surrender to language and to the world. Proceeding, as any modern poet does, from an initial position of alienation, the American poet uses prose not to give evidence of genius and the ability to impose order but instead to create, through attentive receptivity, a space of permission in which the world is allowed to appear through language. In this context the eschewal of verse can be seen as a conscious abnegation of the tremendous "disciplinary" force inherent in verse.[11] Though rhythm, rhyme, and tropes may be as resonantly used by a poet in prose as in verse, the poet who gives up the form of verse knowingly sacrifices a vast and recognizable prestige, one he or she may wish to question, to subsume, or to do without. The excess tempting this prose does not resolve, as one might suppose, to political quietism, for the range of political stances inscribed in poet's prose is as diverse as that reflected in the verse epics of (from right to left) Pound, Williams, Olson, and Zukofsky. It resolves, rather, to the disquieting though often intended sensation one has in reading much of the most experimental prose that the language is writing the poet, instead of the other way around. The "excess," in this case, is a cultivated quality, though, and may mark a virtue in a way that the egotism of certain long poems clearly does not.

The crisis of verse remains such a constant in American poetry that today we find poets of nearly every stripe drawn to the extreme of prose: neosurrealists such as Russell Edson, Robert Bly, W. S. Merwin, and David Ignatow; New York poets of wacky sophistication, such as John Ashbery and James Schuyler; and the followers of Objectivism and Projectivism, such as Robert Creeley, Robert Duncan, and the Language poets – these are a few of the competing camps in contemporary American poetry in which prose plays a significant role. Given the variety of poets writing prose, one wants to know why it has proved so attractive and also whether the texts have any qualities in common. The first, and most traditionally American, value that prose seems to offer our poets is freedom. But freedom, though appropriated into our political cant as a uniformly positive virtue, often masks a negative situation; it presumes reaction to a prior restriction. American poets as a body seem to share something of the complaint of suffering under the tyranny of British verse that led Williams on his lifelong search for a freer, "relative" measure for poetry.[12] Prose, for Williams as for other poets, offers itself as a distancing mechanism from the regulation of verse. Presumably this freedom allows something new to be said, something psychologically or socially repressed by the conventions of verse. As Russell Edson puts it, "Something that needs expression is not being fully released by regular poetry. It may simply be a time of rethinking poetry, the kind of rethinking that cannot be done inside of poetry for a while."[13] On the other hand, any thinking about poetry is going to be governed by rules. What we call freedom, or the breaking of rules, can hide or legitimate the substitution of a new set of rules in a situation where the old set has come to seem unnecessarily restrictive, where the range for play seems too severely limited.

So, once we have noted the impulse toward freedom, the desire to break the rules and to reorganize poetry as a signifying practice, we must move on immediately to consider what new rules are evoked. Consider again the opposing or complementary qualities that we habitually attribute to poetry and prose: succinct / prolix, essential / descriptive, transcendent / mundane. Martin Heidegger essentializes even further this opposition of prose and poetry in his definition of poetic speech:

> The more poetic a poet is – the freer (that is, the more open and ready for the unforeseen) his saying – the greater is the purity with which he submits what he says to an ever more painstaking listening, and the further what he says is from the mere propositional statement that is dealt with solely in regard to its correctness or incorrectness.[14]

American poet's prose, particularly the three texts considered at length in this study, places itself at the service of this more positive freedom, this age-old poetic rule that calls for the poet's receptive listening to guide his or her active saying. Equally, however, American poets employ prose to engage and interrogate what has been thought of as the "antipoetic" realm of fact and argument, which "is dealt with solely in regard to its correctness or incorrectness." While remaining within the precincts of poetry, these poets engage both sides of Heidegger's opposition. In choosing the sentence rather than the line as a unit of composition, a poet not only negates some of the rules of verse (while retaining the principle of poetic listening) but also comes under the sway of rules with a vast, though relatively unexplored, poetic potential. I am speaking not just of the poetic use of grammar and syntax (practiced in verse but heightened in prose): The whole range of mood, tone, and address inherent in the discourse of statement and proposition becomes available in the prose sentence. In other words, the most encompassing freedom that these poets seek is the freedom to construct a poetic entity capable of including what poetry has been told to exclude.

The consequences of this move are manifold and profound. Once a poet feels free to make a statement – to interrogate the realm of truth, rather than merely to present an aesthetic object – then the way is clear for a union of fact and imagination. American poets like Emerson, Whitman, and Pound have ardently sought to promote this union; in pursuing this end, American poet's prose leaves the generic French prose poem behind. The French prose poem is a highly aestheticized, subjective, idiolectal artifact, a paean to the isolated genius. Just as the American idea of the self (as presented, for instance, in "Self-Reliance" and "Song of Myself") posits that experience is shared rather than private, that the self is the center and circumference of democracy, so American poets ask their prose to articulate a shared world in which experience vouches for truth rather than for individual genius.[15]

In writing poet's prose, American poets refuse to separate imagination and intellect, inner experience and the world. In an interview, David Ignatow, reflecting on the extensive body of his poetry in prose, contrasts the range he has discovered in prose with his earlier sense of constriction in writing verse:

> I found my language was responding to the form rather than to my sensibilities. I was getting a little too self-conscious about it. So I decided to cut loose and give emphasis to the imagination rather than to the line. By imagination I mean also the intelligence within the imagination, giving the intelligence its opportunity to explore the imagination as far as it will *go*. Of course it has a form, but it's a form which constantly renews itself because the intelligence is restless. Emotions tend to repeat themselves over and over again, whereas the intelligence is constantly renewing itself, recreating itself. Therefore, I feel in the prose poems the emphasis is on the intelligence with an undercurrent of emotion. In the lyric form the emphasis was on the emotion and the intellect was the undercurrent.[16]

Ignatow, finding his creativity checked by the conventions of verse, wishes to spur his imagination on by giving play to his intelligence. Marjorie Perloff, in *The Poetics of Indeterminacy* and *The Dance of the Intellect*, has stressed the centrality of the intelligence to a whole line of American (and some European) poets, often pointing to poet's prose as a form in which the intelligence is given particularly free rein. While poet's prose is not necessarily more intellectual than verse, Americans have used it to investigate realms of experience and ways of speaking conceived of as antipoetic. Poet's prose and the other avant-garde work that Perloff chronicles manifest an impatience with the narrow range of post-Romantic lyric poetry and a desire to recapture for poetry modes of thought and expression seemingly denied it.[17]

Having made the point that American poets seek to combine in their prose fact and imagination, the subjective and the objective, one must begin to differentiate among the many types of poet's prose. To conceive of the range of types we can imagine a continuum, with the followers of the French prose poem of Baudelaire and Rimbaud at one end and a completely nongeneric prose, such as one finds in the work of contemporary poets like Ron Silliman and Michael Davidson, at the other. At the former end we find a prose influenced by Symbolism and Surrealism, a prose consisting usually of short units that tell a story, a parable, or isolate a timeless moment through descriptive or narrative means. As in Surrealism there are often irrational descriptive and narrative jumps, and the imagery purports to be unconscious. Robert Bly best sums up the position he shares with Merwin, Edson, and Ignatow in his discussion of poetic "leaping":

> That leap can be described as a leap from the conscious to the unconscious and back again, a leap from the known part of the mind to the unknown part and back to the known. . . . Thought of in terms of language, then, leaping is the ability to associate fast. In a great ancient or modern poem, the considerable distance between associations, the distance the spark has to leap, gives the lines their bottomless feeling, their space, and the speed of association increases the excitement of the poetry.[18]

Because this type of prose has so much in common with the European prose poem, it will serve in this study as a point of comparison rather than a major focus. In order to foreground the extrageneric qualities in poet's prose and to argue a particular American derivation for those qualities, I will concentrate upon the more innovative and ambitious works in which they are most prominent.

Moving along the poet's prose spectrum in this direction, one arrives at William Carlos Williams's *Kora in Hell: Improvisations*. Although Ezra Pound, stung by Williams's denunciation of him as an expatriate capitulant to the French, calls *Kora in Hell* an imitation of Rimbaud ("But what the French *real reader* would say to your *Improvisations* is Voui, ç(h)a j(h)ai déjà (f)vu ç(h)a ç(h)a c'est de R(h)imb(h)aud!!"), Mike Weaver sums up Williams's indebtedness to the French most succinctly:

The improvisation was what Williams, as he confessed much later, liked to do most of all. Valéry Larbaud attributed his interest in it to Rimbaud, whose *Illuminations* Helen Rootham had translated, but as Williams informed René Taupin, his knowledge of French culture was visual and not literary.[19]

Williams certainly imbibed the general air of experimentalism wafting over to America from French avant-garde writing and (more pertinently) painting, and this experimental work (or rumors of it, from friends and acquaintances like Pound and Duchamp) provided a general justification and incentive. On the other hand, Williams tenaciously developed an American approach to poet's prose without benefit of a direct European model. While *Kora in Hell* shares some characteristics of the more French-influenced poet's prose, such as the shortness of individual improvisations, the enshrining of an isolate moment, the occasional sense of parable, and the Dada spirit pervading the work, Williams's text also opens the way toward our discussion of the more nongeneric poet's prose being written today through Williams's highly inventive deployment of the sentence as a poetic form.

My discussion of Williams's experiments with the sentence, in Chapter 1, provides the terms for a close reading of the more lengthy and involved writing of Creeley and Ashbery in Chapters 2 and 3. Through a relentless exploration of the generative possibilities of the sentence, Creeley and Ashbery, in *Presences* and *Three Poems*, create a poet's prose of some philosophical subtlety and complexity. Although Creeley's prose maintains a tangential relation to the genre of autobiography and Ashbery's echoes the genre of spiritual meditation, both of these poets step out from the confines of genre into a region where poetry and philosophy come face to face. Many of the fundamental concerns of post-Nietzschean philosophy – the investigation of the relationship between language and experience, the question of the nature of temporality and of presence, the centrality of hermeneutics, and the analysis of modes of discourse – are also primary concerns in American poet's prose. In reading this prose we recognize the ability of poetry to combine, as it has in great poets like Homer, Dante, Shakespeare, and Goethe, an acute and fertile play of language with the asking of questions basic to an age. Because of the unfamiliarity of the form, these long works of prose have been seen as highly eccentric poetry – if poetry at all. When understood correctly, however, the new and skillful poetic appropriation of prose that occurs in *Presences* and *Three Poems* may be seen as central to our time, a moment in which poetry, philosophy, and criticism begin to coalesce. This challenging poetry remains unafraid of ideas and facts, is playful, moving, revelatory, temporally grounded, and critically serious.

The final chapter considers contemporary poets – David Antin, David Bromige, Ron Silliman, and Michael Davidson – who write from beyond the separation of poetry and prose altogether; for them all, poetry is, in David Antin's words, the whole of "the language art."[20] Antin unites poetry, criticism, and philosophy in his "talk poems," actual talks he improvises before an audience, tape-records, and then transcribes in a nonlineated, breath-unit form. He shares the profound hermeneutic and phenomenological concerns of Creeley and Ashbery but expresses these concerns in a form that is neither verse nor prose but something he considers more fundamental: talk. For poets like David Bromige, Ron Silliman, and Michael Davidson, the choice between prose and verse no longer looms as a significant issue; they find no remaining formal tension in the defamiliarization of one form by the other. The use of prose becomes a strategy of the moment, a way of moving, rather than a claim about the correct mode of representation. In their poetry the act of representation is at every point self-aware and self-questioning: No medium or method stands up as a transparent vehicle of truth. Although its American roots and context are crucial, the latest poet's prose contains much that resonates sympathetically with current international thought about language and textuality.

In confronting the American crisis of verse and the continuum of poet's prose that it elicits, one realizes as well a crisis in criticism. Does one, for instance, automatically apply the critical and philosophical methods provided by recent Continental thought to a discussion of poetry that, at times, seems similarly intent upon discovering the ways in which language and texts constitute the fabric of our world? Not necessarily. I take my most important task to be the providing of a model of how to read poet's prose. And while the old-fashioned philological *explication de texte* may not prove wholly satisfactory, neither would current applications of deconstruction; for a deconstructive method that reveals the text as an undecidable play of hidden subtexts works best, it would seem, on texts that are not themselves avowedly engaged in deconstruction.[21] In other words, advanced Continental critical and philosophical methods offer themselves more urgently as analogies in discussing the prose of American poets than as critical tools. My critical method in this book will be exploratory and explanatory, seeking to be neither methodical nor exhaustive, not working within any recognizable critical or philosophical school though drawing on many, and at once practical and theoretical. This is an American, heuristic form of criticism, similar to what Emerson calls a "panharmonicon."

Chapter 1

THE GENERATIVE SENTENCE: WILLIAM CARLOS WILLIAMS'S *KORA IN HELL: IMPROVISATIONS*

WORD VERSUS SYNTAX

Kindly note that all I have ever done has been the one thing. Pound will say that the improvisations are – etc. etc. twenty, forty years late. On the contrary he's all wet. Their excellence is, in major part, the shifting of category. It is the disjointing process.

Williams

Kora in Hell: Improvisations (Boston: Four Seas, 1920) is a unique work for its time and place.[1] For Williams it inaugurated a remarkably fruitful decade of experimentation that is documented in the collection *Imaginations* (ed. Webster Schott [New York: New Directions, 1970]), which contains *Kora in Hell, Spring and All* (1923), *The Great American Novel* (1923), *The Descent of Winter* (1928), and *A Novelette and Other Prose* (1932). For American poetry *Kora in Hell* provided an energetic, attractive, and puzzling model of a native "poet's prose" that has continued to fascinate, especially after it was republished for the first time since 1920 by City Lights (San Francisco) in 1957. The book contains twenty-seven chapters of poet's prose, each consisting normally of three improvisations; following many improvisations is a discursive prose commentary; a long polemical prologue, entitled "The Return of the Sun," begins the book. Written during World War I, the text is itself at war both with poetry as it has been traditionally conceived and with the expatriate wing of American modernism headed by Ezra Pound. In the prologue Williams attacks Pound and T. S. Eliot (and takes mild swipes at H. D. and Wallace Stevens) while defending the nonexpatriate avant-garde that included Marianne Moore, Walter Arensberg, Maxwell Bodenheim, Alfred Kreymborg, and Robert Brown.[2]

But beyond taking sides in an internecine struggle, *Kora in Hell* is a desperate attempt to break open the sacred vessel of poetry, to make it amenable to the truths of daily life. The individual prose improvisations are short skirmishes – usually single paragraphs – that confront the details of mundane existence and engage in battle to wrest from them an understanding of how experience actually happens. The real adversary in this contest turns out to be Death, who has appropriated to himself Desire; Hades has captured Kora (also known as Persephone), and Williams must descend to the Underworld, exploring and acknowledging the chthonic nature of desire, in order to bring her into the open and establish the legitimate grounds for his poetry. The following is one of many improvisations that seek an authentic place for the local and the contingent by exposing the Dionysian world underlying them.

> Giants in the dirt. The gods, the Greek gods, smothered in filth and ignorance. The race is scattered over the world. Where is its home? Find it if you've the genius. Here Hebe with a sick jaw and a cruel husband, – her mother left no place for a brain to grow. Herakles rowing boats on Berry's Creek! Zeus is a country doctor without a taste for coin jingling. Supper is of a bastard nectar   on rare nights   for they will come – the rare nights! The ground lifts and out sally the heroes of Sophocles, of Æschylus. They go seeping down into our hearts, they rain upon us and in the bog they sink again down through the white roots, down – to a saloon back of the rail-road switch where they have that girl, you know, the one that should have been Venus by the lust that's in her. They've got her down there among the railroad men. A crusade couldn't rescue her. Up to jail – or call it down to Limbo – the Chief of Police our Pluto. It's all of the gods, there's nothing else worth writing of. They are the same men they always were – but fallen. Do they dance now, they that danced beside Helicon? They dance much as they did then, only, few have an eye for it, through the dirt and fumes.   (*Imaginations*, 60–1)

In search of a form that would allow elemental forces to dance "through the dirt and fumes" of daily life, Williams chose to work in a muscular and "disjointed" prose, itself a contentious, embattled form. Before giving his book its important-sounding mythological title, Williams referred to it simply as the *Improvisations*. While a verbal improvisation need not appear in prose, the idea of improvisation exerts a strong pull on American poet's prose. An improvisation is offered as an unpremeditated and unprecedented work that breaks forth extemporaneously in a unique moment. Williams characterizes his improvisations as "my day-to-day notations, off the cuff, thoughts put down like a diary in a year of my life."[3] The year was September 1917 to September 1918;[4]

the method was "scribbling in the dark, leaving behind on my desk, often past midnight, the sheets to be filed away later [so that] at the end of a year I had assembled a fairly bulky manuscript" (*Imaginations*, 29).

To speak of one's work as improvisation is to emphasize the spontaneous over the planned, the discovery of form over the formal contract, the new over the traditional. In a penetrating discussion of the improvisation (with special reference to Williams), Gerald L. Bruns presents the following definition:

> From a mildly etymological point of view an improvisation is a species of unforeseen discourse. One cannot predict anything about it. It is discourse that makes no provision for a future, not in a reader's mind nor, certainly, in the writer's; its teleology is entirely in the present. It is discourse whose beginning is what matters, because to improvise is to begin without a second thought, and under the rules there is no turning back. It is discourse that is governed by no provisos, and so differs from nearly every other discourse one can imagine: it is ungeneric almost by definition; it is a close semblance of free speech.[5]

As discourse whose "teleology is entirely in the present" the improvisation has about it a certain timeliness, the stamp of a specific moment. It purports to be the farthest thing from a timeless utterance; it is a meditation upon the moment, with the implication that no later revision is possible. First and foremost a beginning, an improvisation begins from the middle, not from a point of origin.[6] And to the extent that the writer is recalled to the task of improvising, the text continues beginning throughout its length, abjuring the sense of finality through contradiction, paradox, and non sequitur. An improvisation differs from a work of fiction or argument in that the latter two, from the beginning, tend toward an end, while the improvisation tends to go on. An improvisation ends not when it has attained a necessary formal or thematic completion but when it has played itself out.

These observations give a sense of the improvisation's formal requirement of novelty. Although an improvisation is new, abrupt, and particular to a moment, it does not arise *ex nihilo*: It is also a variation. Jazz provides the strongest contemporary association for the word improvisation; in jazz a string of variations is embroidered around an existing musical theme. The excitement of jazz comes from being present (as musician or listener) at the moment of creation; the rigor of jazz inheres in the endless preparation and practice of riffs, of interchangeable stitches with which to embroider the thematic material. The jazz musician establishes an intricately rule-bound domain in which to foster the free play appropriate to a specific occasion. Albert Lord describes a similar process of improvisation in the composition of oral epics: The singer learns verbal formulae that meet certain metrical conditions; during performance, the formulae are freely combined to embroider upon a basic story, making use of the exigencies and creative possibilities of a specific recital.[7]

With the help of Wassily Kandinsky's famous treatise *Concerning the Spiritual in Art,* Williams employs both of these senses of improvisatory form in *Kora in Hell.* Kandinsky distinguishes the improvisation as the middle of three "different sources of inspiration" in art: the "impression," the "improvisation," and the "composition." The first source generates an expression by the artist of visible "outward nature," the second a "spontaneous expression of inner character," and the third a more reasoned, purposeful "expression of a slowly formed inner feeling."[8] The improvisations of *Kora in Hell* are a spontaneous expression of Williams's inner character, especially as it becomes manifest in his roles as physician and husband/lover. The thematic material of the book consists of episodes from his daily life in which these two roles are prominent and upon which he embroiders a fabric of spontaneous expression. As the title suggests, with its reference to the myth of Demeter's daughter Kora, the riffs or formulae that stitch together the thematic material are drawn from classical mythology.

The anecdotes from daily life provide a plot for the improvisations; the mythological allusions constitute a framework upon which to measure everyday life against the energetic, impulsive life of the gods and heroes; and the whole conspires toward a theory of the imagination's operation upon reality. Such a description might apply equally well to other high modernist texts, such as Eliot's *Waste Land,* Pound's *Cantos,* or Joyce's *Ulysses.* These other major works of modernism have received ample annotation and interpretation, but the contemporaneous *Kora in Hell* has proven more resistant to approach than even such famously difficult works.[9] The continued obscurity (in both senses) of *Kora in Hell* may be accounted for in part by its improvisatory nature. As a spontaneous artifact, the improvisation presents its *surface,* upon which the most wide-ranging and resonant invention takes place, as the primary plane for reading ("to explain further what I intended would be tautological, the surface appearance of the whole would please all the ablest I was approaching" [*Imaginations,* 29]). The clarification of allusions and intentions beneath the surface has materially aided our reading of *The Waste Land, The Cantos,* and *Ulysses,* but *Kora in Hell* asks for a reading that pays particular attention to its transitory surface, to the way words and things appear and are linked in the moment of its writing. The short, single-paragraph improvisations strike one as impulsive in their rapid shift of focus and tone; they seem to call for a different pace or stride of reading than one normally pursues in scanning prose.

As an exercise in both careful attention to the surface and in breaking the normal reading pace, we will begin our reading of Williams's text as if examining it under a microscope. Following that, the scope of vision will gradually expand: from the word to the sentence, from the sentence to The Sentence.

In a now-classic statement about the difference between modern and classical poetry, Roland Barthes offers a good point of departure for a microscopic reading. Barthes argues that a radical *disjunction* (or to use Williams's term, quoted at the head of this chapter, "disjointing") occurs in modern poetry, breaking the flow of discourse that any "classical" speech seeks to maintain. The source of this disjunction, he claims, is metaphysical: the Word, the Logos, detaches individual words from the ongoing discourse and establishes each as an immediate and absolute point of origin.

> In classical speech, connections lead the word on, and at once carry it towards a meaning which is an ever-deferred project; in modern poetry, connections are only an extension of the word, it is the Word which is the "dwelling place" . . . Here, connections only fascinate, and it is the Word which gratifies and fulfills like the sudden revelation of a truth . . . It shines with an infinite freedom and prepares to radiate towards innumerable uncertain and possible connections. Fixed connections being abolished, the word is left only with a vertical project, it is like a monolith or a pillar which plunges into a totality of meanings, reflexes and recollections; it is a sign which stands.[10]

Building upon the argument of Sartre's *What Is Literature?* in this early essay, Barthes finds the discontinuity that results from the detachment and apotheosizing of individual words profoundly disturbing. He portrays it as a kind of metaphysical mirror for the condition of absolute alienation. The characterization of words as "vertical projects" reminds one of the singularly vertical, haunted, and hieratic figures of alienation by the sculptor Giacometti.

In contrast to Barthes, Williams finds this abolition of fixed connections and isolation of individual words a welcome development in modern poetry, akin to Cézanne's breakthrough in modern painting. For both the modern writer and painter the materials of the craft become more tangible and at the same time more abstract, since the materials themselves become to a large extent the subject matter. Describing modern painting as "a matter of pigments upon a piece of cloth stretched on a canvas," Williams draws an analogy to what he calls the *tactile* quality in modern poetry: "It is the making of that step, to come over into the tactile qualities, the words themselves beyond the mere thought expressed that distinguishes the modern."[11] The analogy is not an exact one, however, because words are never wholly physical the way the materials of painting may be. Williams means by tactile qualities something more than just the aural or visual aspects of words (and thus differs from e. e. cummings); the words of modern poetry are personal, social, and metaphysical objects that, when detached from ordinary discourse, radiate a "potential." If we think of individual words as instruments for the conduct of our lives, then they take on a palpable character, like tools that are used, cleaned, and then available for use once again. From this perspective, the isolation of single words is somewhat akin to grasping a hammer with one hand and tapping it inquisitively across the palm of the other. When we thus assay words in their given weight and in the potentialities of their use, they do have a tactile quality.

These remarks by Barthes and Williams provide a context for the disjointed, microscopic reading we are about to perform. In order to make the individual words of a sentence from *Kora in Hell* stand out as vertical and tactile objects, I will list them one by one, adducing the kind of associations each might conceivably engender. Then I will join each new word to the ongoing aggregate so that we may experience a sentence being built up of these radiant but resistant forms, "these unrelated objects – words adorned with all the violence of their irruption, the vibration of which, though wholly mechanical, strangely affects the next word, only to die out immediately."[12] The interpretations of these words and their aggregates are given in a voice speaking to itself, engaged in a heuristic rather than explanatory task.

Beautiful

Oh, that old chestnut. Here comes a purely sentimental statement, whose import we can easily disregard. More romantic slush. Well, there were of course writers such as Keats who raised the word "beauty" to a central issue – but "beautiful" is just an adjective, solely an attribution, and probably an unearned one at that.

White

Purity, cleanliness, chastity, virginity; wedding, confirmation, baptismal gown; absence of color – or else all the colors combined; peace, surrender, a white flag; a hospital uniform, sterile, antiseptic, healing, healthy. "White" brings in the visual sense.

Beautiful white

Two adjectives of praise, of sanctification, even of holiness. Could be epithets for the Virgin, for Mary our immaculate mother. Whatever is being described is both beautiful and white, and so we expect a pure beauty, an unsullied perfection.

Corpse

Death. A dead body, spiritless matter, a husk, something left behind. Those who handle corpses are undertakers or physicians. The one reconstructs or preserves them in order to ready them for final rites; the other inspects or dissects them in order to learn which intruder was victorious over the forces of life in the body or else to pursue the study of anatomy. These are the only people who have use for a corpse. To everyone else it is a nuisance, an importunate *memento mori*. The person formerly housed in the corpse now lives in our memory.

Beautiful white corpse

Well, there is certainly a perfection in death, but this makes ironic our sense of the first two words. We were looking for something lovely and pure and have been given something filthy and abhorrent. What we were almost praying to turns out to be that which we fear most. A disturbing oxymoron. But is there a way to reexamine the first two words in an effort to take them straight and still yield a meaningful phrase? Well, "white" is certainly applicable to an absence of life, a pallor, the blood drained from the skin. When something "turns white" it loses "the bloom of life," we say. But in what way could this ghostly white corpse be beautiful? It seems ghastly, horrifying, revolting. There must be a new type of beauty implicit here, one that valorizes even a corpse. Such a beauty would have to stomach things as they are, would have to accept actuality bodily (corpse/corpus) and not turn toward the ideal. Is this possible?

Of

Just a preposition. But wait, what does a preposition do? It's a relational word, like a verb: It acts to hold two things together. "Of" has to do with possession, with one thing belonging to another. The thing before "of" specifies, fits with, owns, holds, is brought into relation with, the thing coming after "of." A glass *of* water. The glass fits, confines, is brought to bear on the water. Water exists in an unconfined shapelessness until it is brought to conform to the shape of a glass – which holds the water.

Beautiful white corpse of

This beautiful white corpse, this *thing,* is about to be brought to bear on something else. It will not be allowed to stand on its own but is about to become dependent upon another. Now, as we feel this phrase in transit, we recall that the word "metaphor" means to transfer, to bring to bear. In metaphor, an image is lifted from its usual context and brought to bear by the imagination upon a new object.

Night

Darkness, sleep, death. Opposite of day, light, awake, life. Blind, ignorant, troubled, despairing – "dark night of the soul." Night connotes everything shadowy, negative, unconscious, unknown, threatening, fearful.

Beautiful white corpse of night

Ah, it's the *night's* "beautiful white corpse"! "Of" has handed this strangely luminous dead thing to the night. But what is beautiful and white that belongs to the night? Stars, for one thing. But somehow the night is dead or contains a dead element. Maybe the stars in the night are the beautiful white corpse. Or maybe it's the "dead" of winter, which we would recognize by the disposition of the constellations. But to imagine the night as a white corpse is to see it differently than we ever really find it: The night is never dead (except when it's "dead quiet" in the "dead of night"), and being dark it is never white. How can such a thing be?

Actually

An adverb. Really, truly, in effect; right now. What's really here, underneath appearances. What's being enacted. What we have to admit is true, though something else seems the case. A condition we're troubled by; something seems in contention. We are in need of reassurance, in a condition of doubt. Modifies a verb, an adjective, or another adverb. Used for emphasis, to focus or insist on something.

Beautiful white corpse of night actually

If "actually" modifies a verb that is still to arrive, then we have the promise of action, of a predicate that completes this "beautiful white corpse of night." If, however, we want to relate this word grammatically to the phrase at hand, it can modify only "beautiful" or "white" or both together. If it modifies "beautiful," then it seems to answer the question we raised when considering "beautiful white corpse": "Such a beauty would have to stomach things as they are, would have to accept actuality bodily . . . and not turn toward the ideal. Is this possible?" The phrase as it stands seems to be saying yes, the white corpse is *actually* beautiful. Beauty resides in actuality, not in ideality. If we let a white corpse be, if we see it as it is, it is beautiful. There is a fullness we alone can grant it by our allowing it to be, a fullness that we lift to the condition of beauty, once we no longer wish the white corpse to be something else but accept it for all it has to say. Then we see that beauty is the condition of full expression, when something has been allowed to say all that it has to say, when we have let it speak through us. Reading the phrase over again, though, "actually" seems a statement about the phrase as a whole. There is such a thing (it seems to be saying) as a "beautiful white corpse of night." But where? We had just been wondering how the night could ever be white. Surely, only in the imagination. And if this metaphorical condition, this "beautiful white corpse of night," is being insisted on, being emphasized by the word "actually," then this is an insistence upon the reality of the things of the imagination. The actuality being claimed must be metaphorical.

!

The exclamation mark. A strong emphasis, a rhapsodic utterance, an absolute statement, something that brooks no cavilling. Indicates raised voice, assertive tone. Is something of a shock, a punch, an explosion, an apotheosis. Has a retroactive effect upon the last word or last few words before it. Changes intonation and emphasis.

Beautiful white corpse of night actually!

The added emphasis, the aggressive punch lands squarely on the last word, "actually." There is a fierce, a polemical insistence that this word be taken seriously. The actuality of imaginary constructs must not be questioned. The sentence so strongly asserts the actuality of this meta-phorical "beautiful white corpse of night" that we must consider it a real entity in the world. This thing, which is only a chain of words, is proposed to be just as real as the material things of the world; they are ontologically equal. But we have always thought of words as a represen-tation or a completion of things in the world; we have never thought of them as possessing the same object status, the same nature as things. This sentence speaks of a new relation of language to being, in which things and words are equals, both as physical (tactile) constructs and as entities that speak. Now we are to "hear" things and "touch" words: so this sentence proposes. And now we come to hear the whole sentence as an exclamation, an excited proclamation of the interpenetration of words and things.

This word-by-word reading of a sentence from the first improvisation in Chapter V of *Kora in Hell,* though an admittedly arbitrary interpretation, is more than a microscopic exercise. By attending to the "vertical" possibilities of these individual words, we have dislodged several propositions that taken together comprise the basis of Williams's aesthetic theory. These propositions arose when we considered the word "actually" and the exclamation point in relation to the rest of the sentence. In order of occurrence, the propositions are (1) that actuality is beautiful; (2) that imaginary constructs are actual; (3) that words are equivalent to things.

Williams begins his self-justifying prologue to *Kora in Hell,* brashly entitled "The Return of the Sun," by casting his mother (The Return of the Son) as a wandering, dispossessed Penelope. Her strength, in this uncharacteristic condition, resides in her powerful imagination: "She might be living in Eden. And indeed she is, an impoverished, ravished Eden but one indestructible as the imagination itself. Whatever is before her is sufficient to itself and so to be valued" (*Imaginations,* 7). Mrs. Williams's defiant faith embodies succinctly the first two propositions. For her the imagination is an actual and a necessary part of life, not a distraction from life, and it includes an acute ability to perceive objects and render them valuable. Williams praises his mother's imaginative acumen and seeks it in himself and others throughout the prologue and body of *Kora in Hell.* He continues:

> Thus, seeing the thing itself without forethought or afterthought but with great intensity of perception, my mother loses her bearings or associates with some disreputable person or translates a dark mood. She is a creature of great imagination. I might say this is her sole remaining quality. She is a despoiled, molted castaway but by this power she still breaks life between her fingers. (*Imaginations,* 8)

This portrait of his mother as methodological example does not include an explicit concept of beauty, but implicit in this avowal is the idea that everything the world holds beautiful is mere illusory daydreaming, while real beauty is found in the imagination's working upon actual things. "The wish would be to see not floating visions of unknown purport but the imaginative qualities of actual things being perceived."[13] The purpose of the exercise of imagination in writing, then, is to place the writer and the reader in direct relation to things, not to other works of literature. This may sound like an extreme form of realism, but Williams carries his objectification beyond the bounds of realism when insisting that the very words the writer employs are things in themselves, rather than transparent signifiers.

The insistence upon the objectification of words coupled with the fidelity to actuality differentiates Williams from many of his American modernist contemporaries. It does ally him, though, with cubist painting technique (as was mentioned above) and with the cubist literary practice of Gertrude Stein.[14] In her experiments with language, Stein provides an important model to American poet's prose. Williams was fascinated by Stein and took her work as a major theoretical exposition of the value of individual words:

> Stein has stressed, as Braque did paint, words. So the significance of her personal motto: A rose is a rose – which printed in a circle means two things: A rose is, to be sure, a rose. But on the other hand the words: A rose is – are words which stand for all words and are very definitely not roses – but are nevertheless subject to arrangement for effect – as are roses.[15]

As things insistent upon their linguistic nature, words can be taken up individually, as we have done in our initial reading of Williams's sentence. One effect of this attempt to experience the tactile qualities of words is a necessary deceleration of reading speed. We cannot regard words as things unless we move at a relatively slow, contemplative pace. When we proceed at this pace, each word, in its singular verticality, produces a series of echoes; these "vibrations" (as Barthes called them) overlap one another somewhat like the overtones one hears in a well-spaced series of sustained piano notes.

Were we to hear a piano sonata performed at this speed, however, we would miss the rhythmic tension that contributes a major element to the music's structure. Likewise, our reading of these words as discrete verticalities muffles the crucial aspect of syntax, which provides certain structural tensions in the sentence. Sentences have an overall thrust based upon syntactic expectations. There is a syntactic rhythm to a sentence (beyond the metrical quantity and stress of the words themselves) that establishes a major element of continuity in our experience of language. Whenever we see words in juxtaposition, our tendency is to attribute a syntax; likewise, the discontinuous elements of modern poetry, or any modern art, are always joined into a new order, though one that preserves the sense of parataxis or heterogeneity among its elements.

The sentence we have been reading, "Beautiful white corpse of night actually!", is clearly held together by syntax – but is it a sentence? To fully answer such a question, one would have to ask whether a sentence is a complete thought, a logical proposition, or a matter of grammar. Let us set this question aside for the moment. For our present purposes we will designate a subject and a verb as the minimal requirements for a sentence. The question concerning Williams's sentence then resolves to the query Where is the verb? There is a strong adverb, "actually," that seems to insist upon the existence of the subject of the sentence. Given that intention one would expect a verb of being, for instance, "Beautiful white corpse of night actually is!" By leaving out the weak copula, Williams in effect converts "actually" into an intransitive verb. This startles the reader and helps strengthen the emphasis upon the actuality of the imaginative subject of the sentence.

This sentence is the first of five in Improvisation V. 1. Having given a disjointed, word-by-word reading to this first sentence, let us now pay close attention to the syntax of the piece as a whole. Rather than stressing the discontinuity of the tactile qualities of words, this reading will concentrate on the ways syntax effects a connection among highly individualized elements (words and phrases).

V.1

Beautiful white corpse of night actually! So the north-west winds of death are mountain sweet after all! All the troubled stars are put to bed now: three bullets from wife's hand none kindlier: in the crown, in the nape and one lower: three starlike holes among a million pocky pores and the moon of your mouth: Venus, Jupiter, Mars, and all the stars melted forthwith into this one good white light over the inquest table, – the traditional moth beating its wings against it – except there are two here. But sweetest are the caresses of the county physician, a little clumsy perhaps – *mais* – ! and the Prosecuting Attorney, Peter Valuzzi and the others, waving green arms of maples to the tinkling of the earliest ragpicker's bells. Otherwise – : kindly stupid hands, kindly coarse voices, infinitely soothing, infinitely detached, infinitely beside the question, restfully babbling of how, where, why   and   night is done and the green edge of yesterday has said all it could.   (*Imaginations*, 38)

The improvisation begins with two exclamatory sentences that bear a strong resemblance to each other. What strikes one immediately about the second sentence is that it begins with "so," as though what follows is a logical consequence of something preceding, yet there is no obvious assertion in the first sentence from which "so" could be deduced. "So" is then reinforced by "after all"; they combine to form the framework for a reply to an argument in which something has been asserted ("The north-west winds of death are mountain sweet") and then denied ("No, they're not"). This sentence seems to be saying that, on the report of new evidence, "the north-west winds of death are mountain sweet after all." The word "actually" in the first sentence operates similarly, insisting on the reality or veracity of the metaphorical condition it represents. There is no prior argument to which the second sentence replies; rather, the

sentence borrows a rhetorical force from the form of such an argument
for the purpose of its singular insistence: "The north-west winds of death
really are mountain sweet."

The third sentence is a long chain of paratactic and appositive phrases.
All of the phrases following the first phrase – "all the troubled stars are
put to bed now" – and ending at the first dash are in apposition to that
phrase (or to each other). They act as a series of metaphorical equivalences:

All the troubled stars put to bed =

three bullets from wife's hand in the crown, in the nape and one
lower =

three starlike holes among a million pocky pores and the moon of
your mouth =

Venus, Jupiter, Mars, and all stars melted into the light over the
inquest table

All four of these phrases elaborate, either descriptively or metaphorical-
ly, upon the three bullet holes visible in the corpse lying on the inquest
table. The bullet holes are "troubled stars" – troubled, no doubt, by
their murderous efficacy, but they need no longer appear troublesome,
since they have been "put to bed" – that is, laid to rest in this corpse. The
next phrase tells us where the bullets came from ("wife's hand") and
then, with the adjectival phrase in apposition, repeats the seemingly
soothing message we heard in "put to bed": "None kindlier."

With this phrase (which is set off by a space and thus functions as a
comment upon what immediately precedes it), the pervasive tone of
irony informing the improvisation becomes manifest. If the hands of the
murderer are described ironically as "kindly," then we must view with
suspicion the other apparently positive attributions in the improvisation
such as "beautiful," "mountain sweet," "put to bed," "good," "sweetest are the caresses," "kindly," "infinitely," and "restfully." But this is
not a simple irony, in which all positive valences are reversed. For such
to be the case we would need a clear indication that the countervailing
values were the true ones: for instance, a report of the wife's unequivo-
cally evil nature. We are not given such an unambiguous moral framework in this improvisation. We know nothing about the relationship of
the husband and wife and thus have no grounds for a moral judgment;
we can imagine a variety of different plots that would place the moral
onus on either or both of these actors. Thus there is a secondary vector of
irony in this improvisation, apparent in such phrases as "none kindlier":
the irony the poet finds in the actual world, where our moral judgments
seem an insignificant posture in the face of such an overwhelming experi-

ence as death. This secondary vector of irony may reverse the direction of the primary vector, though on another level. If death, for instance, in its undeniable actuality, were seen (ironically) as an acceptable condition for humanity, then the corpse might be "beautiful," the wife's hand "kindly," and so forth.

Let us return to the third sentence and the three bullet holes. After seeing them as troubled stars and learning that they originate from the wife's hand, we are told their actual location on the corpse (at least two of the sites are specific). In the next phrase the corpse becomes a metaphorical sky once again, and the following phrase enumerates the three principal planets visible in this sky and then, in a cinematic image, has the corpse/sky dissolve into the light pouring onto it from over the inquest table. This obliteration of stars and planets by light is something like a sunrise in which the "one good white light" of the sun renders the stars invisible. "Good white light" so nearly parallels "beautiful white corpse" that we are forced to return to the first sentence again. A highly complex image seems to be evolving in this improvisation, forging a connection between the corpse, the night, the stars, and the light (and this listing makes clear the rhyming that intertwines the terms). The corpse (death) and the night are customarily images of darkness and negativity; the stars and the light usually form images of lightness and positivity. This is a paradoxical figure, then, in which two pairs of mutually exclusive images, two sets of the basic oppositions that structure our Western cultural assumptions, are somehow being united. Only within the terms of the secondary irony noted above does this make sense. This secondary irony *unites* opposites rather than using one to deny the other; a world in which moral judgments are "infinitely beside the question" (to quote from further on in the improvisation) is one in which oppositions need no longer be held apart and thus may become conflated.

How do we picture this "postoppositional" image, this conflation of the corpse, the night, the stars, and the light? It is awkward to imagine in static terms, so let us think of it as a dynamic image, a transformation, in which the corpse and the night are caught metamorphosing into the stars and the light. This metamorphosis is a special act of the imagination, differing from the figurative union of the corpse with the night or the stars with the light. In this metamorphosis we have the imagination asserting its ability to contradict or conflate the sensuous bases upon which images are customarily formed. The imagination, here, is not under any obligation to represent a world based on the perceptual conventions of Western culture; it is free to construct conceits of bewildering paradoxicality. If we return to our much-explicated initial sentence, we see that this paradoxical image and the claim for its acceptance as actu-

ality (the imagination constructs a world as real as the perceptual world)
are already implicitly stated; the third sentence is an elaboration upon this
image in which the metamorphosis is made more explicit and its process
schematized (though not in a strictly sequential fashion) through a series
of equivalences.

Thus far in the third sentence no phrase has been linked to another by
a coordinate or subordinate conjunction; the phrases are bound by the
almost algebraic colon. Following these appositional equivalences come
two phrases, linked by dashes, that end the sentence. Again we have no
real conjunction, the dashes alerting us to the paratactic connection. The
first phrase, "the traditional moth beating its wings against it," presents
the image of a moth beating its wings against the light over the inquest
table. The moth is traditional both because the image of a moth flying
into a light is a cliché and also because the moth (or butterfly) is a time-
honored image for Psyche. Thus we have the traditional frieze of the soul
hovering over the newly slain body. With the second phrase, "except
there are two here," the ironic use of the term "traditional" becomes
more insistent: The hackneyed image is deflated by the anticlimactic
"except" and by the contradictory fact that there are actually two moths
in attendance. The straw figure of the traditional has been erected and
demolished in short order.

The second section of this sentence makes a claim about representation, through the moth image, that seems at variance with what the first
section claims. The first grants the imagination a special metamorphical
power with respect to reality; the second asserts the primacy of the real
over the habitual. If we look more closely, both sections share a disdain
for the unimaginative, since the first section confounds the common use
of figurative language. Reality and the imagination are both opposed in
this sentence to unthinking tradition. The proper relation of the imagination to reality is one of Williams's primary concerns, while tradition is
associated with fuzzy vision and thought: "The true value is that pecu-
liarity which gives an object a character by itself. The associational or
sentimental [traditional] value is false. Its imposition is due to lack of
imagination, to an easy lateral sliding" (*Imaginations,* 14).

The fourth sentence seems to pick up from the third with the coordinate conjunction "but." But what does "but" coordinate with? In stating
that the sweetest caresses are those of the county physician and the prosecuting attorney, this sentence certainly does not contradict anything just
offered concerning the traditional moth. Rather the conjunction acts as a
kind of grammatical propellant, rushing the reader onward into the next
sentence. The reader assumes that a logical relation justifies the connection and so moves rapidly ahead to complete the promised argument.
Not only does "but" operate in this fashion, but also "so" and "other-

wise": three out of the five sentences in this improvisation begin with conjunctions, part of whose purpose is to trick the reader into assuming the continuation of an argument and thus to propel one into the approaching sentence. This propellant activity and the general lack of subordination help account for the seeming rapidity and montage effect of the improvisation.[16]

The movement of the piece receives a new twist in the second phrase of the fourth sentence, "a little clumsy perhaps – mais – !" The words perform a kind of pantomime in which a comic figure admits a grave fault with a slight gesture and then brushes it aside with an exaggerated shrug of the shoulders and opening of the arms. The speech presents a stock comic situation and introduces an animated quality into the improvisation. Then another character appears: "the Prosecuting Attorney, Peter Valuzzi." Why is this man the only individual cited by name and heralded with a capitalized title? Given the ironic (even sardonic) tone of this improvisation, one is tempted to consider this a dramatic announcement of his insignificance. Possibly. At any rate, the functional, social world of names and titles is promptly transformed into a natural world of dream or myth in which the men change into ineffectual trees, somewhat like Daphne in her metamorphosis, their limbs flapping to the whim of the ragpicker. Peter Valuzzi, the man in charge of this inquest, seeking the facts of a homicide as a representative of the state, is rendered as inconsequential as the anonymous ragpicker – or even placed below him, since the ragpicker may be an Ovidean god in disguise, who transforms Valuzzi and the others into maples. There is also a grotesque pantomime or dance in this second half of the sentence, with the men at the inquest standing stock still but waving their arms like green maple branches to the tinkling of the ragpicker's bells.

The aura of mythical transformation continues into the fifth sentence, where the voices at the inquest change into a babbling brook, flowing along "the green edge of yesterday." This improvisation seems to have little respect for the traditional, certainly as regards technique, yet it continually harks back to classical mythology. As was suggested earlier, the mythological dimension provides the riffs or formulae that embroider upon the daily occurrences, and thus myth has a more integral role in the composition than mere association or sentiment. The gods are emblematic of that metamorphical world of the imagination in which *Kora in Hell* situates itself, where the human, the natural, and the supernatural interpenetrate. The improvisations consistently present the daily occurrences Williams sees, usually on his rounds as a physician, and these banal incidents receive power from the imagination's placing them in an elemental or mythological light. Dissatisfied with his daily life and perceiving a like dissatisfaction in his fellow citizens, Williams perversely seeks perfection in the banal present instead of attempting to escape into an ideal world. Thus, as in Joyce's *Ulysses* – parts of which appeared contemporaneously (1918) with some of Williams's improvisations in *The Little Review* – the mythological and the quotidian coincide.

The classical deity who presides over this improvisation, as he does over Hell itself, is Hades. The scene unfolds under the spell of death, and everything within it is disposed in relation to death. The "north-west winds of death" blow throughout the piece, and their "mountain sweetness" is their imaginative ability to transform a social scene, in all its aggravating contradictions, into a mythical/natural one. In death this corpse is irradiated by an implanation of the moon and three planets, and it is the presence of death (incarnate in the old ragpicker) that changes the busy arms of those attending the inquest into maple boughs. Death, in its overwhelming control of the scene, renders the important functions of the physician and attorney – important in determining the meaning of this event for society – "infinitely beside the question," so that their voices are barely audible within death's loudly rushing winds. Beside the irrevocable reality of death, these clumsy human beings, with their own motives and their search for the motives of others ("how, where, why"), loom pitifully small.

The fifth sentence makes clearest this sense of human insignificance in the face of death. The sarcasm in the litany beginning with "kindly stupid hands" and ending with "restfully babbling" is the most pronounced in the improvisation. The continual diminution of human capability reaches its nadir in the quiet shift to "restfully": By the time this adverb qualifies human activity, there is not enough of such activity in evidence even to provoke contempt. The increasing disdain for human endeavor finally effaces all evidence of humanity and renders the voices a mere natural object. And maybe all along it was only a natural object we listened to: Did we hear the stream of human voices speaking, or was it the "green edge of yesterday," an actual moment of time, that we heard?

In examining this improvisation we have read through five sentences of varying length, noting how a careful attention to the continuity effected by syntax reveals much of the meaning stored in the surface of the text. The five sentences vary markedly both in relation to each other and in respect to normal discursive or narrative prose syntax. Rather than taking the more or less logical order of hypotaxis, the sentences are inventively paratactic, often keeping in suspense the exact relationship between contiguous syntactic units. The compositional continuity forged is on the syntactic level, not the logical or narrative levels, and the ambiguity and propellant quality of the syntax combine to effect what Williams called the "simultaneous" impression of his improvisations, the attempt to evoke a fleeting moment.[17]

When grammar is used for such artful purposes as the complex meta-phorical equations of the third sentence or the propellant conjunctions that tease a reader with a coordination or subordination they never deliver, then grammar is being employed as a primary poetic device. We have discerned and discussed two of the major formal constituents of a poet's prose, syntax and the individual word. Although for the purpose of contrast we have viewed these two elements in opposition, a proper reading takes both into account, since both syntax and the vertical word are elements of composition foregrounded by the poet.

THE GENERATIVE SENTENCE

The stream of things having composed itself into wiry strands that move in one fixed direction, the poet in desperation turns at right angles and cuts across current with startling results to his hangdog mood.

Williams

We have thus far been concerned with words and syntax, which are the components of the sentence, but we have not yet stopped to consider at any length what a sentence is in itself.[18] Once one seriously broaches the question "What is a sentence?" two disciplines, linguistics and philosophy, immediately offer themselves as aids in attaining a rigorous and contemporary definition. Neither, however, renders much assistance. As the science of language, linguistics has striven to become empirical by sloughing off the prescriptive grammar derived from Greek and Latin in favor of a descriptive and theoretical science based upon language as it is actually spoken. From the perspective of speech, linguistics concerns itself primarily with subsentence elements such as phonemes and morphemes, signifiers and signifieds, and transformational generative grammars. The sentence plays a minor, indistinct role in these descriptive and theoretical categories. Philosophy, on the other hand, is primarily conducted in writing, but the sentence is equally auxiliary to its concerns. Philosophy most often examines propositions, not sentences, and a proposition is an assertion for which a truth value is determinable within a logical system. In other words, what is essential to a proposition is not the words or their order but a logical structure, which is often replaceable by a mathematical notation. Before we can understand how the sentence makes use of logic or speech, it is useful to consider it as a separate entity.

A written sentence, with its conventions of spelling, syntax, and punctuation, is not merely a replica of speech, nor is it necessarily confined to a logical structure. But these negations point the way to a positive definition that sees the sentence as sharing something of the essence of writing. The sentence is a primary unit of writing whose purpose is to organize language and thought upon a page. It is also literary in the largest sense: people who speak carefully in complete sentences, especially sentences with hypotactic syntax, wish to appear literate by imitating written prose. The traditional metrical and phonemic patterns of poetry have an oral basis and offer an order addressed to the sense of hearing and the memory (this is Plato's argument in *The Republic*). The sentence, on the other hand, while it does contain rhythmic patterns, has at its core a visual bias.

Likewise, it is important to distinguish the sentence from the proposition. The sentence is not at base a model of a logical or grammatical structure but of a whole or complete literary unit. As such, its most pronounced and indeed defining element is the period. The period posits closure to a string of words; it asks us to regard the words between itself and the preceding period as a unit. Other punctuation marks within a sentence or in place of a period derive their operative character in relation to its full stop. The capital letter, for example, is felt as an insistent beginning to a sentence that overcomes the sense of completion just established by the preceding period.

As a result of this line of thought, a new definition of the sentence is now possible: *The sentence is a literary model of wholeness and completeness.*[19] It is literary instead of linguistic or philosophical. By literary one also means that it is a form of writing and thus primarily a visual rather than an aural means of organization. It is a model in the sense that it exists as a formal paradigm available to writers. It is not a form or genre; rather, it is inherent as a model, whether latent or active, within all literary structuring. A sentence is an ordered string of words with a beginning and an end evincing basic formal relations such as sequence, interdependence of elements, and closure.

Wholeness and *completeness* represent the two modes of order and closure available in a sentence. Though these terms verge on synonymy, I will set them into an opposition necessary for defining the complex intuition of pattern and form that underlies our use of the sentence. The contrary notions of wholeness and completeness can be employed to symbolize various meanings that the word "sentence" has acquired during its history; throughout the rest of this study, *wholeness* will represent organic, implicit, or generative forms of the sentence (often employing parataxis), and *completeness* will represent normative, explicit, or preconceived forms of the sentence (often exhibiting hypotaxis).

Let us say that the sentence enacts a plot. A hypotactic sentence fulfills our normal plot expectations: Whether it begins at the beginning or *in medias res* (for example, with a dependent clause), there is a logical connection and subordination among the grammatical elements of the sentence plot and an outcome in which the plot reaches a denouement or completion. Like any familiar plot, the hypotactic sentence can be dia-grammed hierarchically; it has a logical order. The plot of the paratactic sentence works by a continual sidewise displacement; its wholeness is dependent upon the fraternal bonds of a theoretically endless prolifera-tion of familial resemblances rather than the dynastic bonds of filiation. Thus the conscious sentence writer can subvert, deny, or replace the authority of the hypotactic sentence through the alogical plot and the aural structure of the paratactic sentence. Each of the three poets we will study in depth makes use of paratactic syntax as a way to investigate the relative priorities of wholeness and completeness.

The notion of completeness informs our common definition of the sentence as a "complete thought." This statement is a kind of folklore that measures the sentence against the assumed solidity of thought. As often in folklore this definition reverses the causal order of its terms: It would be more exact to say that since the sentence is a model of com-pleteness, we *call* the thought that it expresses a complete thought. Cer-tainly there is no other way to measure the completeness of, or even divide into discrete units, the highly problematic substance we call thought. But defining the sentence as a complete thought is not merely hopelessly naive; it does point to the public dimension of the sentence. To ask for a complete thought is to ask for a complete assertion, in which something is predicated. To *predicate* meant originally to proclaim, to state something in public. The notion of completeness implies a test of adequacy: Does this assertion meet the conditions of public discourse? We ask a sentence to be a definitive act in itself, as in the judicial sentence, which delivers the last word regarding a case, its resolution and fate.

This sense of completeness or definitiveness, of uttering an assertion that partakes of facticity or poses as the last word on a subject, is one of the primary lures of the sentence for poets writing prose. In the age of the Uncertainty Principle, when all assertions of truth or value are likely to be referred back to the highly relative aspect of their mediation, of how they are said, the sentence is the literary mode par excellence for a radical questioning of such notions as completeness and certainty and their bear-ing upon the representation of truth. The underlying issue raised by this kind of questioning is that of the proper relationship of language to being; Creeley's *Presences* and Ashbery's *Three Poems,* in particular, ad-dress this issue with remarkable insight and artistry. The sentence, as a measuring ground of the adequacy of language to assert or represent with respect to thought or experience, is a ready instrument for this type of questioning. We habitually employ it as our primary tool for grasping facts, for predicating public reality, and thus, in poet's prose the sentence itself becomes implicated in the very questions it asks.

The sentence as a tool of judgment, whether of facticity, completeness, or definitiveness, is a kind of measuring rod of thought and reality. From another perspective, though, we consider the sentence itself a way of thinking, not just as a measure of thoughts and facts. The sentence is active; it generates thoughts. If we follow the etymology of "sentence" back to Latin *sententia*, a way of thinking, an opinion, and from there to *sentire*, to feel, to sense, we see the sentence as a perceiving, generating entity. I have called this aspect of the sentence "wholeness" because the sentence proposes to generate and perceive within an intuition of a whole. The sentence is not a tool of random or disconnected language activity but a model of harmony or a gestalt. This is also the "sententious" aspect of the sentence, its aphoristic character, in which it stands on its own as an image of wholeness, as an analogizing statement. Such a sentence is sufficient unto itself; it disdains the argumentative ramifications of the paragraph in favor of the gnomic character of the aphorism, the maxim, the saying, the proverb, the moral.

As a way of thinking and an image of wholeness, the sentence is generative rather than (as in its aspect of completeness) normative, suggestive instead of definitive, inscriptive not prescriptive. For a writer such as Emerson, whom we shall soon treat, the promise the sentence makes of a structural harmony that lies at least as deep as the rapprochement of subject and object (in both the grammatical and the psychological sense) is a precondition for his deep faith that the words generated in his writing will "discover" the universal harmony. Similarly, for a modern sentence writer such as Williams or Faulkner, the intuitive apprehension of a wholeness inscribed by the sentence allows a seemingly endless freedom to extend the sentence, generating highly complex grammatical relationships that express the intimate movement of thought and perception.

Having developed our definition of the sentence as a literary model of wholeness and completeness, we must return for a moment to clarify the relationship of grammar and syntax to the sentence. Grammar (the way we use words) and syntax (the way words are put together, an aspect of grammar) belong, strictly speaking, to linguistics rather than to the study of sentences; they refer to language (with the genealogical bias towards speech) rather than writing. However, it would be ludicrous to try to separate language and writing in actuality. The words contained in the sentence and most of the relations among them are linguistic. Only the sentence itself is nonlinguistic. The sentence, then, stands as the paradigmatic meeting place of language and writing, where our use of words and our sense of literary wholeness and completeness come together in cooperation or in strife.

Classically, literate men and women endeavored to bring grammar and the sentence as closely into accord as possible. Greek and Latin, in

which our literary sentence developed, have colonized many other languages in the effort to subdue native grammars into forms amenable to
this sentence. The result has been a highly "literary," prescriptive grammar that attempts to extirpate the remnants of speech from a language
seeking to be written. Though Dante struggled heroically with the relationship of speech to writing, it was Wordsworth's intention of writing
"in a selection of language really used by men" that signaled the most
thoroughgoing reopening of this conflict. Eric Havelock, in *Preface to
Plato* (Cambridge, Mass: Harvard Univ. Press, 1963), argues that Plato,
as an advocate of the visual logic of hypotactic syntax, effected the initial
subjection of oral poetry to writing; by Wordsworth's time a sense was
growing that this subjection imposed a restrictive artificiality and a con-
sequent diminution of "natural wisdom" upon post-Classical Europe.
Echoing the democratic claims of the "natural man," poets following
Wordsworth have reopened the battle between speech and writing.

This aspect of the Romantic rebellion against Neoclassicism led directly to the American version of organic form. America presented fertile
ground for the development of an organic form, for both literary and
political reasons. Literarily, American poets have never approached the
accomplishment of their British counterparts in the persuasive and elegant use of traditional genres and forms. Politically, the Rousseauistic
character of American democracy shows itself in the instinctive American faith in the "natural" diction and syntax of vernacular speech. Walt
Whitman, a central proponent of this faith, proclaimed the seminal importance of slang in American thought about language and in American
poetry: "Slang, profoundly consider'd, is the lawless germinal element,
below all words and sentences, and behind all poetry, and proves a
certain perennial rankness and protestantism in speech."[20] Behind Whitman stands Emerson, whose centrality and poetic vision should have
made him the great American poet. Yet Emerson's great works are
written in a special form of prose that borders on but does not satisfy the
claims of theology and philosophy, a form that he and others called *prose
poetry*.[21]

Emerson located the battleground of speech and writing in the sentence rather than, as Wordsworth did, in traditional poetic form, and
thus he launched many later American poets into the species of organic
form that I will call *the generative sentence*. The generative sentence aban-
dons the normative aspect of completeness, often represented by hypotactic syntax, and instead follows the paratactic organization of speech
into an image of the sentence as whole. The generative sentence proceeds
by the method of *discovery*: forms and ideas are held to be at large in the
world (or inside the self) waiting to be discovered. This notion ultimately traces back to the American predilection for typological interpretation,

the tendency to see God at work in the world and nature as revelatory of his presence. The opposite attitude is that forms and ideas are willed and artificial organizers of inchoate experience which valiantly maintain a completeness that is wholly sufficient unto itself (see Poe's "The Philosophy of Composition"). In the nineteenth century Emerson is a point of focus and origin for the reentry of speech into sentences; Williams is a similar locus for the elaboration of the generative sentence in the twentieth century. Before returning to the sentences of *Kora in Hell*, let us look briefly at the influence of Emerson.

Two recent books devoted to Emerson's poetry locate his fullest poetic achievement in the prose of his essays. Both Hyatt Waggoner, in *Emerson as Poet* (Princeton: Princeton Univ. Press, 1974), and David Porter, in *Emerson and Literary Change* (Cambridge, Mass.: Harvard Univ. Press, 1978), agree that Emerson's essays ought to be read as poetic rather than strictly philosophical or religious statements in order to understand their impact and subsequent influence. When read in this way, Emerson's essays are, these writers claim, central to the emergence of modern American poetry. Porter sums up the fullest implications of Emerson's use of prose:

> Debilitated by closed poetry forms, Emerson's poetic sensibility required new possibilities of motion . . . Oratory was a crucial model since it demonstrated a powerful way by which a growing audience was forming its ideas and hearing its own voice, and thus seeing its world. Not less important was the private agony of Emerson the artist as he strove to integrate his imagination, experience, and voice. In seeking a radical reconciliation between experience and expression, undoing that old divorce, Emerson was led inevitably to a unique prosaic form, and thus he set about to pull down the prevailing distinctions between poetry and prose and, in the modernist way, between words themselves and action. (p. 159)

Porter makes reference to two central strands in American discourse that helped Emerson effect a new poetic prose – *oratory* and *meditation* ("private agony"). Both of these strands arose in Puritan New England. The obsession with individual salvation and its attendant compulsive self-questioning gave rise to the poetic meditations of Edward Taylor and the prose meditations of Jonathan Edwards. Though with a contrary goal – that of uniting a fundamentally antinomian group of individuals into a society by rhetorical means – oratory likewise became an important American genre, first in the form of the sermon and then in the political speech and the ubiquitous lecture. In these meditational and oratorical strands, united by the powerful example of Emerson, we can see two of the primary impulses leading into twentieth-century poet's prose.

The relationship of the self-dramatizing, self-questioning prose works we are studying to the meditation is not difficult to perceive. One might question, however, the influence of oratory upon such seemingly private works. Oratory makes it impact upon poet's prose by reasserting the value of speech and its generative effect. The combination of meditation with oratory affirms at a profound level the desire of American poets to raise the experience of the self to a communal expression in their prose. For Emerson, the oration provided a model of an organic form addressed to a specific moment; as a form it breaks through the classical proprieties of diction, of the sentence, and of literary genres. Emerson, anticipating the Ideogrammic Method of Ezra Pound or the Grand Collage of Robert Duncan, calls the oratorical form a *panharmonicon*. The panharmonicon provides an American parallel to Mallarmé's later championing of "individual execution" over the "general organs" of orthodoxy in "The Crisis of Verse."

> Here is all the true orator will ask, for here is a convertible audience & here are no stiff conventions that prescribe a method, a style, a limited quotation of books, & an exact respect to certain books, persons or opinions. No, here everything is admissible, philosophy, ethics, divinity, criticism, poetry, humor, fun, mimicry, anecdotes, jokes, ventriloquism . . . It is a panharmonicon . . . Here is a pulpit that makes other pulpits tame and ineffectual – with their cold, mechanical preparation for a delivery most decorous, – fine things, pretty things, wise things, but no arrows, no axes, no nectar, no growling, no transpiercing, no loving, no enchantment. Here he may lay himself out utterly, large, enormous, prodigal, on the subject of the hour. Here he may dare to hope for ecstasy & eloquence.[22]

A writing that tends toward the panharmonicon (some would call it pandemonium) is poles apart from the formal elegance, the willing submission of the mind to a preestablished order that plays such a large role in European poetry. The panharmonicon is a model of the generative sentence in that speech pushes against the formal bounds of writing and works counter to the tendency of the sentence toward completeness. Speech, as a motivating force, drives the writing onward, postponing endings for the sake of ever-renewed (paratactic) beginnings. Instead of speaking from the authority of an ideal or eternal time, Emerson's orator provides a model of the poet who speaks from the inherently risky moment of lived time, bringing to it a heightened attention to the act of composition. In the very prose that describes this type of writing, Emerson is already producing oratorical sentences that use parataxis and enumeration to counter the judicious completeness the traditional sentence favors:

> Here is a pulpit that makes other pulpits tame and ineffectual – with their cold, mechanical preparation for a delivery most decorous – fine things, pretty things, wise things, but no arrows, no axes, no nectar, no growling, no transpiercing, no loving, no enchantment.

At odds with the notion of completeness, the generative sentence is all the more dependent upon the notion of wholeness. Because this type of sentence chafes against its boundaries does not necessitate that it surrender its claim to wholeness. In fact such restlessness bespeaks Emerson's constant mental habit of analogy with which he intentionally crosses boundaries in search of a universal wholeness. Paradoxically this analogizing isolates rather than blends sentences, stressing an aphoristic instead of a logical or narrative quality. The sentence just quoted, with its restless paratactic syntax in which the dash yokes together successive thoughts, bears a striking resemblance to many of Williams's sentences in *Kora in Hell*; Emerson's sentences, like Williams's, tend to stand detached and isolated. However, because the sentences that make up Emerson's published essays were often drawn individually from notebooks covering a wide span of time, his essays do not usually preserve the sense of overall immediacy or simultaneity of Williams's improvisations. Emerson felt that his individual sentences were microcosmic statements with universal reverberations: When "words are signs of natural facts" and "nature is the symbol of spirit" (as he claims in *Nature*), then a sentence is a statement about relationships that contains a universal truth (an idea perpetuated by Ernest Fenollosa). This aphoristic and discontinuous quality in Emerson's sentences has been noted by F. O. Matthiessen:

> The sentence was his unit, as he recognized when confessing sadly to Carlyle (1838) that his paragraphs were only collections of "infinitely repellent particles." It is significant that he said the same thing when reflecting on society as "an imperfect union": "Every man is an infinitely repellent orb, and holds his individual being on that condition." The sentence was the inevitable unit for the man who could say, "A single thought has no limit to its value."[23]

The equation of organic form with the American political character is an apt way of expressing the dominance of wholeness over completeness in the sentences of Emerson and the poets who follow him. As a nation we have been impatient with the completeness of any order (for example, we keep amending our Constitution); our confidence lies rather in the ultimate perfectibility of man and in the notion that the true forms of the cosmos await discovery within, not imposition upon, the human mind. Poe makes the contrary assertion in "The Philosophy of Composition" – that a poem is an application of formal principles to produce an intended (though "indefinitive") effect. This assertion and the burlesque of poetic form characteristic of his poems act as a kind of reductio ad absurdum of the formalist stance in American poetry, making evident by contrary example the extent to which we bridle against rigid structures.

Whitman, relying upon "the lawless germinal element" of slang, continued and canonized this American rejection of the formal contract and its replacement by generative sentences that take their impetus from spoken language. He championed the struggle of speech to reassert itself within the sentence by allowing its ongoing, generative capacity to rule the long periodic sentences of his poetry. He saw this struggle as in its deepest sense the traditional American vindication of the spirit of the law over the killing letter. Whitman's approach unites literature with politics and religion: It projects the Puritan obsession with biblical hermeneutics onto the homologous American obsession with the rights of the individual as against the claims of the majority; it then applies these principles to poetic form:

> The Real Grammar will be that which declares itself a nucleus of the spirit of the laws, with liberty to all to carry out the spirit of the laws, even by violating them, if necessary. – The English Language is grandly lawless like the race who use it – or, rather, breaks out of the little laws to enter truly the higher ones. It is so instinct with that which underlies laws, and purports of laws, it refuses all petty interruptions in its way.[24]

To break out of the "little laws" of prescriptive grammar, grammar that conforms to the sentence as a literate model of completeness, Whitman proposes to discover the new, higher laws available to the writer of generative sentences; these transcendental laws express an intuition of the organic whole to be discovered simultaneously in language, the self, and reality. In the generative sentences of Whitman's poetry, the reader is witness to the writer's act of discovery; both attend upon the form that is constantly emerging instead of relying upon a form already in place by contract.

Taking the largest measure of American poetry, our greatest successes clearly lie in discovered or panharmonic forms. We are a nation of inventors rather than preservers (though the growing archival impulse threatens to counter that tendency),[25] voluble talkers more often than framers of le mot juste. This is especially true of the two extreme forms our poets have favored, the long poem and poet's prose. It is not difficult to think of many American long poems as extended lyceum lectures; the quirky combination of "philosophy, ethics, divinity, criticism, poetry, humor, fun, mimicry, jokes, ventriloquism" can be found not only in Whitman but in twentieth-century long poems such as Pound's *Cantos,* Eliot's *Waste Land,* Williams's *Paterson,* H. D.'s *Trilogy* and *Helen in Egypt,* Louis Zukofsky's *"A,"* Charles Olson's *Maximus,* Robert Duncan's *Passages,* Edward Dorn's *Gunslinger* and Robert Kelley's *The Loom.* The emphasis on receptive discovery is given an epistemological basis in a statement by Hyatt Waggoner that seems particularly applicable to poet's prose:

> Whitman . . . was taking a characteristically American stance when he said, "No one will get at my verses who insists on viewing them as a literary performance." American poets have typically been very little concerned with what may be called "literary" standards. They have been more concerned, that is, with "discovery" than with "performance" . . . American poets have faced the world armed chiefly with their innocence, their "not knowing." From the beginning, the most representative American poets have anticipated the characteristic that more than anything else distinguishes the American poetry of our own day from that of the past and of other societies: in it *nothing* is known, nothing given, everything is discovered or created, or else remains in doubt.[26]

THE "HEY-DING-DING TOUCH"

I must study my technique, as a Puritan did his Bible, because I cannot get at my emotions in any other way.

                                                                    Williams

With the generative sentence of Emerson and Whitman in mind, we are ready to look again at the sentences of Williams's *Kora in Hell,* which can be seen as a combination of the vernacular style of writers such as Whitman, Twain, and Stein with the improvisatory panharmonicon.[27] The issues expressed by the opposition of the complementary terms we have been examining – *wholeness/completeness, speech/literature,* and *generative/normative* - have a direct bearing upon the improvisations and beyond that the whole of Williams's oeuvre. The values I have described as "wholeness" represented for Williams both a goal and a method of composition, while values I have described as "completeness" represented a repressive style or attitude that threatened to inhibit the composition or frustrate the goal. Williams sought to further, both in and through his writing, an organic sense of wholeness over a preordained measure of completeness such as a metrical contract; he sought to elevate the grammar of speech to a position of formal strength comparable to the traditional metrical and stanzaic forms of literature; and he favored a generative aesthetic, based upon the imaginative fecundity of repeated beginnings, above a normative aesthetic based upon obedience to extrinsic rules. In short, the compositional paradigm I have called "the generative sentence" was a central principle informing his writing.

But what exactly can the generative sentence do as a compositional paradigm? Was Williams's use of it a success, and how can such success be measured? To answer these questions, we will first examine the contribution that the generative sentence makes to the emotional complexity of *Kora in Hell* and then investigate the prosodic function of syntax in the generative sentence and in Williams's verse. By their combination these two lines of inquiry will lead us to an understanding of the intimate relationship between form and content in Williams's prose.

Williams offers a first standard by which we may judge the efficacy and success of his employment of the generative sentence when he says, "I must study my technique, as a Puritan did his Bible, because I cannot get at my emotions in any other way." This admonition, delivered in 1919 (in an article containing a paragraph that also appears in the prologue to *Kora in Hell*), holds that the release or representation of hitherto inaccessible emotions is the end of technique. Williams acknowledges this as a difficult and deadly serious endeavor by invoking the Puritans in his simile. He had deeply ambivalent feelings towards the Puritans (see, for example, *In the American Grain* [1925; rpt. New York: New Directions, 1956] p. 63), and about the Puritan in himself, but his invocation of them here is meant to imbue this project of technical experimentation with the air of a sincere and ardent discipline and also with the sense that this work of discovery was of fundamental importance.

Williams felt so strongly the need for a technique that would reveal his emotions that he spent a major portion of the prologue to *Kora in Hell* defending this technique. He complains, for instance, that in traditional verse "the attention has been held too rigid on the one plane instead of following a more flexible, jagged resort. It is to loosen the attention . . . that I write these improvisations" (*Imaginations,* p. 14). A loosened attention, unfettered by the demand to complete logical and formal structures, escapes the habitual "lateral sliding" and becomes free to follow the momentary impulses that have a greater potential for revealing suppressed emotions. This reliance upon a "more flexible, jagged resort" places Williams at odds with Wallace Stevens, who insists, "Given a fixed point of view, realistic, imagistic or what you will, everything adjusts itself to that point of view . . . But to fidget with

points of view leads always to new beginnings and incessant new beginnings lead to sterility" (Stevens, as quoted by Williams, *Imaginations,* 15).
For Williams, the imperative is in the opposite direction: New beginnings are essential to the generative sentence; also, without continual
new beginnings Williams's poetry, he fears, would be without "true
value" and would lapse into a sentimental sterility. He knows himself
well enough at this point to understand that only by constant attention,
an incessant battering of his own defenses by a generative technique,
would an important and unique poetry arise from the pastiche of Keats,
Shakespeare, and Palgrave's anthology that make up his literary
background.

Marianne Moore, in an early review of *Kora in Hell,* argues against the
facile condemnation of Williams's sinewy prose as flat and formless. She
cites approvingly a statement he made in his own defense in the prologue
and then goes on to extol the daring with which Williams approaches his
technique:

> "The unready would deny tough cords to the wind because they
> cannot split a storm endwise and wrap it on spools." This state-
> ment exemplifies a part of what gives to the work of William
> Carlos Williams, "a character by itself." It is a concise, energetic
> disgust, a kind of intellectual hauteur which one usually associates
> with the French.[28]

It is remarkable that in addition to noting the intellectual integrity informing Williams's stance and associating it with the "tough cords" of
implicit wholeness that cause his generative sentences to cohere, Moore
also pinpoints the contribution of an "energetic disgust." For this emotion cooperates intimately with his technique and is the motivating spur
to his ever-renewed paratactic syntax.

Another of Williams's friends, the poet H. D., was less taken with his
"intellectual hauteur" than was Marianne Moore; to her it was anath-
ema. In 1916 Williams sent a poem to H. D., "Song of the Year," that
she edited, retitled "March," and published in *The Egoist.*[29] In notifying
Williams of the deletions she has made, she refers to a stylistic outgrowth
of the emotion praised by Moore, a stylistic feature that Williams later (in
the prologue to *Kora in Hell*) claimed was "the prototype of the improvisations." She calls it "the hey-ding-ding touch," after a refrain in
Williams's poem:

> I feel in the hey-ding-ding touch running through your poem a
> derivative tendency which, to me, is not *you* – not your very self. It
> is as if you were *ashamed* of your Spirit, ashamed of your inspira-
> tion! – as if you mocked your own song. It's very well to *mock* at

yourself – it is a spiritual sin to mock at your inspiration. (*Imagina-tions*, 13)

Fortunately, "Song of the Year," though unpublished in its original form, is preserved in the Poetry Collection at the State University of New York at Buffalo. The manuscript contains Williams's typescript, H. D.'s corrections, and Williams's recorrections (mostly in the form of heavily underlined explosions of "*STET!*").[30] The poem was published substantially as H. D. revised it at about half its original length. For readers concerned with the development of Williams's writing, the whole of "Song of the Year" bears careful scrutiny, but for our present purposes the first two stanzas of the original poem will suffice:

> Winter is long in this climate
> and spring – a matter of a few days
> only, – a flower or two picked
> from mud or from among wet leaves
> or at best against treacherous
> bitterness of wind, and sky shining
> teasingly, then closing in black
> and sudden, with fierce jaws.
>
> Precarious pretty flowers of
>   spring
> then hey–ding–a–ding!
> God damn winter the more heartily.
> I'm your companion! Then since
> neither of us need shine alone
> – now that we have me – why,
>   Hey–ding–a–ling!
> (now we mock convention)
> Winter has lost his sting
>   his sting!
> (one might equally well say
>   his stink!
> Have we spoilt that first
> fine stanza sufficiently?)

The first stanza begins the published version of the poem; the second stanza, and the other lines and stanzas throughout the poem in the same cocky but self-deprecatory tone, H. D. eliminated. The second stanza is, as she rightly asserts, both derivative and mocking, and beneath the mockery its writer does seem ashamed. The angry, disputatious "jagged resort" offended H. D.'s at that time imagist sensibilities, and as some-one for whom the mocking voice posed a direct and lasting threat to her

ability to write, H. D. felt it necessary to warn Williams of the debilitating effects of such a technique.[31] But Williams, though he agreed with
H. D.'s assessment of the poem and ultimately accepted many of her
corrections, felt that this mockery arose from an authentic impulse: "The
hey-ding-ding touch *was* derivative, but it filled a gap that I did not
know how better to fill at the time. It might be said that that touch is the
prototype of the improvisations" (*Imaginations*, p. 13). There is truth in
this assertion not only because the hey-ding-ding touch operates to dis-
joint the discourse and foreground many poetic practices for the purpose
of ridicule but also because as a technique it gives vent to Williams's
petulance and disgust, the somewhat distasteful but absolutely integral
feelings and attitudes informing both *Kora in Hell* and his own life.

In a letter written in 1920 to his eccentric friend the poet Alva Turner
in reply to Turner's remarks on the newly published *Kora in Hell,*
Williams states, "Disgust is my most moving emotion. Sometimes I
wish it were otherwise, but it is not, so an end of it." The letter ends with
a striking image: "I am always, unhappily, knee deep in blue mud."[32] As
his "most moving emotion," disgust is not what initially sinks him in
depression but rather what arises out of the blue mud and makes possible
the eruption of further emotions. To use the language of boxing, one
could say that Williams leads with his aversion: It is his most capable
defensive punch and also the leading jab of his offense. Whenever he
meets a force that affronts or opposes his own (T. S. Eliot, for instance),
Williams thrusts forth this emotion. Countless times in the *Autobiography*
his disgust breaks into a scene he is recounting, forcing up the taste of
remembered bitterness. His tales of trips to Europe (as an adult) are
especially filled with explosions of bitterness and repugnance at the
worlds of art, literature, and fashion. And yet those travels, which he
recounts in a detail disproportionate to their duration (with respect to the
rest of his life), were germinal for his thinking about and experimenting
with technique. The same pattern is evident in his periodic visits to
Manhattan or the artists' colony at Grantwood: As a sensitive outsider,
Williams continually felt slighted or humiliated by the artists, writers,
and society people he admired; his revenge took the form of a disdainful
hauteur that allowed him to adapt the technical innovations or theories
that excited him without feeling he was copying.

The emotional complex revolving around feelings of disgust is intimately bound up with Williams's technique, and not only as a defense
that allows him to incorporate the gains of others. There is a more
positive sense in which disgust is his most moving emotion: Its entry
into his writing signals the breaking out of a state of repression or depression, of blue mud, so that now other emotions are free to spill forth. The
emotion of disgust provides the generative force in many of Williams's

sentences. Having reached the point of repugnance or self-deprecation, he lets go. Why hold back any longer the impulses that threaten to disrupt the orderly discourse? It no longer matters. With disgust leading the way, divers suppressed emotions arise to consciousness and take form in the sentence. This produces a text of remarkable richness, which has a complexity of feeling and thought unattainable, with such economy, in writing that bows to the normative aspect of the sentence: "Here," as Emerson says, "he may lay himself out utterly."

The second improvisation in Chapter V of *Kora in Hell* illustrates beautifully how technique and emotion converge and how the eruption of disgust drives the sentences onward to discoveries of a compelling density and richness:

V.2

It is the water we drink. It bubbles under every hill. How? Agh, you stop short of the root. Why, caught and the town goes mad. The haggard husband pirouettes in tights. The wolf-lean wife is rolling butter pats: it's a clock striking the hour. Pshaw, they do things better in Bangkok, – here too, if there's heads together. But   up and leap at her throat! Bed's at fault! Yet – I've seen three women prostrate, hands twisted in each other's hair, teeth buried where the hold offered, – not a movement, not a cry more than a low meowling. Oh call me a lady and think you've caged me. Hell's loose every minute, you hear? And the truth is there's not an eye clapped to   either way   but someone comes off the dirtier for it. Who am I to wash hands and stand near the wall? I confess freely there's not a bitch littered in the pound but my skin grows ruddier. Ask and I'll say: curfew for the ladies. Bah, two in the grass is the answer to that gesture. Here's a text for you: Many daughters have done virtuously but thou excellest them all! And so you do, if the manner of a walk means anything. You walk in a different air from the others, – though your husband's the better man   and the charm won't last a fortnight: the street's kiss parried again. But give thought to your daughters' food at mating time, you good men. Send them to hunt spring beauties beneath the sod this winter, – otherwise: hats off to the lady! One can afford to smile.   (*Imaginations,* 39)

The improvisation opens with two declarative sentences. It is true that we are completely uninformed about the referent for the pronoun "it," but the declarative intent of the sentences seems straightforward enough. Next we have a rhetorical question, which, instead of impelling the

seeming narrator to a further disclosure of the workings of the mysterious water, prompts the intrusion of a contradictory voice that utters an
exclamation of antipathy, "agh," and then begins to accuse the first voice
of insufficiently penetrating to, or else concealing, the root of the matter.
The emergence of this second voice, this voice of disdain, signals the
entrance of a Bacchic madness into the improvisation. As we have seen,
throughout *Kora in Hell* the ancient gods reassert their sway in contemporary scenes: "The gods, the Greek gods, smothered in filth and igno-
rance . . . Do they dance now, they that danced beside Helicon? They
dance much as they did then, only, few have an eye for it, through the
dirt and fumes" (*Imaginations*, 60–1). The question "Do they dance now,
they that danced beside Helicon?" might easily have been uttered by
Williams's friend and mentor Ezra Pound, but whereas the gods in *The
Cantos* tend toward an Apollonian manifestation of light (even, for instance, in Canto XVII, with the watery light of Zagreus), Williams
invokes Dionysian gods with roots in the earth. Here, the whole town, a
modern Thebes, is driven mad; a tired husband is metamorphosed into
the transvestite Pentheus, his wife into a menacing maenad. At this point
we can return to the opening sentences, where it becomes evident that
the mysterious "it" stands for something like the mysterious id and that
the water is the wine of desire.

In this improvisation, disgust (especially notable in the exclamations
"agh," "pshaw," and "bah") breaks the metaphorical enclosure around
desire and forces it into the open. The metaphorical continuity of the first
two sentences, in which desire is enclosed in the image of water, is
broken, following the exclamation of antipathy, by a new image of
roots. If Williams had wanted to maintain metaphorical consistency, he
might have directed us to an artesian pool rather than a root, as the
source of the water of desire. The striking (and ever-changing) images of
nearly the first half of the improvisation all suggest desire entrapped, but
the discontinuous clauses, prodded by the disdain evident in the vernacular constructions, keep pressing forth more and more frenzied images
until finally "Hell's loose every minute." Desire erupts onto the earth in
its full Dionysian sovereignty. First all vision is colored by desire ("not
an eye clapped to . . . but someone comes off the dirtier"), then all
conduct ("Who am I to wash hands and stand near the wall?"), and
finally the full, unrepressed, animalian sexuality pushes into the light ("I
confess there's not a bitch littered in the pound but my skin grows
ruddier").

If the phrase "Kora in Hell" can be read as "desire repressed," then
oddly enough it is disgust that functions as the liberating force. We most
often think of disgust as a psychological defense, similar in function to
boredom or frustration. These latter conditions usually signal some emo-

tion or clash of emotions that the ego wishes to keep from consciousness. In the case of Williams, whose puritanical nature we have noted, his repugnance operated in an inverse fashion, countering an initial defensiveness toward desire: having colored desire with his disapproval, Williams then felt free to throw aside propriety and allow the true impulses to emerge and guide his phrasing. We go too far, however, if we imagine this as a process of ultimate liberation. The improvisation tells us that desire must still be inhibited from full expression in life: "the street's kiss parried again." What this process does accomplish is the evocation of a series of powerful images that charge the entire body of Williams's writing: the haggard husband pirouetting in tights, the wolf-lean wife rolling butter pats, the three women locked in combat, the woman who walks with a different air, the street's kiss, the hunting of spring beauties (as Kora does) beneath the sod, all of these images could be traced through repeated manifestations in Williams's poetry and prose.

In this improvisation the technique and the antipathies attend insistently to the underlying emotions and spur Williams to allow the forbidden impulses to reach expression. Williams demanded of his technique that it be a constant goad, hoping that the darker emotions beneath his perceptions would thus emerge. For his courage in persisting through the often embarrassing outbreaks of aversion (such as the hey-ding-ding touch) in order to arrive at deeper emotions, Williams was rewarded by a poetry in which emotion and technique cooperate, each closely attuned to and ready to follow the promptings of the other. As he confesses in the commentary to this improvisation:

> By the brokenness of his composition the poet makes himself master of a certain weapon which he could possess himself of in no other way. The speed of the emotions is such that thrashing about in a thin exaltation or despair many matters are touched but not held, more often broken by contact. (Imaginations, 16)

This commentary, instead of following the improvisation directly as most of the commentaries do, occurs among a block of commentaries in the prologue. The commentaries function in two ways, both as "explanation, often more dense than the first writing" (Imaginations, 29), and as polemic for an aesthetic position. Williams asserts the radical nature of Kora in Hell by displaying his innovative ideas as arising directly from his poetry. The improvisations are thus situated in a hotly contested terrain of truth claims, and, conversely, the polemic is given credence by its seeming derivation from the poetry. Although the improvisations clearly assume primacy in Kora in Hell, the prologue and commentaries are manifestly integral to the book's intent and effect, for Williams makes strenuous metaphysical and, especially, epistemological claims in this book, that he chooses to articulate in a critical prose.

The importance of explanatory and polemical prose in American poetry is a further expression of the crisis of verse. Not surprisingly, the strong desire of American poets to justify and make a place for their poetry leads to repeated resort to manifestos and critical prose. As a consequence we take it as a matter of course to study with as much care the statements as the poetry of American poets. The statements seem to make possible the very grounds for the occurrence of the poetry, staking out for it political, philosophical, and religious territory to an extent far beyond the needs of European poetry. It is hard to imagine American poetry without this critical prose, even the poetry in imagist and objectivist modes whose statements argue (ironically) the absolute quality of poetry. Think, for example, of the importance of Emerson's "The Poet"; Poe's "Philosophy of Composition" and "Poetic Principle"; Whitman's 1855 preface to *Leaves of Grass* and "A Backward Glance"; Pound's many prose texts, such as "A Retrospect," "Cavalcanti," his Fenollosa and *ABC of Reading;* Williams's *Spring and All,* "The Poem as a Field of Action," and "On Measure"; Stevens's *Necessary Angel* and "Adagia"; Eliot's "Tradition and the Individual Talent," "*Hamlet,*" and "The Metaphysical Poets"; and Olson's "Projective Verse" and "Human Universe." An interesting corollary to these prose statements appears in the propositional and sometimes didactic verse of Whitman, Pound, Williams, Stevens, Eliot, Olson, George Oppen, Gary Snyder, William Bronk, and Edward Dorn, among others. Though most of these poets have some association with Imagism or Objectivism, with their oft-repeated injunctions against abstractions and generalization, it seems that in practice the discursive impulse vies with or complements the imagistic one.[33] In the case of poet's prose, the poets who follow Williams have welcomed propositional sentences into their prose, often integrating critical and polemical functions into the poetry.

To complete the investigation of how Williams's technique reveals and expresses emotions, let us look a little more carefully at his prosody. In poet's prose, syntax replaces meter as the basic prosodic determinant; logically this is a consequence of having the sentence rather than the verse line as the basic compositional unit. A sentence demands various kinds of syntactic fulfillment along avenues as codified as (if not more so than) those exacted by the meter of a line. And as meanings particular to poetry arise in verse through the coincidence of a word with a prosodic emphasis (such as placement following a caesura or at the end of a line, or the variation of a meter to fit the natural pronunciation of a word), likewise in poet's prose the coincidence of a word with a grammatical emphasis (usually through the foregrounding of a syntactic practice or the absence of an expected syntactic element) produces what we perceive as poetic meanings in the prose. The special excellence of this prose resides in its ability to produce the heightened experience of language we expect from poetry by making use of the formal patterns of syntax (whether of the generative or normative varieties). It thus works with constraints more deeply embedded in the structure of language and the text making of writing than the metrical constraints that have traditionally bound poetry.[34]

Once this prosodic difference between prose and verse poetry is offered, one must immediately dispel a possible misunderstanding. It is not correct simply to differentiate the two poetries by saying that the former is structured exclusively by syntax, the latter by meter. As Donald Davie has shown through subtle and persuasive argument, syntax is a highly active, crucial element in the composition of verse. Davie argues, in *Articulate Energy* (London: Routledge & Kegan Paul, 1955), that syntax is the "backbone" of poetry; though a poet may choose various methods of employing syntax his poetry cannot "stand up" without a considered use of its resources. We can extend Davie's insight in the opposite direction if we acknowledge that prose qua poetry is still (as Pound would say) "charged language"; as such it evidences (whether accidentally or by calculation) the same rhythmic underpinnings that tend to emerge in any situation in which language becomes charged, from emotional outbursts to oratory, argument, prayer, song, or poetry. Poet's prose, whether in the more highly marked form of the prose poem of Baudelaire and Rimbaud or in the generically more ambiguous forms, is usually as amenable to a sensitive metrical analysis as verse is to the revealing syntactical analysis Donald Davie performs. To take the most ready example: Much of the force of the quizzical exclamation "Beautiful white corpse of night actually!" is a function of its emphatic rhythm and internal rhyming. Though the accents fall in an irregular pattern at first glance,

Béautiful whíte córpse of níght áctually!

the rhyming of "white" with "night" and partial rhyming of "beautiful" with "actually" suggests an underlying symmetry that guides our pronunciation toward a dactyllic foot with closure of its normally open end: $/ \smile \smile /$. If we scan the sentence in this manner, we have three feet, "Beautiful white / corpse of night / actually!," with an elided unstressed syllable in "corpse" and a final accent (provided to some extent by the exclamation point) placed on the last syllable of "actually!"

If we establish the sentence as the basic compositional unit of poet's prose (structured fundamentally by syntax, though not to the exclusion of meter), we can begin to contrast it to the line (structured fundamentally by meter, though not to the exclusion of syntax) as the compositional unit of verse. To do so let us look first at a poem by Williams from *Sour Grapes,* the book following *Kora in Hell.* "The Late Singer" (the opening poem) is roughly contemporaneous with the improvisations and was first published in *The Egoist* (July 1919):

> *The Late Singer*
>
> Here it is spring again
> and I still a young man!
> I am late at my singing.
> The sparrow with the black rain on his breast
> has been at his cadenzas for two weeks past:
> What is it that is dragging at my heart?
> The grass by the back door
> is stiff with sap.
> The old maples are opening
> their branches of brown and yellow moth-flowers.
> A moon hangs in the blue
> in the early afternoons over the marshes.
> I am late at my singing.[35]

This is a slight poem, whose tone of nostalgic lateness is about to pass out of Williams's repertoire, to be replaced more often than not by a tone of urgent earliness. But let us detach three of the more interesting lines from this poem to see how they work metrically:

> The spárrow with the bláck ráin on his bréast
> has béen at his cadénzas for twó weeks pást:
> What ís it that is drágging at my héart?

I have marked the dominant stresses as I hear them in the lines, making a pattern of 4/4/3. In each line the first stress follows an unaccented initial syllable, and the last stress falls on the last syllable. The third line makes it clear that the underlying foot is a kind of elongated (four-syllable) anapest, which also appears in the first two lines. Stuffing an extra syllable into the foot makes the verse sound more colloquial, but the number of syllables per line (10/11/10) and the meter remain fairly constant.

How does this verse form function as a technique for revealing emotions? The key words in this passage, emphasized by meter and near rhyme, are "breast," "past," and "heart." Certainly there is no surprise in finding these three words associated by the rhyme scheme: "breast" and "heart" are here synonymous, and "past" introduces rather complacently the feeling of nostalgia. The most pleasing aspect of this banal rhyming resides in the progressive opening of the vocalics, from e to ă to ä. But this vocalic opening does not mimic a corresponding emotional dilation, and the technique as a whole does little to forward the poet's discovery or expression. The verse line seems on the contrary to enforce a containment of emotion; in Williams's hands little is gained from the tension of this containment. I am not suggesting that containment itself hampers poetic expression but rather that Williams's ability to make use of the poetic possibilities inherent in the prosody of the verse line was undistinguished at this time.

If we turn to an improvisation in *Kora in Hell,* on the other hand, and perceive the constantly innovative syntax Williams employs and its aptness to the lively feelings and diction, we see how congenial the generative sentence was as a compositional paradigm for Williams. By raising expectations of syntactic rather than metrical fulfillment (or other parallel constructions offered by verse), Williams keeps his attention and ours in a constant state of discovery, always on the alert for the grammatical indicators of the relation of one notion to another. We have already examined, for instance, the way the conjunctions in improvisation V.1 arouse certain unfulfilled possibilities of subordination and also act to propel us into the ensuing sentence. Likewise the indefinite reference of pronouns in sentences like "it is the water we drink" (Who drinks what?) keeps one constantly testing other nouns in the vicinity in hopes of locating a referent.

By way of contrast with "The Late Singer," let us look more closely at a sentence from improvisation V.2. The final sentences of the improvisation, the reader will recall, run as follows:

> Here's a text for you: Many daughters have done virtuously but thou excellest them all! And so you do, if the manner of a walk means anything. You walk in a different air from the others, – though your husband's the better man   and the charm won't last a fortnight: the street's kiss parried again. But give thought to your daughters' food at mating time, you good men. Send them to hunt spring beauties beneath the sod this winter, – otherwise: hats off to the lady! One can afford to smile.

Notice first how each sentence stands as a separate unit, beneath even the propellant conjunctions. We can never be sure, from one sentence to the next, whether we are still on the same level of discourse or whether the grammatical indicators really do refer back and forth in the normal way. By the time we reach the third sentence, for example, and are confronted with the third "you," it is not at all certain that this pronoun refers to the same person called "you" in the second sentence, and there's clearly no relation to the "you" in the first sentence (although "thou" could relate to the second "you"). In each sentence the speaker is engaged in dramatic conversation with some interlocutor, but we cannot assume that the person addressed or any of the other characteristics of a dramatic situation hold constant from sentence to sentence.

The third sentence is a particularly striking example of a generative sentence operating under the aegis of wholeness:

> You walk in a different air from the others, – though your husband's the better man   and the charm won't last a fortnight: the street's kiss parried again.

In one swiftly moving sentence we have the entire course of a fantasized affair and the refusal to enact it. The sentence is made up of an independent clause, a dependent clause, a coordinate clause, and another independent clause, but the actual relationship between any of the clauses is always more potential than certain, and thus the syntax is effectively paratactic. The gestures toward subordination and even coordination are imitative of mental reflexes rather than logical connections. These hints of syntactic fastening help to signal the rapidly changing emotions that the sentence chronicles: "Though" indicates hesitancy and self-doubt, while "and" mimics the onset of the panicky logic of someone who has declined to act through fear and then begins to pile up rationalizations.

The nuances of tone achieved in this sentence render gross and hackneyed the verse lines about the bird's cadenza and the poet's heart. When Williams began to work poetically with sentences in the writing of *Kora in Hell,* he discovered the basis for a technique with much greater resources for eliciting and recording emotion than he was able to command in his verse. As he said in reference to *Kora in Hell* (and I assume to its generative sentences), "I had envisaged a new form of poetic composition, a form for the future" (*IWWP,* 30). It may be only now, sixty years later, that we are able to fully give this new form its due, but it was of tremendous consequence for Williams's own writing, and it led to two of his most important stylistic achievements. The first is the organic prose style that infuses all of his prose after *Kora in Hell,* from the experimental texts like *Spring and All* and *In the American Grain* to his works of fiction and even his essays, with the fluidity and syntactic playfulness of the speech-oriented improvisations. Second, and maybe even more important, Williams incorporated into his verse the invigorating use of syntax that the new form taught him. The characteristic toughness of the lines of Williams's subsequent verse is the product of his new facility with syntax, the form of the poem deriving primarily from syntax rather than meter. For example, many of Williams's most memorable poems, such as "The Red Wheelbarrow," "The Young Sycamore," and "Poem" ("As the cat . . ."), consist of a single sentence (or

sentence fragment) that requires the kind of word-by-word care we gave
to the fragment "Beautiful white corpse of night actually!" and that is
structured as a poem by the syntactic tension among words and phrases.

As a single example of the effect of the new form upon Williams's
verse, consider the last poem from *Sour Grapes* (1921):

> *The Great Figure*
>
> Among the rain
> and lights
> I saw the figure 5
> in gold
> on a red
> firetruck
> moving
> tense
> unheeded
> to gong clangs
> siren howls
> and wheels rumbling
> through the dark city.[36]

The poem is a single complex sentence that achieves its form through
tensions created by syntactic relationships. The lines are composed under
no obvious metrical or rhyming arrangement; they take their shape
rather from a syntactic mimesis of the epiphanic vision described. The
simplest sentence, and thus the simplest description of the scene de-
picted, to which the poem can be reduced would read: "I saw the figure 5
moving through the dark city." Upon this simple chassis words and
phrases shift in grammatical weight like the flexible sections of a fire
engine flashing past.

The poem begins as though slightly off balance by giving pride of
place to a prepositional phrase rather than the main clause. "Among the
rain / and lights" is important for locating "I saw the figure 5" in a
mimetic sense, but syntactically it produces a certain tension and anticipation, since we are unsure what to focus on "among the rain and
lights." Throughout the poem Williams plays with this disarrangement
of the relative weights in a hypotactic sentence. For example, we arrive at
the beginning of the most important modifying phrase ("moving") four
lines beyond the main clause, and this modifying phrase is extended and
deferred completion until the last line of the poem. The intervening
words and phrases create an anticipatory tension that seeks a syntactic
fulfillment; this can be compared, somewhat roughly, to the anticipation
of the delayed rhyme in an ABBA rhyme scheme.

The words and phrases that delay this fulfillment, however, are far from neutral elements taking up space. They are like highly reactive ions that begin to work on the grammatical compounds surrounding them. Though the word "moving" is part of the primary sentence that underlies the poem, by its placement in a line between "firetruck" and "tense" it begins to form two other molecules: it works as a participle modifying the fast-moving "firetruck" and is modified in turn by the emotive indicator "tense." The word "rumbling" performs a similar operation, threatening to appropriate to itself the last line of the poem, which is a prepositional phrase orbiting primarily around the participle "moving." Syntactic links are coupled and uncoupled throughout this poem to create a constant syntactical tension and a subtle foregrounding of grammatical relationships.

Our discussion of "The Great Figure" has brought us full circle to the subject of the tactile quality of words. To a large extent the felt presence of any individual word derives from its potentiality for grammatical combination.[37] This tension between the presence of the individual word and the process of grammatical structuring informs all of the poet's prose read in depth in this study. And the sentence is an appropriate location for this interplay between horizontal and vertical elements. As the most basic written field in which our endlessly generative language finds its presentation, the sentence is a fertile matrix where the "vertical project" of the word, the prosodic capacities of syntax, and the literary qualities of wholeness and completeness meet and seek a form.

To understand the distance Williams has come from the generic prose poem by his use of the generative sentence, let us keep in mind improvisations V.1 and V.2 and compare them briefly with a two-part prose poem by Robert Bly (1969).

The Dead Seal near McClure's Beach

I.

Walking north toward the point, I come on a dead seal. From a few feet away, he looks like a brown log. The body is on its back, dead only a few hours. I stand and look at him. A quiver in the dead flesh. My God he is still alive. A shock goes through me, as if a wall of my room had fallen away.

His head is arched back, the small eyes closed, the whiskers sometimes rise and fall. He is dying. This is the oil. Here on its back is the oil that heats our houses so efficiently. Wind blows fine sand back toward the ocean. The flipper near me lies folded over the stomach, looking like an unfinished arm, lightly glazed with sand at the edges. The other flipper lies half underneath.

The seal's skin looks like an old overcoat, scratched here and there . . . by sharp mussels maybe . . .

I reach out and touch him. Suddenly he rears up, turns over. He gives three cries, like those from Christmas toys. He lunges toward me. I am terrified and leap back, although I know there can be no teeth in that jaw. He starts flopping toward the sea. But he falls over, on his face. He does not want to go back to the sea. He looks up at the sky, and he looks like an old lady who has lost her hair.

He puts his chin back down on the sand, arranges his flippers, and waits for me to go. I go.

2.

Today I go back to say goodbye; he's dead now. But he's not – he's a quarter mile farther up the shore. Today he is thinner, squatting on his stomach, head out. The ribs show more – each vertebra on the back under the coat now visible, shiny. He breathes in and out.

He raises himself up, and tucks his flippers under, as if to keep them warm. A wave comes in, touches his nose. He turns and looks at me – the eyes slanted, the crown of his head like a leather jacket. He is taking a long time to die. The whiskers white as porcupine quills, the forehead slopes, goodbye brother, die in the sound of waves, forgive us if we have killed you, long live your race, your innertube race, so uncomfortable on land, so comfortable in the sea. Be comfortable in death then, where the sand will be out of your nostrils, and you can swim in long loops through the pure death, ducking under as assassinations break above you. You don't want to be touched by me. I climb the cliff and go home the other way.[38]

This sentimental poem stands squarely in the tradition of Aloysius Bertrand's imaginary Flemish paintings in *Gaspard de la nuit* (1842) and Baudelaire's fantasies of the city, such as the following fragment:

Above the wave-crests of the rooftops across the way I can see a middle-aged woman, face already wrinkled – a poor woman forever bending over something, who never seems to leave her room. From just her face and her dress, from practically nothing at all, I've recreated this woman's story, or rather her legend; and sometimes I weep while reciting it to myself.[39]

For neither Bly nor Baudelaire is the technique necessary for "getting at" the emotions; the emotions in the poems have already congealed into attitudes that the prose merely sets forth. Against the tense and turbulent syntax of Williams's improvisations, the texts above seem to plod in their description and meditation. Bly adds figurative language to his prose mainly by the inclusion of simple similes: "as if a wall of my room had fallen away," "like an unfinished arm," "like an old overcoat, scratched here and there," "like those from Christmas toys," and "like an old lady who has lost her hair." This is a far cry from the dense play of figures we have discussed in Williams's two improvisations. Bly evinces the American character of his poet's prose by a concern with the objective world, a concern vitiated though by a doctrinaire ecological stance and an imperfectly realized Lawrentian relation to the seal.

The different intensities of their respective investigations of incidents from daily life most clearly distinguishes Williams's prose from Bly's. Although a strain of didacticism runs through each writer's prose, the message of "The Dead Seal" is bald (partially attributable to the incredulous tone) and overstated ("He is taking a long time to die"), giving neither the writer nor the reader impetus for discovery. Williams, on the other hand, draws a moral, often in an oracular voice, and then proceeds to question its pertinence to lived experience. "Here's a text for you," he offers: "Many daughters have done virtuously but thou excellest them all! And so you do, if the manner of a walk means anything." Williams undercuts the pious pronouncement of the first sentence by the innuendo of the second and then submits this already ironic situation to the interrogation of experience in the next sentence about the fantasized affair. Where in these three sentences, one wonders, does the investigation of discourse leave off and the representation of experience begin? Out of a seemingly idle playing with words arises a memorable moment of emotion grasped by an active understanding. To answer the question just posed, there is no discrete break between the playful awareness of language as an arbitrary medium of communication and the serious investigation of the nature of experience. Rather than a poet's prose that comments upon the world, such as that of Bly or Baudelaire, the generative sentence fosters an engagement with language as part of an active attempt at understanding the self and the world; in this poet's prose, as in great works of verse, language interpenetrates experience and understanding.

Chapter 2

"A LIFE TRACKING ITSELF": ROBERT CREELEY'S *PRESENCES: A TEXT FOR MARISOL*

A CONJECTURAL PROSE

Beyond humor, Tristram Shandy *is the narrative of one man's attentions, of what they found to fasten on. That is a defensible comment – there is very clear writing in this book.*

Creeley

Robert Creeley praises *Tristram Shandy* in the context of a review of John Hawkes's *The Beetle Leg* called "How To Write a Novel."[1] The digressive style of *Tristram Shandy* attracts American writers such as Creeley and Hawkes for a number of reasons "beyond humor" and satire; Sterne's writing shares the concern with disposing the relative claims of wholeness and completeness at both the narrative and the sentence levels. In American literature we find the digressive narrative in Thoreau, for example, who proposes in "Walking" a physical and intellectual method he calls "sauntering," a ruminative, meditational stroll, that gives the walker a free rein, enabling one thereby to discover natural law.[2] Narrative digression is also a natural counterpart to the generative sentence, where, as we have seen, grammar leads the writing through a succession of ideas, resisting the gravitational pull of the "complete thought."

There is a second aspect of the digressive narrative found in *Tristram Shandy* that has especially captivated twentieth-century American writers. When Sterne's attention wanders from the so-called plot of his novel, it often "fastens on" a discussion of language or an interrogation of the relationship of language to reality:

The verbs auxiliary we are concerned in here, continued my father, are am; was; have; had; do; did; could; owe; make; made; suffer; shall; should; will; would; can; ought; used; or is wont . . . – or with these questions added to them; – Is it? Was it? Will it be? . . . Or affirmatively . . . – Or chronologically . . . – Or hypo-

thetically . . . – If it was? If it was not? What would follow? – If
the French beat the English? If the Sun should go out of the Zodiac?

This is from Chapter 43 of Volume 5 of *Tristram Shandy* as quoted by
William Carlos Williams in an essay. Williams goes on to give nearly the
entire chapter, which embodies these grammatical lessons in a series of
propositions delivered by Corporal Trim concerning a white bear:
"Would I had seen a white bear! (for how can I imagine it?)." Williams
quotes extensively from and analyzes the prose of Laurence Sterne in
order to demonstrate a point regarding the work of Gertrude Stein: "It
would not be too much to say that Stein's development over a lifetime is
anticipated completely with regard to subject matter, sense and grammar
– in Sterne" (*Imaginations*, 348).

   Northrop Frye has influenced our reading of *Tristram Shandy* by clas-
sifying it as an anatomical novel. We must be careful not to assume that
Creeley, in his comment on the novel, is invoking as a generic precedent
the whole anatomical tradition assembled by Frye, which contains writers such as Petronius, Apuleius, Rabelais, Burton, Swift, and Voltaire.[3]
Creeley is more likely affirming the panharmonic and linguistic preoccupations of his twentieth-century American predecessors such as Stein,
Williams, and Zukofsky. These preoccupations, as Creeley inherits
them, include primarily the generative sentence and the interrogation of
language. What interests none of these American writers but is of vast
importance to the anatomy (and to postmodern fiction) is the parody of
erudition (the humor Creeley wishes to go beyond); American poets in
the Emersonian tradition take much less delight in the hall of mirrors of
intertextual reflections. While previous writers and texts may well be
influences (in Harold Bloom's or anyone else's sense) upon American
poets, the anatomical obsession with past literature seldom appears on
the surface in the Emersonian tradition, except in the case of works like
Walden, where anatomical mock pedantry is replaced by the panharmonic quotation of texts for oratorical effect. In his introduction to the
Riverside edition of *Tristram Shandy* (Boston: Houghton Mifflin, 1965),
Ian Watt notes the qualities of Sterne's prose that would make it attractive to a writer of generative sentences such as Williams: "The manner is
conversational in tone; its diction and syntax are colloquial; we have the
sense not of measured words or pondered clauses but of rapid living
speech" (xxvi). Creeley, as we shall see, takes this generative sentence
and combines it with the Shandean investigation of language such as
Stein performs.[4] By joining the generative sentence inherited from
Williams with a sensitivity acutely attuned to the way language mediates
our conceptions of reality, Creeley uses the generative sentence to create

what I will call a *conjectural* prose, a compelling "narrative of one man's attentions."

Creeley's narrative, *Presences: A Text for Marisol,* is less easily found in the United States than his readily obtainable books of verse. The version now in print, contained in *Mabel: A Story and Other Prose* (London: Marion Boyars, 1976), accurately reproduces the text of the first full edition of *Presences* (New York: Scribners, 1976) but is a markedly different work from the one Creeley and Marisol envisioned. Marisol, a Venezuelan-born Pop sculptor of Creeley's generation, chose him to write the text for a proposed large-format book devoted to her work. Creeley describes his reaction:

> I was delighted, just that her work was most interesting to me, particularly those pieces involved with senses of human interrelation and "presence" . . . What we both wanted, then, was an active complement, rather than a descriptive prose text and/or a sense of illustration in the images themselves.[5]

The book was ultimately rejected by the publisher, Harry Abrams, and then retained by Scribners, Creeley's regular publisher. Marisol remained committed, writing to Creeley, "It is really amazing how you could do something so close to me from seeing me so few times." The book was assembled by Marisol and its designer, William Katz, and interleaves back-to-back photographs of Marisol's sculptures with back-to-back pages of text, so that each page of text faces a photograph. Since the photographs are bled to the edges of the page, the text likewise appears nearly without margins, in large, airy type. One effect of this design is to emphasize the tactile qualities of the words by giving them the implied solidity and presence of sculptural objects. As a unique and imposing collaboration between an artist, a writer, and a designer, the book deserves reprinting.

The text consists of a series of improvisations upon Marisol's images, both sculptural and personal; Creeley's concern with Marisol extends beyond her work to include her distinctive personality and views:

> I felt very free in my own decision therefore, and was primarily involved to explore a diversity of senses of human "presence" in a diversity of modes, e.g., everything from tape "cut ups" to almost nostalgically familiar "narrative" . . . At the root, however, is insistently Marisol's own preoccupation with terms of being human, and its various possible "representations."

In *Presences* Creeley copies, draws from, and improvises upon a wide variety of materials. A few examples should help to give a sense of the diversity of his sources and the inventiveness of his method. The book consists of sixteen prose units (five sections of three units, and a post-script) of varying lengths; the five sections are ordered by a serial per-mutation of the numbers 1, 2, 3 (representing the relative lengths of the units), so that the subsections of the second section, for instance, are in the order 2, 3, 1. In unit V.1, which we will discuss in depth further on, Creeley improvises upon statements by Marisol and lines from a Lorca poem. In IV.2 Creeley constructs a dreamlike narrative around phrases freely translated from a Venezuelan book on Marisol; this book also contains visual images that enter Creeley's prose. For example, from a text in the Venezualan book that reads (one sentence per page),

> ¿Fragiles símbolos de una lumbra incierta?
> ¿Románticas historias . . .
> Acaso el sol terrible de los trópicos iluminó un instante la noche
>   profunda de sus ojos.[6]

Creeley weaves a mysterious narrative:

> Romantic histories? Or fragile symbols of an uncertain light. It is
> not clear to them why the car has stopped so far from the town
> to ask directions, or why it should be of them, so faintly
> apparent from the roadside where the car has been pulled over.
> There seems an invincible arrogance, a secular power, to the
> reason, whatever it may prove to be.
>
> But there are two wings, two wings that go nowhere. To the
> house, or to the castle perhaps. No, it is a bird, that is silent and
> sad, the Dane says. There is no sound from the car as the people
> in it, not quite possible to see clearly, wait for further explana-
> tions. In case the terrible sun of the tropics shines for an instant,
> she wears sun glasses, a profound night of the eyes. This is the
> woman to the left of the driver, hooded figure, they now
> discern, with long talonlike fingers holding the wheel.
>
> (Mabel, 96)

An illustration showing one of Marisol's sculptures, of women with sun glasses, appears beside both the Venezuelan text and Creeley's text. An-other image on the next page of the Venezuelan book shows an auto-mobile with a hooded woman to the left of the driver.

Creeley seldom works so directly with Marisol's images or with words by or about her. The "cut up" that he refers to (III.1) was made from a tape of the voices of Creeley and his friends in Bolinas, California, the artists' colony where Creeley resided for a number of years. Creeley recorded a conversation among the poets Tom Clark and Joanne Kyger,

Magda Welch (widow of poet Lew Welch), Creeley's wife Bobbie (also a writer), and himself. Then, using numerical instructions à la John Cage, Creeley ran the tape forward and backward, transcribing the first articulate statement that occurred each time he stopped. The theme of the resulting improvisation seems to be music (and thus photographs of Marisol's *The Band* accompany it); an excerpt follows:

"A rhythmic experience." "The steady thing."

Making that be your secret guide but not your outspoken guide. Oh, I think so. Beautiful, wise, intuitive sense of where it is. Turned on. Waist deep, amidst the encircling gloom. The intimacy of the sounds in the house were first, like they say, a kind of displacement. Yah. Music interferes, sphere.

"You get here are mostly all your own sounds."

To get it on, but it sounds like. The kind of music that was happening around here when everybody just sits in and tries to make music together. Peter turned me on to African music. To create it if you were particularly serious. I didn't find that experience anything like what I'd think it would be at all.

(*Mabel*, 87)

Creeley achieves a different kind of collage effect in improvisation IV.1, in which he describes a postcard reproduction of Poussin's *L'Inspiration du poète*. The description includes the message on the back of the card and a voice overheard from the radio. As a final example of the sources Creeley draws from in *Presences*, II.1 is devoted almost entirely to a retelling of a Buddhist fable about false security.[7] Through all these various subjects and narrative strategies, Creeley writes a taut prose, reminiscent of Samuel Beckett's lapidary prose, that resolutely submits whatever occurs within it to a lively, scrupulous attention.

In "Placing Creeley's Recent Work: A Poetics of Conjecture" (*b2*, 513–39), Charles Altieri argues that Creeley's poetry, beginning with *Pieces* (1969), and his prose collected in the 1976 volume *Mabel: A Story and Other Prose* (*A Day Book, Presences*, and *Mabel: A Story*) are governed by a poetics of *conjecture*, in which the act of thinking is graphed in its free movement among various conceptual systems: "His is a poetics of conjecture rather than closure, a poetics I see as one whose aim is not so much to interpret experience as to extend it by making a situation simply the focus for overlapping reflexive structures, 'one again / from another one' " (*b2*, 518). Altieri concentrates on the way in which Creeley moves freely from one imaginative context to another, continually testing boundaries. This free play of thinking is what Altieri means by "conjecture," a term that he derived from Creeley's use of it in a 1976 interview:

> Conjecture is a great word. Olson really dug it. I wanted a situation where you could speculate or kind of brood on – not in a depressed sense – but where you could sort of play with something in your head that couldn't be resolved in any simple manner.

The word "conjecture" appears repeatedly in the theoretical writings of Creeley and Charles Olson and is a good choice as a descriptive term, but I believe it carries a larger critical burden in Creeley's prose than Altieri's use of it might indicate. Behind the sense of playful differentiation, of thinking gauging itself, I would like to show another, phenomenological sense of the term "conjecture" by tracing the term back through some of its earlier uses in the writings of Creeley and Olson.[8]

One of Creeley's first essays, "Notes for a New Prose," written in the watershed year of 1950, less than two months after the onset of his correspondence with Olson,[9] already includes the term. The two writers were so intimately involved (through correspondence) in the emergence of each other's characteristic styles, theoretical positions, and even diction that it will not be possible to unravel more conclusively the contributions each one brought to their mutual definitions until the publication of their collected correspondence, now being edited by George Butterick.[10] Creeley had already written all or part of the stories "The Unsuccessful Husband," "In the Summer," "3 Fate Tales," "The Lover," and "The Seance" prior to his contact with Olson, so that his statements about prose, though colored by Olson's sense of the "projective," arise from his own distinctive practice.[11] In the following passage Creeley compares the conjectural prose of his stories with a factual prose, claiming that either method is just as "real" (i.e., nonfictional):

> The swing of ideas, in stasis – is still poetry. But prose is the *projection* of ideas, in time. This does not mean that the projection must be an "actual" one, date by date, etc. The word is law, is the creator, and what it can do, is what any prose can do. There is nothing more real, in essence, about a possible prose than there is about any possible poetry. The ordering of *conjecture* will remain as "real" as the ordering of fact, given the right hand. (*QG*, 13)

Creeley's sense of poetry at this time still included ideas of symmetry and balance ("the swing of ideas in stasis"). His prose, however, as Nathaniel Mackey points out in the "*The Gold Diggers:* Projective Prose" (*b2*, 469–87), was already projective. Olson immediately recognized this. Mackey cites several early laudatory statements from letters by Olson: Creeley is "the most important narrative writer to come on in one hell of a time," and "Creeley's work is extremely important exactly as the push beyond the fictive" (b2, 471). This projective prose did not have to return to the static conditions of parallelism or balance that still dictated verse for Creeley; instead, he could follow the sequential movement of his attention, an attention engaged in complex acts of understanding, and trust that this conjectural motion would be true to the dictates of both language ("the word is law") and reality.

Olson, as the above quotations affirm, was convinced of the seminal importance of Creeley's prose (though more tentative, Mackey suggests, about Creeley's poetry [b2, 471]). Olson made his admiration of the prose clear publicly in his introduction to a selection of Creeley's stories in 1951:

> I take it there is huge gain to square away at narrative now, not as fiction but as RE-ENACTMENT. Taking it this way I see two possibilities:
>
> (1) what I call DOCUMENT simply to emphasize that the events alone do the work, that the narrator stays OUT, functions as pressure not as interpreting person . . . ;
>
> (2) the exact opposite, the NARRATOR IN, the total IN to the above total OUT, total speculation as against the half management, half interpretation, the narrator taking on himself the job of making clear by way of his own person that life *is* preoccupation with itself, taking up the push of his own single intelligence to make it, to be – by his conjectures – so powerful inside the story that he makes the story swing on him, his eye the eye of nature INSIDE (as is the same eye, outside) a lightmaker.[12]

Olson nominates Creeley, "a man putting his hands directly and responsibly to experience which is also our own," as the exemplar of the second method. He finds Creeley responsible to his writing in exactly the manner demanded of a writer of conjectural prose, who must register absolutely faithfully the movement of his or her impulses and thus "re-enact" the "human phenomenology" that is the writer's content.[13] We have noted this fidelity to the impulses that occur in the act of composition in the generative sentence of Williams. For Williams, however, the things of the world and the language of other people are the primary lures to his attention. Creeley follows much more strictly the dictum that "life *is* preoccupation with itself." This does not mean, as we shall see, that Creeley's writing ignores the world of things or other people, but everything "other" arises in his writing through a phenomenological attention, a testing of the other in relation to the self.

Creeley's use of the term "conjecture," then, goes beyond Altieri's conception of conjecture as the playful differentiation among systems and includes hermeneutic and phenomenological speculation.[14] Let us return to the quotation from Creeley with which Altieri introduces the term and follow it on a bit further:

> Conjecture is a great word. Olson really dug it. I wanted a situation where you could speculate or kind of brood on – not in a depressed sense – but where you could sort of play with something in your head that couldn't be resolved in any simple manner. The resolution was something that bored me instantly . . . And then reading Williams's poems . . . [ellipses Creeley's] I really learned a lot from him in the sense that his way of writing relieved my dilemma – simply that I could feel the energy, and I didn't realize before reading Williams that many circumstances of statement had no appropriate conclusion. And I always felt, for example, that as much as I respected him, Donne's love poems, insofar as they do reach this kind of end, so quixotically and beautifully, instantly sort of fell apart at that point, paradoxically. They got to that final clause which brought all the terms into some congruence and conclusion, that's precisely where the attention just didn't want to go with it anymore. And a poem which had that kind of condition of speculative wonder or curiosity was really more attractive. (*APR, 5*)

It is clear that Creeley, like Williams, is troubled by the claims of completeness. But where Williams rebels decisively against traditional notions of completeness, whether in the sentences of *Kora in Hell* or in the variable measure of his poetry, Creeley, as Altieri correctly implies, does not disregard the claims of completeness. Instead, he interrogates them. In the prose of *Presences* Creeley conjectures with various systems and dichotomies, with the ways we measure and understand ourselves and the world, and he offers his prose as instance of this attempt at measuring and understanding, a prose that stays constantly aware of its effect upon the self and its own necessary inadequacy, its sometimes painful incompleteness.

Even in his earlier poetry and prose Creeley never embraced wholeness to the exclusion of completeness. His writing, both early and late, takes place in a tension between these two notions. In his early poetry, collected in *For Love: Poems 1950–1960* (New York: Scribners, 1962), the tension manifests at the levels of the line and of the whole poem. It produces a clash between two senses of form: Creeley's avowed aesthetic, inherited from Williams and reinforced by Olson, insisted upon the openness of a speech-generated wholeness, responsible solely to the demands of the moment of writing; his underlying sense of form, however

– probably the result of his early reading and his education at Harvard –
was still governed by the imperative of completeness. This may be seen
as a collision between the syntax-generated "new form" of Williams and
traditional English prosody. His comments in the *American Poetry Review*
interview (1976) reveal that to a certain extent Creeley was aware of, and
cultivated, this tension:

> It seemed to me that the couplet, which I used a lot in my early
> writing, the disjoint couplet, that that was terrific because you
> could bring two things together as statement and have them seem-
> ingly hold together as a rhetorical situation, and also as a rhyming
> situation, or a rhythm, a parallel situation, but the information
> could be as disjunct as the man in the moon and a cat walking down
> the street . . . And a rhetorical poem could make them seem as
> reasonable as Pope, or at least hold them an instant in the mind as
> though they were reasonable, and then the attention would say,
> "Well, wait a minute now, these two things are not necessarily
> congruous" . . . like "when the sun goes down and it gets dark / I
> saw an animal go into the park," in which you can get disjunct
> syntax or tense, where you're following a line that's not really
> jarring the reader. (*APR*, 5)

Later on in the same interview Creeley seems to indicate that not all
aspects of this clash between wholeness and completeness were fully
intended in his early poetry. He says, somewhat disapprovingly, "For a
long time, when I was younger, I remember I used to have a habit of
wanting to get a punch line, you know, like some way to really lock it
up" (*APR*, 6). In a characteristic poem like "The Letter," the opposition
between wholeness and completeness crops up in a number of ways:

> *The Letter*
>
> I did not expect you
> to stay married to
> one man all your life,
> no matter you were his wife.
>
> I thought the pain was endless –
> but the form existent,
> as it is form,
> and as such I loved it.
>
> I loved you as well
> even as you might tell,
> giving evidence
> as to how much was penitence.[15]

The gestural quality of the lines in the first stanza, the first two ending in mid-syntax, recalls the speech-generated poetry of Williams. But against this sense of openness comes the inevitable rhyme. In the second stanza the rhyming itself produces more tension, since it is nearly absent – though expected – until the near rhyme at the end. The syntax of this stanza is paratactic and clearly gives us the process of thinking rather than a completed thought. The content of this stanza also makes an ironic comment upon the priority of contractual forms, whether of marriage or poetry. The first couplet of the third stanza operates with the same "disjunct syntax" Creeley mentions above: The shifting sense of "I loved you as well / even as you might tell" hinges upon vacillating grammatical locations for the word "even." The last couplet delivers the final ironic punch, which Creeley notes above his inability to resist, to a bitterly ironic poem.

Creeley goes on in the interview to say that not until toward the end of writing *Words* (published 1967) did he begin to loosen his sense of formal necessity, to free ideas and expressions from the imperative of reaching a rested conclusion. He began then to write serial compositions, starting with *Pieces* (1969) and continuing in the three prose books collected in *Mabel,* that investigate propositions of completeness rather than submitting them to the ironic examination employed in "The Letter."

At the same time that Creeley's attitude toward completeness underwent a dramatic change, his reliance upon wholeness shifted as well. A brief look at two passages of prose, one early and one late, will give us the outline of Creeley's transformation in relation to wholeness and completeness. The early prose of his tales (in this case "Mr. Blue," 1951) moves paratactically, employing a generative syntax that tries desperately to capture the movement of thought and the gestures of speech:

> Looked, he looked at me, cut, the hate jagged, and I had gone,
> then, into it and that was almost that. But she said, then, she
> had seen him, earlier, that same day, as he was standing by a
> store, near the door, I think, as it had opened, and she, there,
> across the street, saw him motion, the gesture, then, a dance,
> shuffle, the feet crooked, and the arms, as now, loose, and it was
> before, as before, but not because of this, that made it, or I
> thought, so made it, was it, or was that thing I hung to, when,
> the show over, they motioned us out, and I pushed a way for
> her out through the crowd.[16]

This rapid-fire, speech-generated prose resembles the volatile Williams of *Kora in Hell,* relying exclusively on the notion of wholeness to form the sentences. In a piece of prose of comparable length from *Presences,* the sentences are composed, and operate, in a very different fashion:

Big firemen. Little firemen. In the flames they are dancing. *Fire delights in its form*. Firemen delight in their form? Inform us, policemen. We call upon them to inform us. Hence all the beatings and the shootings and the putting into closed places behind doors. Firemen and snowmen share other fates, the one burning, the one melting. Snow delights in its form, being mutable. It is the immutable that despairs. At least for a time, for any other time, for all time, for bygone times, for times past, for time enough, for in time. Time will tell.

(*Mabel*, 65)

Just as projective verse proposes the line as a scoring for breath and emotion ("the HEAD, by way of the EAR, to the SYLLABLE / the HEART, by way of the BREATH, to the LINE,") according to Olson,[17] so Creeley's projective prose in his early stories used commas for exactly the same purposes. It has often been noted (especially by those who hear him read) that Creeley's verse line graphs a constriction of breath, a constant halting or stumbling, that communicates a raw sense of emotional inadequacy;[18] the same stumbling and the same emotional tenor inform his early prose. The constriction begins to loosen in his novel *The Island* (1963), which is still tight and halting, both formally and emotionally, but the prose in this novel is not as constantly blocked by commas as in the stories of *The Gold Diggers,* where even subject and verb are sometimes disjoined by a comma. The prose works collected in *Mabel* move with much greater fluidity, as in the passage about the firemen, allowing both the heart and mind a freer reign than was afforded by the short emotional and speculative tether of the earlier prose and poetry.

The poet's prose of *Presences* invites the reader's breathing to proceed at its own pace; the pauses indicated by periods are different from those scored by line breaks or commas. Short sentences, many of them fragments or single words, abound, provoking a kind of discontinuity unlike that of the generative sentences of Williams or early Creeley. These short sentences request a full stop, and in doing so they invoke the sentence's claim to completeness and demand the fulfillment of a predication or substantiation. The mind is teased by the necessity for complete grammatical forms and thus comes to question how language works and what it says. The same questioning occurs in relation to propositions, especially those drawn from other sources (Creeley had always spoken for himself in his early tales), such as the Heraclitean "Fire delights in its form."[19] Such propositions are subjected to a careful scrutiny, aimed at discovering what language actually says. In these conjectural sentences Creeley listens carefully to language; in the fireman passage we have the impression that to a large extent language itself is speaking, rather than being beaten somewhat painfully into the shape of Creeley's emotions as in his earlier prose. This kind of acute listening to and questioning of language comes much nearer to the sentences of Gertrude Stein than to those of Williams. Moreover, the prose of *Presences* has an incantatory quality, also similar to Stein, that leaves behind the propellant rush of expectation and simultaneity that we found in Williams's generative sentences. Instead the interrogation of language and of the sentence's claim to completeness moves Creeley's conjectural prose onward.

This discussion of the shift in Creeley's style has left in abeyance the issue of wholeness in the later work. In *Presences,* beyond the sentence, at the level of the narrative, of the movement of the prose from sentence to sentence, there is an implicit sense of wholeness at work. The often discontinuous shifts from one sentence to the next are governed by that same trust in the discovery of form (rather than the imposition of form) that governed Creeley's earlier projective sentences; now, however, this sense of wholeness itself becomes the groundwork for a questioning of kinds of completeness: Is there a complete correspondence between language and the world? Are the body and mind completely congruous? Is complete reciprocation between self and other possible? Questions such as these arise in the sentences of *Presences* and take on the role of themes in the work at large.

The sense of wholeness in Creeley's recent prose also functions at the level of the unit. The numerical structure of the five sections of *Presences* (1, 2, 3; 2, 3, 1; 3, 1, 2; 1, 2, 3; 2, 3, 1) corresponds to the number of typewritten pages in each unit, with three units making up a section. These permutations of the six-page sections were decided upon in advance, so that each time Creeley sat down to compose a unit he knew exactly how much he would be writing.[20] These a priori, arbitrary limits to the possibility of writing do not offer any promise of completeness; instead, they operate upon Creeley's intuition of wholeness, forcing him to explore the total context of a given situation within the space allotted, ensuring a discovered rather than a balanced or symmetrical ending.

> Somehow that sense of page length frees me to be as various and speculative as I want to be within the period designed. It frees me from some writing sense that I've got to worry about how this is going to end or where it's going to get to. It somehow always does end intuitively where it should, where the physical limit occurs. (*APR, 6*)

This intuition of a wholeness achieved at the level of the unit presents an exact analogy to the wholeness achieved in the generative sentence in Williams's practice, as we observed it in the sentence about the woman who walks "in a different air." Creeley transposes the aspect of wholeness directly from the generative sentence to the full unit.

I have chosen *Presences* from among the three prose works collected in *Mabel: A Story and Other Prose* because in it the conjectural prose is most fully explored and presents itself most distinctly as a contribution to the developing possibilities of poet's prose. *A Day Book* and *Mabel: A Story*, also included in the 1976 volume, depend upon other prose forms – the journal and the story, respectively – to determine (if loosely) their narrative directions. *A Day Book* records the thoughts and activities of thirty literal days, each on a single page (of the typescript). In *Mabel: A Story* Creeley seeks to understand his relationship to women and sexuality through anecdotes, memories, and conjectures about a conglomerate woman he calls Mabel.[21] *Presences*, with its loose relationship to the sculptures of Marisol (an occasion for improvisation analogous to the mythological scaffolding of *Kora in Hell*), is more nakedly involved in conjectural narratives per se. The subject matter of *Presences* is probably the least predetermined of any of the three texts, and the interrogation of and listening to language the most acute. To appreciate fully the philosophical seriousness of this questioning and listening, we must turn for a while to several modern philosophers whose treatment of the issues of form and content that arise in *Presences* will help make clear its distinctive achievement and provide further insight into the philosophical concerns of American poet's prose in general.

REPETITION AND APPEARANCE

> *How wonderful and new and yet how gruesome and ironic I find my position vis-à-vis the whole of existence in the light of my insight! I have discovered for myself that the human and animal past, indeed the whole primal age and past of all sentient being continues in me to invent, to love, to hate, and to infer. I suddenly woke up in the midst of this dream, but only to the consciousness that I am dreaming and that I must go on dreaming lest I perish – as a somnambulist must go on dreaming lest he fall. What is "appearance" for me now? Certainly not the opposite of some essence: what could I say about any essence except to name the attributes of its appearance! Certainly not a dead mask that one could place on an unknown x or remove from it!*
>
> *Nietzsche*

With his genealogical method and his origination of the concepts of the death of God, the *Uebermensch*, the will to power, and eternal recurrence, Friedrich Nietzsche raised some fundamental questions about ways of thinking that had been taken for granted for centuries.[22] By applying his own radical analysis to the traditional problems of philosophy, Nietzsche broke down the age-old categories of metaphysics, ethics, and epistemology; in their wake he left the individual human being confronting himself, language, and the world. Nietzsche recorded not only the death of God and the death of man (the "last man" will be replaced by a new species, the *Uebermensch*) but also the death of philosophy; he purposely wrote a "last philosophy." To those who come after this "last philosophy, " the relation of language to being is a basic issue. To what extent does language imitate or refer to reality, and to what extent does it create reality? Is language a tool whose meaning is determined merely by its use, or does language "house" being? Is any kind of understanding possible outside of language? These major questions of twentieth-century philosophy arose after the demise of idealism, which Nietzsche in large measure effected: When the stable categories around which we organize our world dissolve, men are thrown back on the medium that creates those categories – language – and find themselves trying with great earnestness to articulate "what can be said." As we shall see, these questions of the operation of language with respect to being, reality, or language itself are important not only to modern philosophy but also to writing that proceeds philosophically, such as American poet's prose.

Aside from his more general role as "last philosopher," Nietzsche provides us with a concept of great importance to our reading of *Presences*. He calls it "the eternal recurrence of the same," and though philosophically a highly complex and possibly contradictory notion, it can be broken for our present purposes into two ideas – repetition and appearance. To provide a context for these terms, we will look briefly at Nietzsche's discovery of the eternal recurrence.

During the writing of *The Gay Science* (August 1881), Nietzsche underwent a kind of conversion experience on a walk in the mountains.[23] This experience involved the idea of eternal recurrence, so that the concept itself has an existential component. The first major exposition of the idea occurs in section 341 of *The Gay Science*:

> What, if some day or night a demon were to steal after you into your loneliest loneliness and say to you: "This life as you now live it and have lived it, you will have to live once more and innumerable times more; and there will be nothing new in it, but every pain and every joy and every thought and sigh and everything unutteraby small or great in your life will have to return to you, all in the same succession and sequence – even this spider and this moonlight between the trees, and even this moment and I myself. The eternal hourglass of existence is turned upside down again and again, and you with it, speck of dust!"
>
> Would you not throw yourself down and gnash your teeth and curse the demon who spoke thus? Or have you once experienced a

tremendous moment when you would have answered him: "You are a god and never have I heard anything more divine." (GS, 273–74)

To one who analyzes experience as relentlessly as Nietzsche, the recognition of an ironclad determinism or a self-referential circularity can be overwhelming. Likewise, Creeley (for whom Valéry's *Monsieur Teste* has been called a "bible from the late forties until he rejected it in the mid sixties")[24] engaged in and felt the often crippling consequences of this kind of rigorous scrutiny. As Nietzsche says, the recognition of the constant repetition of life, the lack of a transcendental realm or eschatological direction to human life, will in most cases create a shuddering revulsion – but it may also prompt an astonishing affirmation. The affirmation does not actually oppose the revulsion but rather arises out of it by means of a further recognition: that one may choose to accept reality unconditionally in its moment of appearance ("even this spider and this moonlight between the trees, and even this moment and I myself") and thus, by this gambit of acceptance, attain what Nietzsche calls *amor fati*, loving one's fate.

> The question in each and every thing, "Do you desire this once more and innumerable times more?" would lie upon your actions as the greatest weight. Or how well disposed would you have to become to yourself and to life to crave nothing more fervently than this ultimate eternal confirmation and seal? (GS, 274)

The question becomes, for both Nietzsche and Creeley, "Can I let the present be all?" Knowing that there is no way out of the continuity of cause and effect, can one become reconciled to the seemingly discontinuous appearances that constitute the present, to a world with no assurances beyond the moment, in which one is paradoxically aware of the repetition of all systems? This antithetical yoking of the desire to exist completely in the present with an acute awareness of the mediation of systems ("of valuation, habit, complex organic data, the weather, and so on" [WTRP, 5]) forms the crux of the conjecture in Creeley's later writing and looms as the central issue in *Presences*.

For Nietzsche, eternal recurrence brings a dramatic reversal of idealist conceptions: "What is 'appearance' for me now? Certainly not the opposite of some essence: What could I say about any essence except to name the attributes of its appearance! Certainly not a dead mask that one could place on an unknown x or remove from it!" (GS, 116). Once eternal recurrence is experienced, there is no longer a hidden depth, a privileged essence or a transcendental signified that stands behind all of existence. Rather, things just appear, and their appearance itself manifests a totality of being. So far, says Nietzsche, only "we daredevils of the spirit" have reached the ultimate goal of humanity, acceptance of this reality, but when he wants to cite predecessors he inevitably enlists the Greeks: "Oh, those Greeks! They knew how to live. What is required for that is to stop courageously at the surface, the fold, the skin, to adore appearance, to believe in forms, tones, words, in the whole Olympus of appearance. Those Greeks were superficial – out of profundity" (*GS*, 38).

We have already noted the primacy of the surface in the improvisations of *Kora in Hell*. Creeley insists even more emphatically upon the knowing superficiality that Nietzsche would cultivate. The literal appearances of words and images on the present surface they create form the subject of Creeley's writing: His words and images are not masks or correlatives for "an unknown *x*." Creeley's choice of the term "presences" as the title for the work reflects this bias toward the literal. Though the word carries a metaphysical charge, the first sense in which one is likely to take it, since the text conjectures about Marisol's posed, masklike sculptures, is as "attitude" or "bearing," as a term for the qualities a person displays in social situations. This is a valid assessment of the term, for *Presences* does concern itself with ethical questions of attitude or bearing; for example, the fireman passage evaluates firemen and policemen as people hiding behind uniforms ("It is their way of dress that disarms that which stands as us. They can't stand us?" [*Mabel*, 64]) – the uniform is an *affront* that wholly contains its wearer's presence (*Mabel*, 64–66, *WTRP*, 54–58).

But in addition to this ethical sense of "presence," which includes an evaluation of the extent to which people *are present*, Creeley also uses the term as a synonym for "appearances," as in this statement from an interview conducted in 1971, shortly after he completed *Presences*:

> I was again thinking of Bacon, Francis Bacon, the presences of the images that one finds in his painting are surreal, to put it mildly, but their impact on consciousness comes from the fact that they are a literal reality. They're not about something.[25]

The word "appearances" could be substituted in this statement for "presences" without change of meaning. Creeley insists that the surrealistic appearances of Bacon's images constitute a literal reality (the paintings do not contain the symbolic surrealism of, say, Magritte or Delvaux), in order to claim that the "many surreal situations" in *Presences* "are literal": "I'm by nature and circumstance a very literal man."[26] When Creeley refers to himself as literal (a favorite adjective), he does not mean that his approach is objective but rather phenomenological. As the "NARRATOR IN," he engages in "the study of all possible appearances in human experience" (to borrow from the definition of phenomenology in the *American Heritage Dictionary*), not in the objective stance of the narrator "OUT." We will continue to examine in greater detail the way appearances arise on the literal surface of *Presences* and how Creeley links appearances to the constant confrontation with repetition. Aiding us in this discussion will be the figures of Wittgenstein and Heidegger, who will represent respectively these two aspects of eternal recurrence: repetition (interrogation of language) and appearance (listening to language).

One obvious way in which repetition occurs in *Presences* is by the frequent reiteration of words and phrases. Take, for instance, the passage we spoke of earlier:

> Big firemen. Little firemen. In the flames they are dancing. *Fire delights in its form.* Firemen delight in their form? Inform us, policemen. We call upon them to inform us. Hence all the beatings and the shootings and the putting into closed places behind doors. Firemen and snowmen share other fates, the one burning, the one melting. Snow delights in its form, being mutable. It is the immutable which despairs. At least for a time, for any other time, for all time, for bygone times, for times past, for time enough, for in time. Time will tell.

Besides the aural effects of rhyme or incantation, what is the purpose of repeating words and phrases, often with slight variations, in a passage such as this? A brief look at the activities of Ludwig Wittgenstein, whose later philosophy indulged in just such "language games," will assist us.[27]

Wittgenstein's philosophy may be roughly divided into two complementary stages: the first, culminating in the *Tractatus Logico-Philosophicus* (1921), consists of a masterful logical critique of what *cannot* be said, ending with the famous conclusion "What we cannot speak about we must pass over in silence";[28] the second stage, culminating in the unfinished *Philosophical Investigations* (1953), is an inquiry, by means of language games, into what *can* be said. This second stage took Wittgenstein into language investigations that Creeley also pursues, trying to understand what language says, what it means, and how by examining ordinary language (rather than using specialized terminology) one can attack fundamental problems. In his language games, endeavoring to tease out exactly what we mean by what we say, Wittgenstein is as careful in his use of words – as precise, suggestive, playful, and aware of nuances – as a poet.[29]

Wittgenstein's most important contribution to our understanding of poet's prose consists in his expanded notion of grammar, in which he combines the meaning, the function, and the use of words:

> The explanation of the meaning explains the use of the word.
> The use of the word in the language is its meaning.
> Grammar describes the use of words in the language.[30]

The object of philosophy, and of prose such as Creeley writes, by this definition, becomes an investigation of grammar. Both writers explore propositional language in order to see how grammar (the way words are used) and thinking are interrelated.

The fireman passage from *Presences* conducts a kind of grammatical investigation. Creeley submits a proposition – "Fire delights in its form" – to the careful scrutiny of a language game. Under what conditions, one might ask, could such a statement be made? Do we mean, for example, that "delight" is used here as a term for human enjoyment? If so, then we could say, "Firemen delight in their form." The question mark after the proposition, however, alerts us to the absurdity of this use of the word, given the context provided by the first proposition. If we take the question on its own grounds, however, then we are asking whether firemen enjoy their form – that is, whether they take delight in being firemen. But then one wonders if that is all that is meant by "form." The present sense of the word denotes a passive state or concretion; if we change the word slightly to make it a verb, then *form*ing becomes an activity, something that is per*form*ed or delivered (in*form*ation). What do we learn about the meaning of "form" by making it into a verb? We open up other contexts of its usage: We ask authorities, such as the police, for "information" regarding critical circumstances, and yet these same policemen are informed by informers who contribute to the brutal treatment and incarceration some of us face.

The permutations, the inquiries into how language speaks and how we use it continue: If some people reach a form of containment and stasis (prison), others persist in the Heraclitean transmutation of form: "The one burning, the one melting." Then we repeat the initial proposition, substituting "snow" for "fire" and adding an explanatory phrase: "Snow delights in its form, being mutable." Does this explanation help us to understand what kind of delight is being spoken of? One tries a reversal, using "despair" – the antonym of "delight" – to see if this yields greater understanding. To a certain extent it does, reminding us that people in immutable conditions, whether incarcerated in a prison or contained in a uni*form*, can be said to experience despair. Though not always: "At least for a time, for any other time, for all time, for bygone times, for times past, for time enough, for in time." Even understanding is mutable. This sentence interrogates the grammar of "time" through both normal and absurd uses. It also raises the issue of the relation of time to change and fixity. And finally, the paragraph ends with a reminder that ultimately only language speaks: "Language must speak for itself," says Wittgenstein,[31] and Creeley concludes, "Time will tell."

By sketching out the areas of grammatical inquiry, we have partially explicated the conjectural prose of this passage. A fuller treatment would relate "Big firemen. Little firemen" to the terms of measure with which *Presences* opens: "Big things. And little things" (*Mabel*, 63). It would situate this passage in the body of its unit (I.2), which is concerned with fire, with policemen, with calling for help, and with civic or political determinations. A broader discussion would also include Olson's affinity for and uses of Heraclitus (Robert Duncan's, too) and a favorite Creeley quotation from Norbert Wiener's *The Human Use of Human Beings*: "The individuality of the body is that of a flame rather than of a stone, of a form rather than of a bit of substance" (*QG*, 213). Finally one could make reference to a fascinating discussion by Creeley (*WTRP*, 54–8) in the lecture "Inside Out" (1973 – a year after *Presences*) of the way uniforms and the assumption of a generalized condition of "We-ness" remove people from their true individual experiences, causing "despair":

> The sculptor Marisol speaks of using herself over and over, in her work. "When I show myself as I am I return to reality." When one wears a uniform or otherwise generalizes the condition of one's experience of oneself, that "reality" is most difficult to enter. There was, sadly, a professor employed at the University of New Mexico who one time began a lecture with the statement: As I was shaving this morning, seeing myself in the mirror, Professor Jones, I said . . . [ellipsis Creeley's] That is the end of the story, no one else otherwise home. (*WTRP*, 57)

I list these considerations to give a fuller sense of the part language games play in the thematic and narrative extension of *Presences*. This repetitive questioning of grammar reflects not only ethical but also epistemological and metaphysical considerations. Grammar is use, and use is action. So when Wittgenstein says, "We ask 'How do you use the word, what do you do with it' – that will tell us how you understand it,"[32] the understanding he and Creeley strive for is a pragmatic one. This grammar of speech in action (or speech as action) interrogates the seeming completeness of sentences. Is "Fire delights in its form" a complete thought? That is impossible to determine without understanding what we mean by this sentence, that is, how it would be employed in a given context. Wittgenstein, Olson, and Creeley all concur on the vital test of use: There is no other way to evaluate statements. For Wittgenstein, this means that no separation is possible between grammar and semantics.

For Creeley and Olson the criterion of use extends to the ethical domain;
all acts of language are judged with reference to their usefulness in living.
For instance, in the following passage Creeley quotes several lines from
The Maximus Poems to point out how Olson subjects all knowledge to
the criterion of use:

> What belongs to art and reason is
> > the knowledge of
> > > consequences . . .

It is a sense of *use,* which believes knowledge to be necessarily an
active form of relation to term, with the corollary that *all* exists in
such relation, itself natural to the conditions. It is not, then, knowledge as a junkheap, or purposeless accumulation of mere detail . . . It is knowledge used as a means to relate, not separate –
which senses must, *per se,* prove very different. That is why the
term, *use,* is to be met with so frequently in Olson's writing. (*QG*,
168–9)

Against this concern with the "use" of language, though complementing rather than contradicting it, stands a more passive relation to
language; it was hinted at above, in reference to the proposition "Time
will tell," by calling attention to the fact that language itself speaks. For
Wittgenstein, the statement "Language must speak for itself" is an in-
junction to set aside our categorical assumptions and listen to language in
context. For Martin Heidegger, the act of listening to language proves
essential to any authentic human speech. Only by listening carefully,
while letting language itself speak, can the poet create a location in which
Being may appear:

> Man acts as though he were the shaper and master of language,
> while in fact language remains the master of man. When this rela-
> tion of dominance gets inverted, man hits upon strange maneuvers.
> Language becomes the means of expression . . . Strictly, it is lan-
> guage which speaks. Man first speaks when, and only when he
> responds to language by listening to its appeal . . . The responding
> in which man authentically listens to the appeal of language is that
> which speaks in the element of poetry. The more poetic a poet is –
> the freer (that is, the more open and ready for the unforeseen) his
> saying – the greater is the purity with which he submits what he
> says to an ever more painstaking listening, and the further what he
> says is from the mere propositional statement that is dealt with
> solely in regard to its correctness or incorrectness.[33]

Beyond the testing and interrogation of grammar that we noted in the
fireman passage, within *Presences* we can also discover the careful listen-

ing, the freedom to follow the promptings of language, that Heidegger attributes to poetry. The passage moves more quickly and with greater metaphorical leaps than a mere investigation, and clearly it is language itself and Creeley's sensitivity to it that leads the poetry from one sentence to the next. The words "fire," "delight," "form," and "time" acquire a rich density in a short space that gives them primacy as language and reminds us of their tactile qualities. By the standards he invokes, Heidegger's own prose moves poetically, too. Proceeding according to this same listening to language, remaining sensitive to the tactile qualities of words that acquire greater and greater density in his use of them, Heidegger writes a prose markedly akin to a poet's prose. The pull of individual words against the ongoing sense guarded by the syntax, in a characteristic sentence such as the following, displays the interplay of continuity and discontinuity with which we are already familiar: "If speaking, as the listening to language, lets Saying be said to it, this letting can obtain only in so far – and so near – as our own nature has been admitted and entered into Saying" (*OWL*, 124).

Saying is important for Heidegger because it partakes of the essence of language as disclosure: "*The essential being of language is Saying as Showing*" (*OWL*, 123). Showing takes place in appearance through presence and absence (both necessary to appearance), and thus language is most intimately concerned with appearance. "Language speaks in that it, as showing, reaching into all regions of presences, summons whatever is present to appear and to fade" (*OWL*, 124). At its base, then, language, as "the house of Being" (*OWL*, 135), gathers presences, bringing things into appearance and letting them fade. This deep intuition of the relation of language to Being resonates throughout Robert Creeley's writing as well and gives to the term "presences" its privileged entitlement. The task of the writer is to open a clearing in which things may appear. This phenomenological stance denies both that the work of art is an object and also that it is merely subjective expression. As Octavio Paz says,

> Criticism of the object and of the subject intersect in our time: the art object dissolves in the instantaneous act, the subject is a somewhat fortuitous crystallization of language . . . Criticism of the object prepares the way for the resurrection of the work of art, not as something to be possessed, but as a presence to be contemplated. The work is not an end in itself nor does it exist in its own right: the work is a bridge, an intermediary.[34]

We must be careful, when in the rhapsodic presence of presence, not to lose sight of the fact that such writing is not merely self-reflexive but presents things. One critic, Robert Kern, has given an admirable account of Creeley's poetics yet misses this crucial point. "Creeley's position, then," he says, "is one which allows no temporal gap between writing and experience . . . What a poem is *about* is literally its own making or unfolding. The poet, in such a conception, is *inside* the act of composition, which is entirely self-limiting, a record of the circumstances of its own occasion" (*b2*, 213–14). The poet may be inside the act of composition and keenly aware of the temporal nature of its occasion without the poem's becoming entirely self-limiting. To insist on this limitation is to miss the essential activity of Creeley's writing, which seeks to effect an actual opening in the present in which *things* are invited to appear to both writer and reader. Rather than offering a literal or metaphorical description of the process of composition (a favorite modernist approach), Creeley attends unswervingly to the unfolding of his writing in order to maintain the opening that allows things to occur. What results is not "subject matter" but rather a heightened awareness in both the writer and the reader to appearances in the present. In other words, Creeley creates a kind of negative space through his writing that asks us to fill it up with the world of our experience as we read.

Charles Olson sums up best this phenomenological aspect of Creeley's writing in his 1951 "Introduction to Robert Creeley":

> For "things" are what writers get inside their work, or the work, poem or story, perishes. Things are the way force is exchanged. On things communication rests. And the writer, though he is the control (or art is nothing) is, still, no more than – but just as much as – another "thing," and as such, is in, inside or out . . . I take it that these stories are . . . of the writer putting himself all the way in – taking that risk . . . and, by the depth and sureness of his speculating, making it pay, making you–me believe, that we are here in the presence of a man putting his hands directly and responsibly to experience which is also our own . . . For his presence is the energy. And the instant? That, too, is he, given such methodology. For his urgency, his confrontation is "time," which is, when he makes it, ours, the now. He is time, he is now, the force.[35]

The role of appearance and repetition in Creeley's conjectural prose reveals the philosophical subtlety of this writing. We have seen that the idea of repetition recognizes the circularity of experience within systemic restraints and that it results in an interrogation of the mediation of systems; language, as the primordial mediator, receives Creeley's most sustained conjectures regarding its claim to completeness. Appearance, on the other hand, occurs at the surface of the text, in the insistence by Creeley and Nietzsche that surface appearances in the present are already sufficiently profound; moreover, by listening to language, the conjectural prose maintains a clearing in which presences may appear.

The complementary notions of repetition and appearance can be read back into American literature and culture, suggesting that the American idea of presence has always supposed these dual components. As an offspring of the Reformation, America comes into being inheriting the conflict between the mediate and the immediate. The Reformation in general, and Puritan dissenters in particular, rebelled against the mediation of the Church between man and God, endeavoring to foster an immediate relationship. What had come to seem natural (because culturally embedded) – the Church – was declared unnatural, setting in motion the search for what Emerson calls, in *Nature,* "an original relation to the universe." The immediate does not, however, reveal itself once and forever but forms the goal of a quest beyond the acknowledged ubiquity of the mediate. Americans begin from an acknowledged condition of *différence* (spatial difference plus temporal deferral) and belatedness, and when we speak of presence we invoke an ardently sought regeneration, a desire to "make it new."

When French critics such as Barthes, Derrida, and Foucault speak of absence, they are contrasting it to the unquestioned assumption that tradition is natural. These critics argue that language is a disruptive, deferring medium of representation as against the traditional conviction that it re-presents immediately. In America, where the crisis of verse could actually be pushed back to the first settlement, tradition and the efficacy of the word are in doubt from the beginning; exile and absence are our native conditions. Rather than a naive trust in tradition, the American cry for presence and speech already includes within it and does not deny the experience of absence. Tradition acts as if no mediation exists between Now and the Beginning, and thus resists the hermeneutic and historical nature of writing; Americans are not Adamic but regenerative and thus see writing as profoundly hermeneutic and historical. When we deny or investigate the traditional claim to completeness, we do so not in a spirit of nihilism but to propose a new, provisional wholeness that stands more resiliently in the present than the bounded completeness assumed from the past. While attending to the endless and systematic repetition of differences, we look to the present as a free and inexhaustible source for conjecture, transformation, and authentication.[36]

"A LIFE TRACKING ITSELF"

Auto-bio-graphy *I translate as a life tracking itself.*

Creeley

Life is *preoccupation with itself.*

Olson

In a lecture delivered a year after the composition of *Presences,* "Inside Out," Robert Creeley delineates the mode of autobiography in a way that points to *Presences* as an instance of that mode:[37]

> You begin at any point, and move from that point forward or
> backward, up or down – or in a direction you yourself choose. In
> and out of the system, as Buckminster Fuller would say. It's a
> system – of valuation, habit, complex organic data, the weather,
> and so on. Usually the choice is to track it backward, that is, most
> autobiographical impulse tends to follow this course. One can
> think of one's life as not worth remembering, in fact one can want
> to forget it – but if what has constituted it, the things "of which it
> was made up," as William Carlos Williams says, are dear to your
> memory and experience of them, then it may well be a record of
> them, a graph of their activity as "your life," is an act you would
> like to perform. (*WTRP*, 51)

Creeley proposes autobiography as a type of conjecture, "in and out of
the system . . . of valuation, habit, complex organic data, the weather,
and so on." In the autobiographical mode the recurrent systems of
thought, value, emotion, sensation, and memory are subjected to investigation by the "things" that appear in the act of writing. Autobiography, for Creeley, is an active, continual testing of the self against time
and space, memory and location.

> This mode of autobiography is close to our usual senses of history,
> *his story* as we said in fourth grade, and it is also useful to note
> *history* comes from a Greek root, '*istorin*: to go find out for yourself.
> This was Charles Olson's clear point of emphasis in his own pro-
> cedures, that *self-action* – the middle voice – was crucial in human
> existence. Why he so insisted, I think, comes of his belief that
> humans get truly lost in thought and language insofar as no sub-
> stantiating act, particularly from and of and to the human itself,
> takes place.[38]

Autobiography, in this case, would be the most authentic history (or
art) that puts all evidence accumulated to the test of the writer's present
concerns. The final locus of value, Creeley and Olson insist, resides in
the individual: "Why not speak for yourself. Sooner or later you'll have
to. There are no sure investments. Watch the dollar do the dirty float –
like a mind, a dead idea, fading" (*WTRP*, 55–6). There are no values, no
"investments" of human energy that guarantee a stability beyond the
present conditions of the self. As Creeley says in his introduction to
Olson's *Selected Writings,*

Even the most sympathetic ordering of human effects and intelligence leads to unavoidable assumptions and the test – which is the reality of one's quite literal being – denies any investment of reality prior to its fact.

> There are no hierarchies, no infinite, no such
>   many as mass, there are only
> eyes in all heads
> to be looked out of ("Letter 6")   (QG, 182–3)

Creeley applies this test to a variety of autobiographical situations. As a quick overview of the range of these situations, I offer descriptive titles for each of the units of *Presences*:

I.1	Situating the thing
I.2	Authorities and the Heraclitean fire
I.3	Remembering being with a woman in a park
II.2	Mommy comes home
II.3	The size of human bodies on a transatlantic voyage
II.1	Fable: monsters in the desert
III.3	School days, boys as boys
III.1	Stoned music
III.2	Mabel, after forty years
IV.1	Painting: *The Inspiration of the Poet*
IV.2	The death car leaves the Dane's castle behind
IV.3	The stay in a villa, doubting wife's love
V.2	Teeth
V.3	Remembering the idea of being on that farm
V.1	Accepting and using the self
Postscript	Death as absence

These titles are not exhaustive thematic analyses, but they do give an inkling of the types of autobiographical narrative in *Presences*, a subject to which we will return.

Creeley shares this mode of autobiographical valuation with Marisol, and this shared method forms the basis of his admiration of her work. Just as Creeley sees all his writing as ultimately autobiographical, Marisol sees all her sculpture as self-portraiture; even the portraits of other objects or people are tacitly measured against the self:

> I'm always there (in my studio) when I'm working. I work very often late at night. I can't call up a friend at one in the morning to make a cast of his face. But when I make a cast of my own face, I file it down or alter it by sandpapering. Whatever the artist makes is always a kind of self-portrait. Even if he paints a picture of an apple

or makes an abstraction. When I do a well-known person like John
Wayne, I am really doing myself.[39]

This type of autobiography presents the self not for purposes of asserting
the ego but as a measure of honesty or sincerity. Until tested against the
artist's sense of self, a work of art cannot claim authenticity; for any
knowledge to become authentic, it must be measured against self-knowl-
edge. The artist, as knower, strives to achieve a kind of congruity between the "inside" and the "out." Creeley recognizes this task of equilibration in Marisol's work: "The sculptor Marisol speaks of using
herself, over and over, in her work. 'When I show myself as I am I return
to reality' " (*WTRP*, 57). Though Creeley has often been accused of
solipsism, Marisol's statement of equilibration between self and world,
"When I show myself as I am I return to reality," could be taken as his
motto.[40] In fact Creeley uses this and several other statements by Marisol
as the basis for the final unit of *Presences* (V.1):

> Voices from the silence. Silencio immenso. Darkness falls from
> the air. When I show myself as I am, I return to reality. Vestida
> con mantos negros. Somewhere else, sometime. Walking in the
> rain.
>
> When I show myself as I am, I return to reality. Piensa que el
> mundo es chiquito. Goes green, goes white. Weather falls out,
> raining. Applause at the edges. Seeing wind. When I show
> myself as I am, I return to reality. People should think of
> themselves when they live alone. Goes white.
> . . . .
> Piensa que el mundo es chiquito. Small. Little. Not very much. I
> would learn about myself. I used myself. I show myself as I am.
> Goes green, goes white. The heart. Y el corazon es immenso.
> Large. Immense. Sees rain. A hand at the end of an arm.
>
> I was very sad. I was very happy. I was thinking of rain,
> walking. People should think of themselves. I started doing
> something funny. I need a lot of affection. I return to reality. I
> had no other model. I used myself over and over. I put things
> where they belong. I show myself as I am. I started doing
> something funny so I would become happier. People I met were
> so depressing. And it worked. You are your own best friend.
> Vestida con mantos negros.   (*Mabel*, 111–12)

I have copied the first two and last two paragraphs; the four paragraphs in between continue the permutations on substantially the same
set of phrases. Charles Altieri misreads this unit, seeing in it "a fairly
contented egotist simultaneously serious and self-parodic" who vacillates

between the serious and self-parodic treatments of "popular psychological slogans" (*b2*, 535). Altieri's reading is at once too clever and misinformed. He inventively argues that Creeley, by simultaneously accepting and parodying these statements about the self, is able to sidestep the centrality of the I. But this overly rationalized reading is unnecessary when one realizes that most of the statements the I makes here are attributable to Marisol. Rather than self-parody, Creeley's prose conjectures with the possibilities of autobiographical art as he and Marisol understand it.

These conjectural sentences become incantatory, as often happens in *Presences,* reminding one of the incantatory sentences of Gertrude Stein. The interweaving of Spanish phrases among Marisol's pronouncements enhances the magical aspect of incantation. As a Venezuelan (born in Paris in 1930), Marisol's native language is Spanish; this might have suggested Creeley's use of Spanish here. The words, however, are Lorca's and were also quoted by Creeley as the epigraph to his early story "A Death." Here is their source, Lorca's poem "La Soleá," flanked by Paul Blackburn's translation:

La Soleá	*The Recluse*
Vestida con mantos negros piensa que el mundo es chiquito y el corazón es inmenso.	Rigged out in black veils she thinks the world is tiny & that the heart is immense.
Vestida con mantos negros.	BLACK VEILS
Piensa que el suspiro tierno y el grito, desaparecen en la corriente del viento.	She thinks the delicate sigh & the scream will disappear in the wind-flow
Vestida con mantos negros.	THOSE BLACK VEILS
Se dejó el balcón abierto y al alba, por el balcón desembocó todo el cielo.	Balcón was left open & at dawn, the whole sky rushed in at the balcony
¡*Ay yayayayay,* *Que vestida con mantos negros!*	MIGOD, WHAT A WAY TO DRESS! BLACK VEILS![41]

Not only does the phrase "vestida con mantos negros" (dressed in black veils or mantles) describe the mantlelike coiffures of the women (each bearing Marisol's face) who lean against each other and the wall in the sculpture (*Women Leaning*) that accompanies the Scribners text, but the stanza as a whole evokes Marisol's isolation and the quality of her work that might be called "feelings writ large upon the world." In

Marisol's sculpture, the conventional representation of proportion gives
way to distortions that project single, "immense" emotional states onto
blocklike human figures. The figures lose their variety of planes and
features and present highly discrete emotions as planar absolutes. There
is much for Creeley to identify with in Marisol's art: the isolation, the
immensity of the heart, the repetition of frontality, and the constant use
of the self. Neither artist is devoid of masks (appearances), but the masks
are masks of the self that take on a concrete density in their presence.

The figures in *Women Leaning* share another feature with "La Soleá":
the tone of impending death in the poem, which may find accomplishment in the last stanza; the sky seems to rush into the vacuum created by
the recluse leaping out of her balcony. In the related illustration showing
a close-up of *Women Leaning,* the face looks like a death mask of the
sculptor surrounded by a solid, veiling mass of black hair. This tone is
likewise apparent in the quiet urgency of Creeley's prose. Rather than
self-parodic, the permutations he works upon these phrases from Marisol and Lorca are tenderly playful; the self asserts itself tentatively in the
face of threatening darkness (and the world's immensity). Though some
of these phrases may initially strike one as clichés (and Creeley cherishes
the familiar and the banal), through repetitious conjecture the poet invests these phrases with a reverberant dignity that asks the reader to
listen closely and hear them as a revelatory "saying." These clichés about
the self are of the same order as the broken cliché (from "I Know a
Man"), "the darkness sur- / rounds us,"[42] and in both cases Creeley
foregrounds the phrases in such a way that they begin to carry the weight
of authentic speech and offer a tentative, if interrogative, affirmation of
human possibility in the midst of elemental and man-made doom.[43]

An autobiographical art, whether Creeley's or Marisol's, that is so
attentive to its own limitations does not seek to convert the world to its
own viewpoint or ask for admiration of its technical accomplishment;
instead it bears witness to the problems of knowledge and action through
the vehicle of the "I" and has as its ultimate goal an exemplary wisdom
that will be of use to others. Creeley sees this wisdom as the prerogative
of those who have lived long and fully:

> The grandfathers, and grandmothers, are the great storytellers –
> and in societies alert to that human need they are of course so used.
> They tell a life of *I* that becomes more than singular consciousness
> in isolations of intent or assertive energy. They are, as it were,
> taking the *I* back to its center. Olson once told me that the initial
> sign for the pronoun *I* was a boat. Insofar as *I* is a vehicle of passage
> or transformation, its powers are clear. Realized as will or person-
> ality, that "mealy seal" as Olson called it, the power vitiates as

soon as the energy necessary to sustain it exhausts itself. "L'état c'est moi" is truly the end of a period. (*WTRP*, 60)

The autobiographical prose from *Presences* V. 1 that we have been reading proceeds by a method of grammatical transformation. The passage we read earlier concerning the Heraclitean fire also moved via transformations. Three other narrative modes, or conjectural directions, can be found (usually in combination) in the poet's prose of *Presences*. I call these the *occasional*, the *memorial*, and the *fabulous* narratives, and each is a mode of tracking, an act of measurement of the self in relation to a variety of presences. The occasional narrative is almost purely phenomenological; using it, Creeley tries to locate himself as human being in a present situation. The memorial narrative is concerned with memory or history; Creeley uses it to locate his present condition with reference to a distant or recent past. The fabulous narrative presents mythical or magical situations, which Creeley employs as fables that measure the literal present against a numinous realm. The fourth narrative mode, the transformational, that we have already discussed to some degree, investigates grammar through puns, clichés, collage, and rhymes, rendering words as corporeal presences. Each of these narrative modes participates in the autobiographical purpose of tracking, of measuring the self among the various realms of presences: the physical world, memories, the numinous world, and language. Before speaking further of the importance of the act of measurement in *Presences,* let us consider a brief example of each of the first three modes.

In addition to terms like "literal," "presence," "measure," and "possibility," one of the key words in Creeley's vocabulary is "occasion," which denotes the actual time and space in which things happen. The occasional narrative in *Presences* consists in an attempt to place the self in a given situation and to understand the parameters of measurement by which such location is possible. At its most basic level, the occasional narrative opens a clearing in the present in which things may appear:

Big things. And little things. The weight, the lightness of it. The place it takes. Walking around, it comes forward, or to the side, or sides, or backward, on a foot, on feet, on several feet.

There is a top, and a bottom. From the one to the other may be a distance. Equally it may be so dense, or vaporous, so tangential to touch, that an inextricable time passes in the simplest way. If it were to fall, either over, or up, or down, what spaces were there to accomplish would be of necessity measured later. Time runs to keep up, in other words. Already days have apparently gone by in the presence of one. (I.1, in *Mabel*, 63)

The memorial narrative, as Creeley noted above, is the more familiar autobiographical mode, though in *Presences* Creeley characteristically uses it for the specific purpose of understanding how events in the past still remain present to the self. In the following passage the memories are associated with the onset of the very sense of self:

> *Myself* is what one comes to think of, then, letting the well fill up, things happen. Others out there, like June Welsh, who was a welfare kid living on the DeSouza farm up from where we did. Beauteous June, round faced, short bob, so tough and so tender. She caught one's heart with her human vulnerability and to walk home with her was to enter such deep pride and confusion. Or Helen, seemingly tall, Scandinavian, her brother for a time my sister's boyfriend so that she and I were likewise linked. Tilda, whose brother was my own friend and whose father thought I should devote myself to Latin, and the outwitting of the Catholic conspiracy. Days and nights no doubt forever.   (III.3, in *Mabel*, 85)

The magical activities in the fabulous narrative are often associated with death. When we leave our present condition and seek to outwit the future (and death) by magical controls, we end up fooling ourselves, losing track of ourselves. The fable from which the following excerpt is taken ends disastrously, as it inevitably must:

> There are monsters in the desert, who prey on the unwary. Tales record as much as such ever leaves behind. Windy bones bleaching, like they say. This time they got wise, they thought, and made extensive preparations so as not to let these monsters have their way with them, however many there were in fact in the company. Forty, say. More like two hundred. At least a very distinct number of these people. What they do is get lots of water in big casks and water bags and all that sort of container and they load the mules and the camels, all that they have to hoist this stuff forward into the desert of their desire. They have the monsters completely buffaloed, so they figure, because they are not going to run out of water out there and drop down on their knees in the sand with their tongues going black and their eyes popping out, etc.   (II.1, in *Mabel*, 79–80)

By placing himself in relation to things, memories, fables, and words, Creeley opens up many levels of conjecture. The texture of the prose owes its characteristic movement to the intersection of continuous narrative modes (memorial and fabulous) with discontinuous modes (occasional and transformational). The interplay of continuity and discontinuity at the narrative level gives the conjecture a multivalent density and richness. Every narrative mode, though, promotes specific acts of measurement in which the self finds its scale and place among all the other presences that appear. The repetition of acts of measurement likewise signals an interrogation of the very systems that allow measure: "Time runs to keep up, in other words." Of this aspect of Creeley's conjectural prose Michael Davidson says,

> In *Presences,* more than anywhere else, Creeley incurs the limits that mediate experience. By pointing endlessly to size and scale, to boundary and limit, he investigates a continually shifting perspective which attempts at each moment to establish a realm of value for that instant. Perhaps the most important single word in the book is "scale" since it appropriates ideas of big and small, density and opacity, background and foreground into the world of human concern.[44]

It may at first seem curious for a prose that forgoes the traditional measures of poetry to invoke terms of measurement so insistently. However, although so many modern American poets have rejected traditional meter as an a priori determinant for the form of poetry, paradoxically the rejected concept of measure becomes transposed and reasserts itself as a central area of inquiry for these poets. This is a large subject, worthy in itself of extended treatment, and there is time here for only a broad sketch of the background for Creeley's radical concern with measure.

We begin with Ezra Pound in his imagist phase, and some statements from his "Credo":

> *Rhythm.* – I believe in an "absolute rhythm," a rhythm, that is, in poetry which corresponds exactly to the emotion or shade of emotion to be expressed. A man's rhythm must be interpretative, it will be, therefore, in the end, his own, uncounterfeiting, uncounterfeitable.

and

> *Technique.* – I believe in technique as the test of a man's sincerity; in law when it is ascertainable; in the trampling down of every convention that impedes or obscures the determination of the law, or the precise rendering of the impulse.[45]

In the notions of an " 'absolute rhythm' . . . which corresponds exactly to the emotion" and of the sincerity required for "the precise rendering of the impulse" Pound sets the stage for both the variable meter, determined by the impulse, and a moral concern for the formal sincerity with which an impulse or emotion is rendered.

After Pound comes Williams, who pursued a lifelong, passionate quest for measure. Williams searched continuously for a basis of measurement in poetry that would reflect the relative measures proposed by modern physics and mathematics:

> Relativity gives us the cue. So, again, mathematics comes to the rescue of the arts. Measure, an ancient word in poetry, something we have almost forgotten in its literal significance as something measured, becomes related again with the poetic. We have today to do with the poetic, as always, but a *relatively* stable foot, not a rigid one. That is all the difference. It is that which must become the object of our search.[46]

Toward the end of his life he finally reached the variable foot, a convention that has seemed to nearly everyone a wish-fulfilling compromise with the terms of his search for a relative measure, however splendid the poems it produced. Earlier, though, his insistence on a measure intrinsic to the subject matter of the poem led him to an association with Objectivism in both philosophy and poetry. After Imagism the objectivist moment (the twenties and thirties) provides the clearest focus for the developing concept of measure. The term "objectivist," referring to a philosophical position that holds objects and subjects as equal participants in the world, received its first important formulation in the writings of A. N. Whitehead. A controversy still surrounds Louis Zukofsky's derivation of the term, which he first used in the "'Objectivists' 1931" issue of *Poetry* (37, no. 5 [February 1931]), but Williams regarded his own reading of Whitehead's *Science and the Modern World* as "a milestone surely in my career."[47]

Rather than navigate the historical and doctrinal complexities of Objectivism in poetry (as F. T. Sharp has done in "Objectivists 1927–1934," Ph.D. diss., Stanford University [1982]), let us simply examine the generally Whiteheadean ideas underlying the objectivist sense of measure. The new space–time physics of Einstein, Whitehead, Heisenberg, and similar thinkers teaches that no measurement is a neutral act; all such acts are affected by the measuring subject and the measuring instrument. Thus in Whitehead's epistemology all we may know is the event, which, in the case of measurement, is the coincidence of the measurer, the thing measured, and the measure. In poetry this would mean that the writer (measurer), the world (what is measured), and language (the measure) are all integral and specific ("objective") to the single event of the poem. This new measure would hold ideally that all three components are equally important to the poem (though of course this varies in practice from writer to writer and poem to poem) and that they are inseparable. To consider, for instance, the measure of the poem apart from what it measures would be to violate the terms of a necessary interdependence.

An objectivist poet such as Williams conceives of the traditional poetic meters as the application of arbitrary numerical standards to language in which language acts as a kind of ruler for measuring experience. This rigidifies and overemphasizes the measuring device at the expense of the measurer and the thing measured, fitting them both into a deformative mold. By breaking this mold and returning all three components to a position of relative equality, objectivist poetry becomes an effective instrument in the apprehension and understanding of reality. Keeping in mind the equivalent priority of these three terms, we can account for the impression of flatness in objectivist writing. When one believes that an event is constructed of all the elements in a given space at a given time, there is no need to suggest a symbolic depth that begs us to penetrate appearances and ferret out essences.[48]

Though not articulated in precisely this manner by any individual poet, this summary sketchily delineates the underlying sense of measure in poets who derive their practice from Objectivism – Williams, Zukofsky, George Oppen, Charles Reznikoff, Carl Rakosi, Lorine Niedecker; Charles Olson, Robert Creeley, Robert Duncan, Edward Dorn, Denise Levertov, Larry Eigner, and Paul Blackburn. The projectivist verse of Olson and Creeley continues and refines this objectivist sense of measure. Its most succinct expression, Creeley's dictum that "form is never more than an extension of content," derives from Zukofsky's extension of Pound's concept of *sincerity* – that the words used fit exactly the things invoked – and *objectification* – that the poem appear as a "rested totality," that is, an object.[49]

Objectivist poetics, through notions like sincerity and objectification, breaks down the barrier between the subjective and the objective and brings together the self and the world of fact. Prose, as the traditional mode for statements of fact, affords American poets of an objectivist bent a ready-made tool for such an integrative poetry. Not only Creeley but poets in the generation following his such as David Bromige, Ron Silliman, Barrett Watten, and Barbara Einzig construct what Michael Davidson calls a "prose of fact" as a means to effect this union. The third element in this objectivist triangle, the measure, likewise spurs these younger poets to varied and sustained investigations of language itself.

THE MORALITY OF MEASURE

I want to give witness not to the thought of myself – that specious concept of identity – but, rather, to what I am as simple agency, a thing evidently alive by virtue of such activity. I want, as Charles Olson says, to come into the world. Measure, then, is my testament. What uses me is what I use and in that complex measure is the issue.

Creeley

For Creeley, the concept of measure unites the formal issues of writing with other, more philosophical notions.[50] In his later writing in general and especially in *Presences*, Creeley seeks to conflate ontology with epistemology. To the question "How do we know something?" Creeley answers, "By being with it," by allowing ourselves to exist alongside the thing we would know and thus measuring ourselves in relation to it. In the sentence "Already days have apparently gone by in the presence of one" (*Mabel*, 63), the ambiguous use of "one" reveals that one thing and one's self are inextricably entangled in experience. But one does not become present merely by existing; the extent to which one pays attention and brings all one's powers to bear upon the present situation determines how much one may know. Creeley deepens the notion of sincerity into a measurement of the ability to "presence" (Heidegger's verb): The degree to which one is present in the act of writing determines how present the things of the writing may become, how present they may be to a reader.

Edward Dorn has similar philosophical interests. To illustrate the union of ontology with epistemology, Dorn, in *Gunslinger* (Berkeley: Wingbow Press, 1975), arranges a comic masque in which the "semi-dios" Gunslinger gets the "drop" on a Stranger by the exercise of his impeccable attention; he then draws his gun and "describes" the Stranger: "a plain, unassorted white citizen." The observer of this disabling description (which traps the Stranger in a "general" condition, that is, robs him of his presence) is called "I." "I" has yet to understand the relation of presence to knowledge:

> What does the foregoing mean?
> I asked. Mean?
> my Gunslinger laughed
> *Mean?*
> Questioner, you got some strange
> obsessions, you want to know
> what something *means* after you've
> seen it, after you've *been* there
> or were you *out* during
> that time? No.
> And you want some *reason.*
> How fast are you
> by the way? No local offense
> asking that is there?
> No.   (Book I, n.p.)

"I" is clearly none too fast, in Gunslinger's terms, which are divulged on the next page:

To eliminate the draw
permits an unmatchable Speed
a syzygy which hangs tight
just back of the curtain
of the reality theater
down the street,
speed is not necessarily fast.
Bullets are not necessarily specific.
When the act is
so self contained
and so dazzling in itself
the target then
can disappear
in the heated tension
which is an area between here
and formerly
In some parts of the western world
men have mistakenly
called that phenomenology –   (Book I, n.p.)

"To eliminate the draw" in poetry is to be so present to both language
and appearances that dualities cease to conflict and the writing becomes
its own measure. When opposing terms such as here and there, subject
and object, body and mind, self and other, one and many, big and small,
are brought into equilibration by attention to appearances in the present,
then "the act is / so self contained / and so dazzling in itself" that the
object (of description) "can disappear / in the heated" presence. This
coincides exactly with the poetic stance expressed earlier by Octavio Paz:
"The art object dissolves in the instantaneous act . . . [into] a presence to
be contemplated. The work is not an end in itself nor does it exist in its
own right: the work is a bridge, an intermediary." "The work is a
bridge, an intermediary" that exists "between here / and formerly"
(mixing terms for space and time); it is that "vehicle of passage or transformation" that Creeley calls autobiography. The work is not in the final
analysis phenomenology but poetry, since poetry of the variety here
contemplated must totally embody its occasion in language, whereas
phenomenology may remain merely descriptive.

Throughout *Presences,* Creeley invokes coordinates of measurement,
such as here/there, big/small, now/then, one/many, self/other. In the
turnings of his conjectural prose a coordinate seldom remains stationary
and often invokes its opposite, leaving us finally to listen primarily to
language:

You are very big, you think. You were small, a speck merely, a
twinkle in the universe. You have come here to continue and

will never stop again. You think it all goes on forever and will
go insistently with it. Here, there, you run back and forth. You
are in love again.   (*Mabel*, 78)

Through conjecture about bodily size and scale, the "you" turns to ideas
about time and space and then becomes aware of being in love. The
course of this conjecture, from conditions of bigness to love, enacts
another instance of sincerity, in which the body and spirit are no longer
in opposition but are intimately connected. Language is then the incarnation of this fact, itself a perceptible presence.

Like the phenomenologist Maurice Merleau-Ponty and like Olson in
his essay "Proprioception,"[51] Creeley holds that experience is corporeal
and that perception is a relation of the body to the world. Speaking of
"Proprioception" (the body's internal perception of itself), Creeley notes
that Olson "makes evident the content of any man as literal experience in
and of his *body*" (*QG*, 193). In *Presences* the body places and measures as a
vulnerable organ that feels itself constantly in the midst of other things.
The body has necessary reactions, such as affection, hostility, fear, and
longing, that it applies instantly to anything felt as present, whether
literally or in the imagination. These reactions comprise a necessary facet
of the registration of presence in writing.[52]

Even language, in its tactile qualities, produces bodily reactions.
Often in *Presences* Creeley takes a metaphorical phrase at face value (that
is, with the same frontality found in Marisol's sculptures) and then draws
out the implications of linguistic assertion as it bears upon the body:

What was he doing on the beach? No, it was a chair he sat in.
He continued to sit in the chair. As if he had been thrown there.
He had been thrown there. His small, unobtrusive body lay
crumpled against one of the arm rests and his eyes, photographic
blurs of grey, were pleading, mutely. In a book of the same
order, so to speak, of the ungenerous kinds of people who do
not love but nonetheless expect to be loved. Why was he
foresaken? He was not. He was placed, in a place.

She picked him up and threw him into another place. His little
seersucker suit tightly hugged the space under his arms, his
armpits, and his diminutive body became rumpled with the
impact of being elsewhere. His tie, however, fell straight, un-
disturbed. Always the gentleman. Being alive, she felt contempt
but moved away from it to get some ice from the refrigerator.
This, as one says, she put into glasses which she then filled with
gin.   (*Mabel*, 63–4)

"As if he had been thrown there" is a figure of speech that Creeley
conjectures with as a literal possibility. Likewise he imagines the collo-

quial expression "I'm in another place" (that is, not attentive) as literal in the sentence "She picked him up and threw him into another place." But this interrogation of language is done not merely for the purpose of humor or to dramatize self-pity, but to reveal the assertive objectifications that language performs and in which we participate unconsciously. A double helplessness is represented here: on the one hand, the retreat from presence, the way one chooses to be absent ("as if thrown there") or allows oneself to be "thrown" by the more powerful presence of another person; on the other hand, the overassertiveness of language, which in its potency often overstates what one would say.[53]

Another autobiographer, Roland Barthes, in *Roland Barthes* (1975), an autobiography as original in form and content as Creeley's *Presences*, criticizes his critical texts, focusing on the role his body plays in his works. Like Creeley, Barthes experiences the assertive power of language:

Vérité et assertion – Truth and assertion

His (sometimes acute) discomfort – mounting some evenings, after writing the whole day, to a kind of fear – was generated by his sense of producing a double discourse, whose mode overreached its aim, somehow: for the aim of his discourse is not truth, and yet this discourse is assertive.

(This kind of embarrassment started, for him, very early; he strives to master it – for otherwise he would have to stop writing – by reminding himself that it is language which is assertive, not he. An absurd remedy, everyone would surely agree, to add to each sentence some little phrase of uncertainty, as if anything that came out of language could make language tremble.)

(By much the same sense, he imagines, each time he writes something, that he will hurt one of his friends – never the same one: it changes.)[54]

This type of autobiographical writing, with its sensitivity to and investigation of the way language speaks, goes beyond the intentions of the ego and de-authorizes the author. Recounting an anecdote of Richard Alpert's about his experience of ego loss the first time he tried LSD, Creeley challenges the reader and any would-be autobiographer: "Can you melt yourself, 'autobiographically,' can you stand, literally, not to be some absent dream of glory, just what your mother always wanted" (*WTRP*, 56).

Although *Presences*, as autobiographical writing, does not strictly belong to the prophetic tradition of American autobiography delineated in G.

Thomas Couser's *American Autobiography: The Prophetic Mode* (Amherst: Univ. of Massachusetts Press, 1979), Creeley admits the "Puritan" impulse to confess painful secrets as an autobiographical motive (*WTRP*, 58). More important, the writing proceeds from and proposes a definite ethical stance based upon the enabling criterion of *use*: Just as Creeley's autobiographical conjectures make use of anything present in mind or space, so the text is meant to be of use to a reader in the actual living of life. "What the autobiographic does, primarily, is to specify *person*" (*WTRP*, 55), to focus on the individual's actual experience rather than the imagination of some general condition. Generalization is the assumption of a stable identity outside of time (the moment of composition/presence); this falsifies experience and yields a text (or mind) available to external manipulation. For Creeley, the critical manipulation of the text that deforms it into abstract categories is tantamount to the physical manipulation of persons by officials (who are individuals assuming the mantle of a general role or corporate entity):

> When the New York Police Department has persons within it who will literally threaten to run other persons down with trucks in order to gain their compliance, no matter how "guilty" those threatened may be, one cannot accept the agency. Realize that the *general,* the *we-ness* proposed in various realities, may well prove to be this kind. (*WTRP*, 54)

Similar to generalization is abstraction, which Creeley and Olson, following in the path of Imagism and Objectivism, see as a dangerous type of synecdoche in which a part of experience becomes reified and then stands in the way of authentic action in a given context. As Creeley says, "To discover a precision in this situation, to act in the specific context, takes all the wit and alertness anyone of us can bring to it" (*WTRP*, 54). Creeley's vocabulary, which appears so abstract, with its reliance upon a nonspecific use of pronouns (here/there, one/it, and so forth), is not meant to reify or categorize experience but rather to open a clearing in the present (of both writing and reading) in which one can live authentically. In that sense all of his pronouns are demonstrative: They point to the actual world in which beings constantly approach and retreat.[55]

The commitments Creeley shares with Olson to presence and to process can easily be confused (and possibly were so confused by each of them in the late sixties) with a prevalent strain of amorality abroad in American society in which "anything goes." This confusion masks the deeply moral commitment of each man as a writer. Though Creeley does not share the prescriptive and proscriptive moral certitude of Olson (one of whose favorite words, reflecting his Catholic background, is "dogma"), he constantly probes moral questions throughout his writing, especially in his prose. The preface to *The Gold Diggers* opens with an ambivalent expression of his strong moral impulse:

Had I lived some years ago, I think I would have been a moralist, i.e., one who lays down, so to speak, rules of behavior with no small amount of self-satisfaction. But the writer isn't allowed that function anymore, or no man can take the job on very happily, being aware (as he must be) of what precisely that will make him. (QG, 3)

Finding himself unwilling to prescribe moral conduct, Creeley deflects the burden of his ethical concern to the domain of form. Michael Davidson comments on the moral element in *A Day Book* and *Presences*:

Like his earlier prose, the new work investigates the conditions under which moral decisions are made; "to look at it is more / than it was" remains a crucial index of ethical choice. But in his more recent work, Creeley embodies the ethical choice in his form; the open-ended, exploratory style with its lack of closure and its awareness of contextual frames becomes a kind of moral condition in itself. (b2, 563)

In the autobiographical writing that Creeley advocates, authenticity offers an implied criterion that can be used to gauge the ethical choice embodied in form. To the extent that one remains true to the moment of writing (process) and to what arises in that moment (presences), one envinces moral rectitude in authentic writing.

From the beginnings of their association, Olson, Creeley, and the other members of the Black Mountain School shared an ethical commitment to process in the form of "composition by field." This moral stance provides the rationale for the remarkable degree of opprobrium these writers have poured upon other writers for whom composition is the realization of prior intentions rather than the recognition of form and content as they arise. In his union of process with presence, Creeley may be the most implacable and single-minded of these writers: Not only must the composition form itself by a discovery of its contents, but these contents must be continually tested against the phenomenological reality in which the writer stands. Of the other Black Mountain writers, Robert Duncan, for instance, makes little effort to adhere to the ethic of presence, feeling free to wander into any absent realm whatsoever as long as his composition remains true to the dictates of process.

The ethic of presence ramifies further in Creeley's rejection of fiction. The fictional is the unreal, what is not actual or present, and thus the writer of fiction lapses from the autobiographical responsibility to mea-

sure oneself against what arises in one's writing. All of Creeley's "tales,"
from *The Gold Diggers* to *The Island* to *Mabel: A Story,* shun the fictional
by insisting on the conjectural. In this context, recall Olson's praise of
Creeley's antifictional stance, in which Olson nominates Creeley as "the
push beyond the fictive," whose tales should be read "not as fiction but
as RE-ENACTMENT." Fiction (in league with the similarly proscribed
simile) partakes of the realm of *as if,* which Creeley opposes diametrically
to his chosen realm of *it is*: "One path only is left for us to speak of,
namely, that *It is.*" This statement opens into a virtual credo that uses
metaphysics to imply an imperative ethics of presence: "In this path are
very many tokens that what is is uncreated and indestructible; for it is
complete, immoveable, and without end. Nor was it ever, nor will it be;
for now *it is,* all at once, a continuous one" (*Mabel,* 25). Not only does
this unidentified quotation from Parmenides (Diels, Fr. 8) place Creeley
in opposition to Robert Duncan – who is so certain of the centrality of
fiction to his writing that he has titled a book of his essays and autobiographical writing promised from New Directions *Fictive Certainties* –
but Edward Dorn, too, has felt himself in conflict with this moral abso-
lutism. Dorn noted in conversation that Creeley (as well as Olson) disap-
proved of the fictional aspect of *Gunslinger* and that Dorn's next book,
Recollections of Gran Apachería, was written using factual material as a
homage to Creeley (to whom the book is dedicated).

This discussion of the morality of form locates an interesting paradox
in Robert Creeley as man and writer: The supreme value he places upon
openness, both in form and in living, confronts a moral essentialism that
demands strict adherence to the absolute actuality of the moment. The
paradox of such openness (in which he courageously maintains a nakedness nearly unprecedented in American writing) confronting such a willful constriction accounts in large measure for the particular intensity of
Creeley's writing.[56] By its openness his conjectural prose risks an un-
focused, associational wandering, but by its scrupulous attention to the
living implications of what appears it continually returns us to the heroic
demands of an absolute present, "complete, immoveable, and without
end."

A short consideration of Robert Duncan's prose will illustrate the
extremity of Creeley's position by comparing it with that of a projectivist writer with whom Creeley has maintained a fraternal relationship
over a period of three decades. In his ongoing *Structure of Rime* sequence,
Duncan combines the European-inspired prose poem with aspects of the
more innovative poet's prose. His prose is unconcerned with fact or
presence but instead uses the generative sentence to create an ongoing
fiction about the process of self-reflective poetic thought. Propositions
abound, making romantic proposals of a doctrine of correspondences

(Rime) that turns the world into poetry. For Duncan, the essence of poetry is Rime, which encompasses both the likeness and difference of sounds and the correspondence and uniqueness of images: "An absolute scale of resemblance and disresemblance establishes measures that are music in the actual world." The *Structure of Rime* sequence explores the workings of Rime within a version of the generative sentence that sees the sentence itself as an ideal entity, a mythical person, who summons the possibilities of Rime. As a summoner of Rime, the sentence (the paradigm, as we have seen, of writing) calls forth verse as well as prose, extending itself through continual overlappings of sound and image.

The Structure of Rime I

I ask the unyielding Sentence that shows Itself forth in the language as I make it,

Speak! For I name myself your master, who come to serve. Writing is first a search in obedience.

There is a woman who resembles the sentence. She has a place in memory that moves language. Her voice comes across the waters from a shore I don't know to a shore I know, and is translated into words belonging to the poem:

Have heart, the text reads,
  you that were heartless.
Suffering joy or despair
you will suffer the sentence
a law of words moving
seeking their right period.

I saw a snake-like beauty in the living changes of syntax.

Wake up, she cried.
Jacob wrestled with Sleep – you who fall into nothingness and
    dread sleep.
He wrestled with Sleep like a man reading a strong sentence.

I will not take the actual world for granted, I said.

Why not? she replied.
Do I not withhold the song of the birds from you?
Do I not withhold the penetrations of red from you?
Do I not withhold the weight of mountains from you?
Do I not withhold the hearts of men from you?

I alone long for your demand.
I alone measure your desire.

O Lasting Sentence,
sentence after sentence I make in your image. In the feet that
measure the dance of my pages I hear cosmic intoxications of the
man I will be.

> *Cheat at this game? she cries.*
> *The world is what you are.*
>   *Stand then*
> *so I can see you, a fierce destroyer of images.*
>
> *Will you drive me to madness*
>   *only there to know me?*
> *vomiting images into the place of the Law!*[57]

In his "Notes on the Structure of Rime," Duncan specifies influences
upon his prose: St.-John Perse, Mallarmé, Rimbaud, Poe, Charles Henri
Ford, Philip Lamantia, Nietzsche's *Zarathustra,* George MacDonald,
Blake, and the Zohar.[58] This heady hermetic and surrealistic crew leads
Duncan to an opaquely prophetic prose, full of striking images and
vague intuitions, a fictive prose that "will not take the actual world for
granted" and yet will demythologize as "a fierce destroyer of images." I
find this style most appealing in the way the dense pattern of rhyming
leads the syntax into ever-new twists and turns; as he says, "I saw a
snake-like beauty in the living changes of syntax." This ravelling and
unravelling of sense approximates Ashbery's even more enigmatic syntax in *Three Poems* or the convolute circlings of Heidegger's tautological
prose. Duncan works this syntax to masterful effect in his later poem
"The Museum" (1973), which begins

> Grand Architecture that the Muses command! my heart and
> breathing lungs mount the ascending tones in which your pillars
> swell, sound, and soar, above the struggling mind. In the
> treasure room enclosed in sound, Muse upon Muse turns to gaze
> into the radiant space in building.
>   In certain designs they are most present, and in their presence
> I come, I realize, into their design. What I see now is a
> shadowed space, a shell in time, a silent alcove in thunder, in
> which the stony everlasting gaze loses itself in my coming into
> its plan. It is an horizon coming in from what we cannot see to
> sound in sight that is female. Moving toward an orison of the
> visible. From the carving out in thought of an arrival, the figure
> of a womanly grace invades the sound of the heart that beats for
> her, and, in number, repeats in a run of alcoves – shadowd
> radiance upon shadowd radiance – beyond the body of this
> Woman, the body of these women. In the Museum – as in the

labyrinth at Knossos, the Minotaur; as in the head of the Great
God, the hawk Horus returning – a Woman that is a Company
of Women moves.[59]

The prose employs copulas, prepositional phrases, and the grammatical
oscillations of nouns and verbs to multiply the frames around statements,
creating a synesthetic echo chamber of sound and sense. The room of the
muses that Duncan creates in the poem is a scene of translation or understanding in which the muse's function is hermeneutic: "It is an horizon
coming in from what we cannot see to sound in sight that is female."
Duncan uses his prose to represent the emergence of understanding
rather than to test statements of fact. "Her voice comes across the waters
from a shore I don't know, and is translated into words belonging to the
poem."

Although Creeley and Duncan have remained in close correspondence
for thirty years, both engaged in "composition by field," differences
between them abound. Duncan is committed to process, to the endless
play of identity and difference, whether psychological, metaphorical, or
auditory; though he stands squarely in the lineage of Emerson and Whitman, Duncan is equally at home in the avant-garde European tradition,
from Baudelaire, Rimbaud, and Mallarmé to Surrealism and the cabalistic fictions of textuality of Edmond Jabès. For Creeley, process is a
means of access to presence; the interplay of identity and difference yields
to the interplay of repetition and appearance. Although both poets investigate with boldness and sophistication the hermeneutic realm of understanding, Creeley does so from a phenomenological perspective, while
Duncan's investigations (though employing terms like "horizon" and
"presence") proceed through erecting a fiction of language and textuality, engaging the quasi-theological Persons of language in the play of
the text.

Creeley offers a "last word" about fiction in his postscript to *Presences*:

> "My death," said a certain ogre, "is far from here and hard to
> find, on the wide ocean. In that sea is an island, and on the
> island there grows a green oak, and beneath the oak is an iron
> chest, and in the chest is a small basket, and in the basket is a
> hare, and in the hare is a duck, and in the duck is an egg; and he
> who finds the egg and breaks it, kills me at the same time."
>
> (*Mabel,* 113)

This fable about the endless process of differentiation reads as a discovery
rather than an invention by Creeley. As it turns out, Creeley found this
tale in Joseph Campbell's *The Hero with a Thousand Faces* (175), and he
repeats it verbatim. In Campbell's book this tale occurs in the context of

a discussion of ego doubles and the desire for immortality, achieved here,
so Campbell says, by placing a spirit double of the ego at a safe remove
from death. Creeley's repetition of the tale in *Presences* would seem to
invert Campbell's interpretation and to present the tale as a fable of
process gone wrong, of the career taken by ego-interested writing further and further into absence and finally to death. The unfolding of
differences that hide an identity, a process so fascinating to Duncan, leads
in this instance to an absolute absence. Creeley seems to offer the post-
script as a parable of the dangers of fiction, contrasting the absence it
creates to the path of presence enunciated in *Presences*.

Chapter 3

"HE CHOSE TO INCLUDE": JOHN ASHBERY'S *THREE POEMS*

A TRANSLATIVE PROSE

It is usually not events which interest Miss Stein, rather it is their "way of happening," and the story of Stanzas in Meditation *is a general, all-purpose model which each reader can adapt to fit his own set of particulars.*

Ashbery

Just as Robert Creeley's early reference to *Tristram Shandy* provided clues to the nature of his conjectural prose, so John Ashbery's early review of Gertrude Stein's *Stanzas in Meditation* offers several avenues of entry into his own poet's prose.[1] Stein's writing stands as an important example for the prose of all three of the poets examined at length in this study: To Williams, she provides a model for the determined use of the tactile qualities of words; to Creeley, she offers the model of a sustained and relentless investigation of language, which also takes on the intonation and cadence of incantation; to Ashbery, she embodies in writing "the way things happen," a special kind of mimesis. And for the poets to be discussed in the final chapter, Stein also provides a significant example and impetus.

In his review of *Stanzas in Meditation*, entitled "The Impossible," Ashbery describes aspects of Stein's poetry that recur in his own meditative poetry, especially the three long meditative prose pieces that constitute *Three Poems*: "The New Spirit," "The System," and "The Recital." Of the two strands in American writing leading up to poet's prose – oratory and meditation – we have thus far focused more consistently upon the former, which has a special bearing upon the issues of speech and wholeness. With Ashbery's *Three Poems* we arrive at a predominantly meditative prose, though one still sensitive to the action of speech upon diction and sentence structure. In Gertrude Stein's unending investigations of consciousness in the ongoing present, Ashbery discovers many of the terms for his own meditative practice.

One of the first qualities one notices upon reading either Stein or Ashbery is the relative invariance of tone; one is confronted by a seemingly undifferentiated flow. In his review Ashbery defends the relative monotone in Stein, admitting, "There is certainly plenty of monotony in the 150-page title poem [of *Stanzas in Meditation*] . . . but it is the fertile kind, which generates excitement as water monotonously flowing over a dam generates electrical power" (250). Ashbery's simile emphasizes both the monotony and the dynamism of this kind of writing. Like Stein, Ashbery cultivates a flatness and sameness of tone in order to induce a certain double-edged reading experience. Speaking of the second of his own *Three Poems,* "The System," Ashbery comments in an interview:

> Just as one may be depressed by reading the fine print in the 11th edition of the *Encyclopedia Britannica,* with long prose passages in eight point type, and feel as if one is drowning in a sea of unintelligible print – and yet this is one's favorite ocean, just as drowning is said to be delicious when one stops struggling, so I tried to reproduce that delicious sensation.[2]

Should this inducement to drown be seen as a willful abuse of the reader, a mere teasing with the monotony of incomprehension? If one looks closely, the repetition and tonal invariance of the writing (both Stein's and Ashbery's) break up into what Ashbery calls an "endless process of elaboration," of differentiation. It is this continual process of differentiation, of attention to the minute alterations that define the moment, that Ashbery claims as mimetic of the experience of life, its "way of happening." To illustrate this point Ashbery compares *Stanzas in Meditation* to Henry James's *The Golden Bowl*:

> If these works are highly complex and, for some, unreadable, it is not only because of the complicatedness of life, the subject, but also because they actually imitate its rhythm, its way of happening, in an attempt to draw our attention to another aspect of its true nature. Just as life is being constantly altered by each breath one draws, just as each second of life seems to alter the whole of what has gone before, so the endless process of elaboration which gives the work of these two writers a texture of bewildering luxuriance – that of a tropical rain-forest of ideas – seems to obey some rhythmic impulse at the heart of all happening. (252)

Ashbery takes quite seriously this aesthetic analogue to experience. Just as understanding our experience and determining how to act upon it are primary epistemological and ethical questions of life, so the writing of Stein, James, and Ashbery raises these kinds of questions by its endeavor to reproduce the dilemmas of living:

The almost physical pain with which we strive to accompany the evolving thought of one of James's or Gertrude Stein's characters is perhaps a counterpart of the painful projection of the individual into life. As in life, perseverance has its rewards – moments when we emerge suddenly on a high plateau with a view of the whole distance we have come. In Miss Stein's work the sudden inrush of clarity is likely to be an aesthetic experience, but (and this seems to be another of her "points") the description of that experience applies also to "real-life" situations, the aesthetic problem being a microcosm of all human problems. (252)

The creation of an artistic experience analogous to the rigors of living forms one of the heroic goals of the modern arts. In theory one spurns the conventional fictions of representation (perspective in art, the story in literature, melody in music, and so forth) and instead endeavors to present an artistic experience that corresponds to the multiphasic, incomplete, discontinuous experience of life. This attempt to present unmediated experience ultimately comes up against the bounds of the medium used for presentation. Language, for instance, will always convey to us an experience structured by its own characteristic means: No work of writing can evade its status as writing and reach us as mere reality. Though this perfect mimesis of experience is finally unattainable, that does not make it any the less enticing as a goal. If the aesthetic problem is a microcosm of all human problems, then, Ashbery says, this one in particular is worthy of pursuit:

> Donald Sutherland, who has supplied the introduction for [Stanzas in Meditation], has elsewhere quoted Miss Stein as saying, "If it can be done why do it?" Stanzas in Meditation is no doubt the most successful of her attempts to do what can't be done, to create a counterfeit of reality more real than reality. And if, on laying the book aside, we feel it is still impossible to accomplish the impossible, we are also left with the conviction that it is the only thing worth trying to do. (253–4)

In the course of this brief characterization of Gertrude Stein's Stanzas in Meditation, John Ashbery also describes many of the salient features of his own Three Poems, such as the flatness and sameness of tone in a meditation; the mysterious energy generated by the persistence and seeming monotony of incomprehension; the presentation of life's "way of happening" – the experience of experience; the conviction that "the aesthetic problem [is] a microcosm of all human problems"; the attempt to reach the impossible goal of total mimesis. These five features provide a loose framework for the exposition that follows.

If one wishes to state what *Three Poems* is "about," however, one encounters problems. In a brief discussion of his own work in the reference text *Contemporary Poets* (ed. James Vinson [New York: St. Martin's Press, 1975], p. 36), Ashbery claims, "There are no themes or subjects in the usual sense, except the very broad one of an individual consciousness confronting or confronted by a world of external phenomena. The work is a very complex but, I hope, clear and concrete transcript of the impressions left by these phenomena on the consciousness . . . Characteristic devices are ellipses, frequent changes of tone, voice (that is, the narrator's voice), point of view, to give an impression of flux." The best way I have found to approach Ashbery's admittedly complex prose is through a consideration of the compositional process. Out of this analysis will arise a number of the major questions Ashbery entertains in *Three Poems* – which may be as close as one can arrive to "themes or subjects."[3]

> Only out of such "perfectly useless concentration" can emerge the one thing
> that is useful for us: our coming to know ourselves as the necessarily inaccurate
> transcribers of the life that is always on the point of coming into being.
>   Ashbery

The adjective that almost invariably appears whenever critics begin to characterize John Ashbery's writing is "difficult."[4] Richard Kostelanetz, for instance, entitled his 1976 article on Ashbery in the *New York Times Magazine* "How To Be a Difficult Poet."[5] The sense of difficulty seems to be evoked by the reader's perception of the "perfectly useless concentration" underlying Ashbery's poetry. Qualities of fortuitousness and discontinuity combine with a clearly evident attentiveness; this combination usually provokes one of two opposing reactions in critics: either to defend the meaningfulness of "pure play" or to deprecate the uselessness of such "nonsense." Marjorie Perloff, for instance, in *The Poetry of Indeterminacy: Rimbaud to Cage* (Princeton: Princeton Univ. Press, 1981), speaks for the indeterminacy in Ashbery and a number of other writers and contrasts its playful proliferation of meanings (in which no meaning is primary) to the limited and resolvable ambiguity of poets writing in the dominant Symbolist mode, beginning in Baudelaire and codified in Anglo-American poetry by T. S. Eliot. What Perloff celebrates as the poetry of indeterminacy, Charles Molesworth, in *The Fierce Embrace: A Study of Contemporary American Poetry* (Columbia: Univ. of Missouri Press, 1979) castigates as the "poetry of inconsequence" (p. 163), capturing in one term his frustration with both the discontinuity and the lack of primary meaning in much of Ashbery's poetry. These swings between critical appreciation and rejection of Ashbery's difficulty can become so extreme that even as staunch a supporter of Ashbery as Harold Bloom damns the long poem "Europe" as a "fearful disaster," while Richard Kostelanetz praises it as his "favorite Ashbery poem."[6]

The storms of advocacy and opprobrium that wash over Ashbery's poetry leave us with little insight into the nature of the difficulties caused by his "perfectly useless concentration." His own statement quoted above helps because it tells the purpose of such attention: By its exercise poets gain knowledge of their vocation as "the necessarily inaccurate transcribers of the life that is always on the point of coming into being." We can recognize immediately in this statement the impossible mimetic goal of representing life's way of happening. But why is the poet a "necessarily inaccurate transcriber"? Necessarily inaccurate transcription would seem to characterize a secondary operation rather than primary composition, something like a translation instead of an original presentation. It sounds similar to Robert Duncan's statement in "The Structure of Rime I": "Her voice comes across the waters from a shore I don't know to a shore I know, and is translated into words belonging to the poem." If the necessary inaccuracy of translation is analogous to Ashbery's way of writing, then an inquiry into the process of translation may illuminate Ashbery's difficulty.

Most writing about translation frustrates the reader in search of theory by never arriving at any general principles. The perpetual oscillation between norms of fidelity and freedom provides no insight into translation as such; these debates at best merely sensitize the translator to the domain of issues that invariably arise in the act of translating and that would seem to require pragmatic solutions. The only original theorist in the field of translation, the only person who tries to give translation itself an ontological grounding rather than assuming its derivation from literary creation, is the modern German critic Walter Benjamin. His essay "The Task of the Translator," written as an introduction to his translation of Baudelaire's *Tableaux parisiens,* is the founding work of the theory of translation, a theory still in its infancy.[7]

Looking steadily at the nature of translation, Benjamin notes an intriguing difference between an original work and a translation: "While content and language form a certain unity in the original, like a fruit and its skin, the language of the translation envelops its content like a royal robe with ample folds" (*ILL,* 75). Benjamin asserts that this variance arises from the contrasting goals of creation and translation; creation tries to say something but translation tries to approximate a Mallarméan "pure language." Pure language is the creative, structuring aspect at the base of all languages that makes expression and signification possible; it is the "true language" that united men and God prior to the destruction of the Tower of Babel. If the pure language were ever again uttered, claims Mallarmé, it "would materialize as truth" (*ILL,* 77). The goal of translation, then, is not a communication of the sense of the original but a revelation of a facet of pure language:

> It is the task of the translator to release in his own language that pure language which is under the spell of another, to liberate the language imprisoned in a work in his re-creation of that work. For the sake of pure language he breaks through decayed barriers of his own language. (*ILL*, 80)

Benjamin states that the more "poetic" a work is – the less it is confined to mere sense – the more it demands translation, for buried within the poetic element is the pure language. Though at first sight this concept of pure language seems a highly idealistic, even cabalistic conception, one finds that Benjamin often uses transcendental expressions as a way to characterize more material phenomena. He explains that pure language inheres in the "mode of signification" (*ILL*, 77), the way words mean or make sense, and that different languages have developed different modes of signification over time. The translator endeavors to carry the mode of signification employed by a given writer from one language to another. Benjamin describes this process as one in which the translator finds in his own language the pure language in another language. As guardian of the manifestation of pure language, translation has a special role in the understanding and even functioning of language and leads language toward its messianic, Mallarméan goal:

> If there is such a thing as a language of truth, the tensionless and even silent depository of the ultimate truth which all thought strives for, then this language of truth is – the true language. And this very language, whose divination and description is the only perfection a philosopher can hope for, is concealed in concentrated fashion in translations. (*ILL*, 77)

For the sake of his argument Benjamin posits a clear distinction between poetry and translation: "The intention of the poet is spontaneous, primary, graphic; that of the translator is derivative, ultimate, ideational" (*ILL*, 76–7). This distinction is helpful as a way of understanding translation and giving it an ontological grounding, but it is easy to think of modern poets – Mallarmé himself, for example – who combine both functions in their writing. John Ashbery, as a poet, leans heavily toward the translative half of Benjamin's distinction, especially in the prose of *Three Poems*. Ashbery's sentences are much more ideational than they are concrete or graphic; rather than presenting the primary sensations of experience, he presents the experience of experience, the ultimate sensations and ideas one encounters when trying to gauge experience (how it happens and how it changes); though the composition is spontaneous,

the moment itself never arrives, and so in this sense the writing is continuously derivative and never immediate.

Given this definition of translation, it is not difficult to see John Ashbery as a necessarily inaccurate transcriber of pure language in *Three
Poems*. The dilemma that begins the book and that runs throughout it
illustrates exactly this impossibility of incarnating the true language in
human expression: "I thought that if I could put it all down, that would
be one way. And next the thought came to me that to leave all out would
be another, and truer, way" (*Three Poems*, 3). Pure language is a "supreme fiction" (in Wallace Stevens's words), a means of bringing accord
between language and reality, and as such unattainable in pure form
within writing. The issue of selectivity, how much to put in or leave out,
is a question about the mode of signification. Ashbery would like to
show language's relation to experience, how our ways of speaking structure how we think about what happens, rather than describe specific
experiences. This explains, for example, his use of clichés and jargon not
primarily for parody or satire but as a means of interrogating the mode of
signification:

> What moves me is the irregular form – the flawed words and
> stubborn sounds, as Stevens said, that affect us whenever we try to
> say something that is important to us – more than the meaning of
> what we are saying at a particular moment . . . The inaccuracies
> and anomalies of common speech are particularly poignant to me.
> This essence of communication is what interests me in poetry.[8]

Ashbery makes it clear that the essence of communication is not a matter
of a hidden message but of the mode of signification. For him the essence
of communication has become the essence of poetry:

> I guess what interests me in poetry is the difference, the ways in
> which the prose sense of a poem gets transformed in poetry and this
> I think is the area that I write in to the exclusion of a formal theme
> or topic. I find one can say very much more by advancing immedi-
> ately to the poetry in the poem.[9]

Uniting Ashbery's and Benjamin's notions, we could say that Ashbery reverses, though with similar intent, Frost's dictum: Poetry is what
gets found in translation. As a translative writer Ashbery even acknowledges the characteristic of his text that Benjamin noted as the hallmark of
a translation: Its language "envelops its content like a royal robe with
ample folds" instead of fitting around the content "like a fruit and its
skin" (*ILL*, 76). Ashbery calls it "an overflowing of meaning": "Saying
a very big thing in place of what might originally have been a much
shorter and more concise one" (*COP*, 124). Elaboration and differentia-

tion are more characteristic operations in *Three Poems* than is the more usual poetic quality of compression.

The salient feature of this translative writing is its relation to pure language, the way a poet surrenders to a virtual language and attempts to transcribe it. How does a writer know when he or she engages with pure language? Since pure language is not a matter of "prose sense" (an interestingly unconscious use by Ashbery of the term "prose" to mean denotative or communicative), I would contend – though it may at first sound paradoxical – that one must enter a state of "not-understanding" in order to write in this mode. Not-understanding is a positive experience available to translators, writers, readers, or anyone involved in a complex hermeneutic activity. Not-understanding of this sort is a pleasurable, relaxed, receptive state (what Ashbery calls the delicious sensation of drowning) in which a feeling of strangeness or mystery hints that certain ineffable thoughts or connections may be possible. It is the prelude to a new understanding. This state occurs in relation to language, whether spoken, written, or about to be composed; around the language hovers a kind of aura that we invest with unexpressed feelings, desires, or insights, hoping that they may find form in this language. It is always possible for this to take place if we allow ourselves to dwell in not-understanding. If one does not do so resolutely, the will to understand is so strong that it may imperiously dispel the aura and with it the new content one hoped would appear. We often experience the vagaries of this unstable procedure when returning to words that "meant so much" to us, seeking a reaffirmation of this fugitive content and finding it fled – in its place the dead weight of fully analyzed understanding.

The state of not-understanding is available any time we trust in a meaning beyond our present understanding, and it manifests as an aura around language. For a writer such as Ashbery this aura appears as a sign of being engaged in writing. It remains present, calling words and phrases up to fit its inarticulate content and, upon relinquishing them back into the formative syntax, gives them its own direction. So that the aura leads the writing, ever at oblique angles, toward the unattainable pure language; the aura contains "the life that is always on the point of coming into being." In "The System," Ashbery gives a humorous description of how not–understanding prepares the way for a partial revelation of truth:

> And as the discourse continues and you think you are not getting anything out of it, as you yawn and rub your eyes and pick your nose or scratch your head, or nudge your neighbor on the hard wooden bench, this knowledge is getting through to you, and taking just the forms it needs to impress itself upon you, the

forms of your inattention and incapacity or unwillingness to
understand.   (*Three Poems,* 80)

The knowledge to be communicated here concerns a "latent happiness"
(71) in which the truth, or "new spirit," is always immanent but never
wholly present. This truth takes the "forms" of not-understanding as the
means for its partial expression just as a translation is a means for the
partial incarnation of pure language.

Ashbery is quite straightforward about his effort to incorporate not-
understanding into his writing, not to deceive the reader but because he
believes that this epistemological dilemma is a crucial aspect of experience:

> It seems to me that my poetry sometimes proceeds as though an
> argument were suddenly derailed and something that started out
> clearly suddenly becomes opaque. It's a kind of mimesis of how
> experience comes to me: as one is listening to someone else – a
> lecturer, for instance – who's making perfect sense but suddenly
> slides into something that eludes one. What I am probably trying to
> do is to illustrate opacity and how it can suddenly descend over us,
> rather than trying to be willfully obscure.[10]

In another context he speaks favorably of seeing silent films without
captions: "You would know only somewhat what was happening. In a
way it was more beautiful. Something was being communicated, but
you didn't know what it was."[11] The metaphor that Ashbery has developed most fully for describing his means of composition through not-
understanding comes from music:

> I think that the forms of music are deeper than the forms of most
> poetry. They have evolved . . . [Ashbery's ellipsis] Why exactly
> did the sonata form turn out the way it did? It's really the result of
> an instinctual feeling that that's what music should sound like –
> rather than a lucid elaboration on an idea such as one might find in a
> Milton sonnet. And it satisfies us. A sonata or a symphony starts
> with a hypothesis, which is developed and tested by argument, and
> then brought round to a resolution, although nobody can say ex-
> actly how this is done. That's what I'd like to do in poetry.[12]

By writing a translative prose that aims at a pure, musical language of
structuration through an adherence to not-understanding, Ashbery operates clearly within the Emersonian realm of discovery that we discussed
first in connection with Williams's generative sentence. Like the sentences of *Kora in Hell,* Ashbery's sentences are often long and convoluted, filled with clauses whose grammatical connections are not al-

ways clear. But whereas Williams's sentences seem propelled by the speech-oriented syntax that produces a paratactic wholeness, Ashbery's sentences are even more complex, often containing paratactic units of some length within a larger hypotactic structure. In Ashbery's sentences one sees a completeness of logical predication that seems, however, unreliable; on the other hand, one intuits a sense of wholeness through the seemingly disjointed parataxis of what, in the end, may turn out to be a logical, hypotactic sentence. It is the translative element to these sentences that places the reader in this quandary: As each new clause begins, neither the writer nor the reader knows for certain where this new clause will come to rest in the ongoing way of happening of the sentence. One could make identical points about *Three Poems* at the level of structure or argument: Each of the three sections proposes arguments that become so riddled with paratactic intrusions that one has no way of deciding finally whether the argument reaches a conclusion; the book as a whole incorporates the same interplay of wholeness and completeness in evidence at the level of the sentence. Because the sentence is our most highly developed tool for argument, its employment by Ashbery in the form of prose allows him to investigate argumentative and philosophical realms more intensively than in his extremely elliptical verse. Though frame shifting characterizes both his prose and his verse, the shifting of frames is less dramatic in the prose, inviting him to a more sustained inquiry into a whole region of discourse.

The following sentence, one of the longer sentences in *Three Poems,* provides a clear sense of writing into unknown territory; its subject matter (and a central issue of the book) is the tricky incarnation in life of a content available only through not-understanding:

> For just as we begin our lives as mere babes with the imprint of
> nothing in our heads, except lingering traces of a previous
> existence which grow fainter and fainter as we progress until we
> have forgotten them entirely, only by this time other notions
> have imposed themselves so that our infant minds are never a
> complete *tabula rasa,* but there is always something fading out or
> just coming into focus, and this whatever-it-is is always project-
> ing itself on us, escalating its troops, prying open the shut gates
> of sensibility and pouring in to augment its forces that have
> begun to take over our naked consciousness and driving away
> those shreds of another consciousness (although not, perhaps,
> forever – nothing is permanent – but perhaps until our last days
> when their forces shall again mass on the borders of our field of
> perception to remind us of that other old existence which we are
> now called to rejoin) so that for a moment, between the fleeing

and the pursuing armies there is almost a moment of peace, of
purity in which what we are meant to perceive could almost take
shape in the empty air, if only there were time enough, and yet
in the time it takes to perceive the dimness of its outline we can
if we are quick enough seize the meaning of that assurance,
before returning to the business at hand – just, I say, as we
begin each day in this state of threatened blankness which is
wiped away so soon, but which leaves certain illegible traces,
like chalk dust on a blackboard after it has been erased, so we
must learn to recognize it as the form – the only one – in which
such fragments of the true learning as we are destined to receive
will be vouchsafed to us, if at all.   (*Three Poems*, 78–9)

The model for this sentence seems to be the epic simile, in the form of
"just as . . . , so . . ." After a long series of phrases delineating the first
half of the simile, the speaker comes to a summation marked by "just, I
say, as" and then finally arrives at the "so" several lines further on. Thus
the sentence would seem to be grounded firmly in the rules of rhetoric.
In this case, however, the summation given of the first half of the simile
does not exactly fit what has gone before; the simile begins as a Wordsworthian birth image ("trailing clouds of glory"), but its summation is
presented in terms of waking up each day. The latter image, while equa-
table with the former, actually refers to the sentence before the one we
are reading: "The answer is in our morning waking." Within the simile-
tic continuity of our sentence, then, there is a metaphorical disjunction. It
is in this somewhat compromised rhetorical "form [that] such fragments
of the true learning as we are destined to receive will be vouchsafed to us,
if at all."

Though based on the structure of the epic simile, even to the extent of
employing the Homeric image of armies, this sentence presents a rather
equivocal, tentative comparison. For one thing, the imagery keeps shifting. This happens from one image to the next and also within images. At
the outset, we have a Wordsworthian Platonism opposed to Locke's
tabula rasa. The sentence seems to begin on Locke's side ("we begin our
lives as mere babes with the imprint of nothing in our heads") but
immediately qualifies this position with a diffident nod in Wordsworth's
direction ("except lingering traces of a previous existence"). Both of
these positions are progressively deflated until they merge in the flat
perceptual generality of "there is always something fading out or just
coming into focus." From the flat description of this nameless "what-
ever-it-is" (a designation for primal otherness), Ashbery builds up another elaborate metaphor of epistemological process through the image
of clashing armies. The army of the world (the army of otherness) be-

comes the image for the Lockean impressions that enter our consciousness from outside, while inside we are defended by the Wordsworthian
army of "original" consciousness. But in the midst of the clash of these
armies "there is almost a moment of peace," we learn, and though we
receive no assurance that it actually arrives, we are supposed to prize it as
the only truth we may hope to know. This equivocal truth, finally, is
presented in the image of traces left on a blackboard by chalk that has
been erased. Is the blackboard the tabula rasa? And if so, are the remaining traces original or merely learned?

Within the shifting terms of the imagery of this simile, the comparison
loses its clarity; the two image complexes of the Wordsworth–Locke
controversy and the skirmish of the internal and external armies do not
exactly elucidate the final, more mundane image of a day beginning as a
palimpsest. This direction of comparison, from the grand to the mundane, is characteristic of *Three Poems,* where the terms of comparison are
constantly inverting or overcompensating. Rather than exalting the
quotidian by expressing it in terms of a high-flown philosophical or
mythological image, Ashbery throughout the book reverses the normal
rhetorical figure and ground by making the course of a day the primary
image for the course of spiritual activity. Whenever mythological or
romantic figures arise, they are referred back to the issue of dailiness and
the domestic situation. By doing this Ashbery keeps the ordinary and the
transcendental in a constant state of equilibrated flux, refusing to un-
tangle the interpenetrating strands of imagination and reality. This invites an attitude of creative not-understanding in which both the writer
and the reader are implicated in the creation of an ongoing fiction of
reality from "lingering traces." The poetry is radically performative:
The "truth" it yields inheres in the performance of the text, just as a play
yields its truth only in a dramatic performance. If we read the text for
condensed images extractable from its surface, for meaning separable as a
kind of talisman (a profound idea captured in a striking image molded by
beautiful language), we will be disappointed. Instead of this one may find
during reading a creative pleasure and a certain wisdom through participating in a journey of experience and understanding.

Before leaving this sentence, let us examine the diction and syntax a
bit further. The diction is markedly inconsistent, including philosophical
Latin ("tabula rasa"), poeticisms ("mere babes"), the commonplace diction of clichés ("nothing is permanent"), and ungrammatical contemporary cant ("escalating its troops"). When asked in an interview what
varieties of diction he incorporates in his poetry, Ashbery replied,

As many kinds as I can think of. In "The System," for example,
there's an almost pedantic, philosophical language and lecturing

quality and the poetry keeps running afoul of clichés and pedestrian turns of phrase; again these are the result of my wish to reflect the maximum of my experience when I'm writing; these are ways in which one finds oneself talking to oneself or to someone else. (*COP*, 128)

The one type of diction noted above that Ashbery neglects to mention is the poetic, which, like the exalted images referred to in the previous paragraph, must fend for itself within this complex mélange. Many readers have mistakenly felt that this heterogeneous diction is meant for parody and therefore implies a satirical tone. As Ashbery's comment about his diction makes clear, he is abundantly aware of its humorous qualities, but he denies that parody and satire are directing motives:

It's not so much satirical as really trying to revitalize some way of expression that may have fallen into disrepute. Again, just because it's a way that we frequently have of speaking it deserves our attention and we should find out what it is that makes us talk that way and why it is that we do that, there's a good reason I think each time. (*COP*, 129)

As Hugh Kenner argues in *The Counterfeiters*, all of modern discourse contains an element of parody within it.[13] Rather than emphasizing this parodic quality and using it for ironic distancing, Ashbery accepts the counterfeit nature of his language and endeavors to translate this nearly exhausted diction into a provisionally adequate discourse. Ashbery's revitalization differs from that of modernists like Williams and Stein; where they attempt to strip words of their tattered connotations, Ashbery operates directly upon the equivocal language he finds lying about him. Though his diction is often quite abstract, his acceptance of the present condition of language also lends a subtle historicity to *Three Poems*. The two phrases at the beginning of the warring armies metaphor, for instance, "escalating its troops" and "prying open the shut gates of sensibility," refer to the historical moment in which Ashbery was writing, 1969–71.[14] During the Vietnam War the term "escalation," arising from U.S. military tactics, acquired such general currency that one might easily have overheard the ungrammatical and absurd locution "escalating its troops," meaning to increase their number. Likewise, drug consumption drew attention as the other pressing social phenomenon besides the war, and the phrase "prying open the shut gates of our sensibility" alludes to Aldous Huxley's then popular use of Blake's phrase "the doors of perception" to describe the perceptual expansion Huxley experienced under the influence of mescaline.[15]

Recognizing that language and experience are irrevocably inter-

twined, Ashbery employs the common language of our time to depict
the experience of our time. Instead of offering us the heightened diction
of an individual genius (which may be more in evidence in his verse,
although one could argue that the heightened diction is merely a use of
poeticisms rather than an attempt to exalt an individual sensibility), Ashbery makes the profoundly historical gesture of translating the way we
speak and think into a representation of how it presently feels to be alive:
the possibilities, hopes, temptations, sufferings, elations, of anyone's
ongoing attempts to understand the world. The farther we move in time
from the moment Ashbery has incarnated, the more we are likely to
value the historical nature of *Three Poems*. In this sense *Three Poems* unites
the two extreme forms of American poetry, the long poem and poet's
prose. Through its "negative" virtue of surrendering to the time of its
composition, *Three Poems* makes a fitting complement to the aggressive
American long poems of the twentieth century.

Turning to the syntax of this sentence, we find it characterized by
many parenthetical phrases, often parentheses within parentheses; this
proliferation of parentheses continually breaks up the hypotactic syntax
with paratactic elements. There is a kind of Chinese box effect to the
syntax, the beginning and ending of the simile operating as the outer-
most box. One source for this parenthetical syntax is the French writer
Raymond Roussel, whom Ashbery studied extensively as the subject for
an uncompleted doctoral dissertation. Ashbery describes this syntax in a
discussion of Roussel's *Nouvelles impressions d'Afrique*:

> *Nouvelles impressions d'Afrique* (1932) is Roussel's masterpiece. It is a
> long poem in four cantos which bear the names of African curi-
> osities. Each canto starts off innocently to describe the scene in
> question, but the narrative is constantly interrupted by a paren-
> thetical thought. New words suggest new parentheses; sometimes
> as many as five pairs of parentheses (((((()))))) isolate one idea buried
> in the surrounding verbiage like the central sphere of a Chinese
> puzzle. In order to finish the first sentence one must turn ahead to
> the last line of the canto, and by working backward and forward
> one can at last piece the poem together.[16]

Though the syntax of *Three Poems* is not so maniacally calculating as
this, it clearly makes use of the parenthetical mode as a way of applying
shifting frames. This is an aspect of Ashbery's preoccupation with illusory forms of completeness, placing him closer to such masters of the
shifting frame as Kafka, Borges, or Calvino than to Creeley or Williams.
Ashbery's poet's prose is the prosiest, the most discursive of the three
Americans, eschewing the abrupt transitions and elisions of *Kora in Hell*
and the puns, rhyme, and repetition that enhance the aural effects of

Presences. But the hypotactic indicators of completeness vie in Ashbery's sentences with paratactic gestures toward wholeness; this oscillation reflects Ashbery's primary syntactic and semantic concern – probing modes of signification. As a translative writer, Ashbery skillfully weaves together a constantly metamorphosing fabric of such modes, giving priority to none but allowing each syntactic configuration to modify its predecessor while seemingly stating its own assertive proposition. This results in a continual inversion of semantic figure and ground, the same type of inversion Benjamin proposes by directing the translator away from the sense and toward the pure language concealed in the mode of signification.

This is not to say, however, that the sense is wholly neglected, that *Three Poems* is purely abstract poetry. The use of parenthetical syntax, for instance, not only probes modes of signification through the shifting of syntactical frames; it also represents an epistemological dilemma that characterizes much of American writing. Ezra Pound, in an interview in *The Paris Review,* insists upon what he calls the "Jamesian parenthesis" (recall Ashbery's citation of the *The Golden Bowl*) as an effort by the American writer to lead the reader to an understanding of subtle or recalcitrant ideas:

> I'll tell you a thing that I think *is* an American form, and that is the Jamesian parenthesis. You realize that the person you are talking to hasn't got the different steps, and you go back over them. In fact, the Jamesian parenthesis has immensely increased now. That I think is something that is definitely American. The struggle one has when one meets another man who has a lot of experience to find the point where the two experiences touch, so that he really knows what you are talking about.[17]

We have been examining this long sentence of John Ashbery's as an instance of the difficulty of his style. By now it should be apparent that this difficulty is not sufficiently explained by concepts like "play" or "inconsequence." Ashbery speaks of "trying to duplicate or, rather, reproduce" in his poetry "the dilemma of understanding," to produce "in a sort of concrete way something that is unintelligible as well as some things that are intelligible" (*CON,* 95). He realizes that this makes a difficult writing for both the writer and the reader, and he accepts this condition as inherent in his position as a "necessarily inaccurate transcriber":

> The difficulty of my poetry isn't there for its own sake, it is meant to reflect the difficulty of living, the ever-changing, minute adjustments that go on around us and which we respond to from mo-

ment to moment – the difficulty of living in passing time, which is
both difficult and automatic, since we all somehow manage it.[18]

By writing a difficult prose that investigates modes of signification as
instances of pure language, Ashbery by no means turns his back on the
reader; he merely asks the reader to participate with him at the same
demanding activity of gauging experience through a translative prose
grounded in not-understanding:

> I think every poem before it's written is something unknown and
> the poem that isn't wouldn't be worth writing. My poetry is often
> criticized for a failure to communicate, but I take issue with this;
> my intention is to communicate and my feeling is that a poem that
> communicates something that's already known by the reader is not
> really communicating anything to him and in fact shows a lack of
> respect for him.[19]

One of the things we normally expect a writer to communicate is his
or her personality. In *Three Poems,* however, there is no single personality in evidence, yet senses of self and other constantly arise, often
suggesting the most intimate relationship of lovers. One way Ashbery
dissolves any accretion of personality is by the shifting of personal pronouns, so that any person (first, second, third; singular or plural) can be
the "subject" of the prose. Conscious of this effect, Ashbery gives an
illuminating explanation of it:

> The personal pronouns in my work very often seem to be like
> variables in an equation. "You" can be myself or it can be another
> person, someone whom I'm addressing, and so can "he" and "she"
> for that matter and "we"; . . . we are somehow all aspects of a
> consciousness giving rise to the poem and the fact of addressing
> someone, myself or someone else, is what's the important thing at
> that particular moment . . . I guess I don't have a very strong sense
> of my own identity and I find it very easy to move from one person
> in the sense of a pronoun to another and this again helps to produce
> a kind of polyphony in my poetry which I again feel is a means
> toward greater naturalism. (*COP,* 123–4)

Rather than creating a muddle of persons, this pronoun strategy
brings self and other into a large imaginative and social arena where the
fictive roles we play are given a communal coherence. Ashbery operates
from the central American premise that the self is a shared entity, that
through language, consciousness is both individual and collective. The
use of "you" is particularly effective in dissolving the ego and projecting
the sense of self outward toward a global circumference (compare Emer-

son's "transparent eyeball"), for in *Three Poems* "you" can legitimately refer to an aspect of the self, to a lover, to the reader, to a deity, or to the world, and "we" can include any of these "others" within the speaking consciousness. By what I called in the introduction a heroic accommodation to language and to the world, Ashbery's prose enacts the negative capability partially inherent in Emerson's self-reliance; both poets constantly translate between the Me and the Not-Me. Emerson's "Experience," with its valuation of experience as the greatest truth (over abstractions), its easy residence within contradictions, and its insistence upon not-understanding, would make a fitting companion to *Three Poems*. Speaking of "The Self in Postmodern American Poetry" (in an address given in 1979),[20] Robert Creeley, after mentioning approvingly the "flexible cliché brilliance" of *Three Poems*, its high intellectuality and its echoes of Wordsworth ("an acknowledged saint in this dimension"), offered a remarkable judgment of the book: He called it "as near a communal self as I've witnessed" and recommended it as a possible way out of the postmodern dilemma of the self, in which writing no longer speaks for the self as a social entity.[21]

"HE CHOSE TO INCLUDE"

The nothingness was a nakedness, a point

Beyond which thought could not progress as thought.
He had to choose. But it was not a choice
Between excluding things. It was not a choice

Between, but of. He chose to include the things
That in each other are included, the whole,
The complicate, the amassing harmony.

                                              Stevens

If Wallace Stevens had been alive in 1972, one might well assume that these lines had been written then to describe the dilemma and method of John Ashbery's *Three Poems*, even down to the complicated, completion-ridden wholeness of his sentences.[22] This assertion sounds perilously close to Harold Bloom's contention that Ashbery's successful "misprision" of Stevens makes us read Stevens now in Ashbery's voice.[23] I do not believe that Ashbery has wholly engulfed and then disgorged Stevens nor that he has fundamentally changed our way of reading Stevens; however, *Three Poems* is surely Ashbery's disquisition on the nature of "supreme fictions" ("a kind of fiction that developed parallel to the classic truths of daily life" [*Three Poems*, 55]), and the issue of choice that Stevens raises in the lines above runs as a central thread throughout *Three Poems*: "I thought that if I could put it all down, that would be one way.

And next the thought came to me that to leave all out would be another, and truer, way" (*Three Poems,* 3).

The question of whether to put it all down or leave all out is described by Ashbery on the back cover of *Three Poems* as "the author's dilemma over selectivity in his work," which becomes a "metaphor for man's ability to act either with or upon his destiny."[24] The dilemma over selectivity results in a moral investigation of the human will and the ability to chose; for advice, Ashbery seems to counsel a Rilkean active passivity with regard to one's destiny. The issue of inclusion versus elision also raises a mimetic question: How much of reality can be represented in art, and by what means; and what is the proper relationship of imagination to reality?

These central questions are set within a mid-life spiritual meditation that has affinities to both Dante's *La Vita Nuova* (compare "The New Spirit") and the *Commedia* ("the middle of the journey, before the sands are reversed" [*Three Poems,* 4]). From the vantage point of a person living through his late thirties and early forties, Ashbery tries to judge the course of his life, gauging how things have gone in the past and attempting to determine what he may hope for in the future. This involves him in classic meditational questions: What and how do we understand? What is life's way of happening? How does one experience time, and what is the proper attitude toward past, present, and future? Is happiness possible, and what is the best route to its attainment? The object of these meditational questions is the essentially religious question, How does one incorporate the moment of grace (the new spirit) into everyday life?

I have listed these philosophical questions as if they were themes or propositions developed in the work; however, Ashbery never states an unequivocal proposition or sets forth an unambiguous theme. In fact, he works against all unilateral notions by antithesis or by constant undermining, inversion, or overcompensation. In his attitude toward oppositions, Ashbery provides another instance of the choice not "between, but of." The constant oppositions in *Three Poems* function not as negations or contraries (as in Blake), nor as dialectic (as in Hegel or Whitman – "opposite equals advance"), but as inextricably intertwined facets of one process (as in Heidegger or Derrida). For example, in the course of a sustained consideration of "two kinds of happiness . . . : the frontal and the latent" Ashbery chooses the latter, only to find that "this second kind of happiness is merely a fleshed-out, realized version of that ideal first kind"; note how, in a typical reversal, "ideal" refers to "the frontal" while "realized" refers to "the latent" (*Three Poems,* 71–86). This makes it particularly treacherous to quote from *Three Poems,* since whatever proposition seems affirmed in any one statement may be modified or subverted by what follows or precedes it. Ashbery sees this kind of difficulty as mimetic of "the dilemma of understanding" (*CON*, 95) and illuminates its operation within the text itself. In "The System" (p. 85) he arrives at a "truth" remarkably akin to Nietzsche's eternal recurrence (if one reads the word "must" as referring to future necessity): "whatever was, is, and must be." Eight pages later we find the following passage:

> "Whatever was, is, and must be" – these words occur again to you now, though in a different register, transported from a major into a minor key. Yet they are the same words as before. Their meaning is the same, only you have changed: you are viewing it all from a different angle, perhaps not more nor less accurate than the previous one, but in any case a necessary one no doubt for the in-the-round effect to be achieved.
>
> (*Three Poems*, 93)

This passage not only illustrates the problem of asserting a univocal interpretation for a proposition in *Three Poems;* it also hints (through the musical metaphors) at the tricky matter of tone in this text. The overall tone of *Three Poems* is the controlled flatness of a monologue, whether interior or delivered to another. At certain times elation, regret, and nostalgia slip through, but none of these becomes a dominant tone; there are touches of humor, irony, and satire, especially in "The System," but, as was shown before, Ashbery's preoccupation with redeeming any present method of speech overshadows the parodic tone that may arise in a given passage. The issue of tone distinguishes Ashbery's poet's prose sharply from that of Creeley and Williams. Like Creeley, for example, Ashbery practices a meditative self-reflection, but Creeley is extremely emphatic, both in his reading style and in the stress he places upon key words, while Ashbery is absolutely unemphatic both in his writing and his reading style, giving equal emphasis to each word and keeping them all at a slight distance by use of his subtle wit.[25] The tone of *Three Poems*, however, need not appear to a reader merely flat and dull. It partakes, rather, of a kind of fruitful neutrality that allows the reader to project varying emphases onto the text. As Ashbery says, from one reading to the next a reader may find that the same words change tone, "transposed from a major into a minor key," and in fact Ashbery seems to encourage these changes of tone as "necessary . . . for the in-the-round effect to be achieved."

With these problems of explication in mind, let us look at some specific passages from *Three Poems* that illustrate the thematic and stylistic richness of Ashbery's poet's prose. Any passage chosen from such an intricately woven fabric will have echoes in other passages, and many of the major preoccupations are present in any specific section. The first passage is a short one occurring near the beginning of the book, in "The New Spirit" (all ellipses are Ashbery's):

> Then, quietly, it would be as objects placed along the top of a wall: a battery jar, a rusted pulley, shapeless wooden boxes, an open can of axle grease, two lengths of pipe . . . We see this moment from outside as within. There is no need to offer proof. It's funny . . . The cold, external factors are inside us at last, growing in us for our improvement, asking nothing, not even a commemorative thought. And what about what was there before?
>   (*Three Poems*, 5)

This passage announces a complex of issues that fall under the rubric of "man's ability to act either with or upon his destiny," such as the relation of inside to outside, the influence of the other in one's life, and the possibilities of growth and change. As I mentioned before, Ashbery seems to counsel a Rilkean active passivity as the wisest course for the human will in its encounter with its own destiny. Even the grammar of much of *Three Poems* works by active passivity, often rendering action in the passive voice. In the following passage from *Letters to a Young Poet*, Rilke uses sadness as a vehicle to discuss the relation between inside and outside in a manner remarkably akin to Ashbery's, both in the passage above and throughout *Three Poems*:

> Were it possible for us to see further than our knowledge reaches, and yet a little way beyond the outworks of our divining, perhaps we would endure our sadnesses with greater confidence than our joys. For they are the moments when something new has entered into us, something unknown . . .
> I believe that almost all our sadnesses are moments of tension that we find paralyzing because we no longer hear our surprised feelings living. Because we are alone with the alien thing that has entered into our self; because everything intimate and accustomed is for an instant taken away; because we stand in the middle of a transition where we cannot remain standing. For this reason the sadness too passes: the new thing in us, this added thing, has entered into our heart, has gone into its inmost chamber and is not even there any more, – is already in our blood. And we do not learn what it was. We could easily believe that nothing has happened, and yet we have changed, as a house changes into which a guest has entered. We cannot say who has come, perhaps we shall never know, but many signs indicate that the future enters into us in this way in order to transform itself in us long before it happens.

And this is why . . . when on some later day it "happens" (that is, steps forth out of us to others), we shall feel in our inmost selves akin and near to it . . . We have already had to rethink so many of our concepts of motion, we will also gradually learn to realize that that which we call destiny goes forth from within people, not from without into them.[26]

We are lucky to have so skilled a reader as Rilke to help us explicate our passage from *Three Poems*. Rilke's reading is so strong because it also anticipates some of the further ramifications growing out of the notions of destiny, change, and the inside/outside dialectic throughout *Three Poems*. The passage about the warring armies that we read earlier, for instance, uses the image of the armies and the Wordsworth–Locke dialectic to speak of our resistance to incursions of "the new thing" (the new spirit) and also speaks of the "moment of peace" (*Three Poems*, 79) when we can almost see our destiny as it enters us.

To return to the passage about the "objects placed along the top of a wall," another Rilkean aspect of the passage appears in the things that enter from outside, "the cold, external factors": "a battery jar, a rusted pulley, shapeless wooden boxes, an open can of axle grease, two lengths of pipe." These are not random objects or a series of interchangeable metaphors; these are the things that Rilke, in the ninth of the *Duino Elegies,* counsels us to show to the angel: "So show / him some simple thing shaped for generation after generation / until it lives in our hands and in our eyes, and it's ours." The act of incorporating these things in order to be able to speak of them is for Rilke the supreme purpose of human life: "Maybe we're here only to say: *house, / bridge, well, gate, jug, olive tree, window.*"[27] These "cold, external" things recur in *Three Poems* at a dramatic moment towards the end of "The System." Everyone is waiting for the answer to the question of being, when "suddenly you realize that you have been talking for a long time without listening to yourself; you must have said *it* a long way back" (*Three Poems*, 95). Realizing that this "buried word" (compare Matthew Arnold's poem "The Buried Life") is always already spoken, one comes into a balanced accord with the world:

> Meanwhile it is possible to know just enough, and this is all we
> were supposed to know, toward which we have been straining
> all our lives. We are to read this in outward things: the spoons
> and greasy tables in this room, the wooden shelves, the
> flyspecked ceiling merging into gloom – good and happy things,
> nevertheless, that tell us little of themselves and more about
> ourselves than we ever imagined it was possible to know. They
> have become the fabric of life.   (*Three Poems*, 95–6)

It has taken nearly the whole book to arrive at the measured wisdom that affirms "It is possible to know just enough." Reminding us of the "superficial profundity" that Nietzsche recommends (*GS,* 38), this wisdom is a compromise between the urges to "put it all down" and "leave all out" that Harold Bloom calls "Ashbery's two contradictory spiritual temptations":

> To believe that one's own self, like the poem, can be found in "all things everywhere," or to believe that "there is still only I who can be in me." The first temptation will be productive of a rhetoric that puts it all in, and so must try to re-vitalize every relevant cliché. The second temptation rhetorically is gratified by ellipsis, thus leaving it all out.[28]

Ashbery has been aware of these spiritual temptations at least since the poem "The Skaters," where he offers a kind of *Ars Poetica* outlining the basic issues of his poetry.[29] The stanza most germane to our present discussion contrasts "this leaving-out business" to "the costly stuff of explanation":

> It is time now for a general understanding of
> The meaning of all this. The meaning of Helga, importance of
>   the setting, etc.
> A description of the blues. Labels on bottles
> And all kinds of discarded objects that ought to be described.
> But can one ever be sure of which ones?
> Isn't this a death-trap, wanting to put too much in
> So the floor sags, as under the weight of the piano, or a piano-
>   legged girl
> And the whole house of cards comes dinning down around one's
>   ears!
> But this is an important aspect of the question
> Which I am not ready to discuss, am not at all ready to,
> This leaving-out business. On it hinges the very importance of
>   what's novel
> Or autocratic, or dense or silly. It is as well to call attention
> To it by exaggeration, perhaps. But calling attention
> Isn't the same thing as explaining, and as I said I am not ready
> To line phrases with the costly stuff of explanation, and shall
>   not,
> Will not do so for the moment. Except to say that the
>   carnivorous
> Way of these lines is to devour their own nature, leaving

Nothing but a bitter impression of absence, which as we know
    involves presence, but still.
Nevertheless these are fundamental absences, struggling to get
    up and be off themselves.[30]

In his quest for understanding, Ashbery is wary of explaining the
meaning of things and people by attempting a minute description. To do
so would be to burden the imagination so heavily with reality that "the
whole house of cards comes dinning down." If one realizes that a poem
could never sustain the whole burden of a literal reality, then how does
one choose what to leave out? The difficulty with leaving things out is
that this promotes exaggeration, both in what is spoken of and in what is
ignored. The only resolution achievable by Ashbery in "The Skaters" to
this debate about representation in "supreme fictions" is to note that
underlying the debate is the "fundamental absence" of any animating
truth.

In *Three Poems,* as we have seen, this issue of mimesis and selectivity is
more than a mere aesthetic question; Ashbery raises it to the central
problem of ethics and epistemology and follows it relentlessly until it
becomes, like an enigmatic Zen koan, the very landscape of living and
dying:

Because life is short
We must remember to keep asking it the same question
Until the repeated question and the same silence become answer
In words broken open and pressed to the mouth
And the last silence reveal the lining
Until at last this thing exist separately
At all levels of the landscape and in the sky
And in the people who timidly inhabit it
The locked name for which is open, to dust and to no thoughts
Even of dying, the fuzzy first thought that gets started in you
    and then there's no stopping it.
It is so much debris of living, and as such cannot be transmitted
Into another, usable substance, but is irreducible
From these glares and stony silences and sharp-elbowed protests.
But it is your landscape, the proof that you are there,
To deal with or be lost in
In which the silent changes might occur.   (*Three Poems,* 6–7)

By employing the "royal robe with ample folds" (*ILL,* 75) of a translative prose in *Three Poems,* Ashbery seems ready to "line phrases with the
costly stuff of explanation," but the explanation is not sufficient to nail

down forever the meaning of experience and becomes itself a mode of
questioning, as the lines above from "The New Spirit" make clear.

In the last section of "The New Spirit," this prose that "explains as it
uses it" (*Three Poems,* 50) is represented by the image of the Tower of
Babel:

> But it dawned on him all of a sudden that there was another
> way, that this horrible vision of the completed Tower of Babel,
> flushed in the sunset as the last ceramic brick was triumphantly
> fitted into place, perfect in its vulgarity, an eternal reminder of
> the advantages of industry and cleverness – that the terror could
> be shut out – and really shut out – simply by turning one's back
> on it.   (*Three Poems,* 50)

The Tower of Babel has always symbolized the misuse of pure language,
the attempt at an absolute representation of reality that would take precedence over, or even the place of, what it represents. The punishment for
this mimetic transgression (a kind of idolatry) was the fall into the myr-
iad ordinary languages that require translation to lift them again, always
provisionally, toward the pure language. For Ashbery this mistaken attempt at absolute representation is "perfect in its vulgarity, an eternal
reminder of the advantages of industry and cleverness" – something like
a miracle plastic, a genetic clone, or a computer simulation. There is a
prideful vulgarity in having a representation – a mere metaphor – become so concrete that it overshadows reality. And a vulgar indelicacy
also appears in the relentless refusal of technology to allow us to forget. If
everything that happens is put down into value-free computer memory,
then the selective forgetting that comprises an essential leaving out in the
human process of evaluation is lost. Without choice (whether "of" or
"between"), the possibility of value and judgment collapses.

What happens when one turns away from this technological terror of
putting it all in?

> As soon as it was not looked at it ceased to exist. In the other
> direction one saw the desert and drooping above it the constella-
> tions that had presided impassively over the building of the
> metaphor that seemed about to erase them from the skies. Yet
> they were in no way implicated in the success or failure,
> depending on your viewpoint, of the project, as became clear the
> minute you caught sight of the Archer, languidly stretching his
> bow, aiming at a still higher and smaller portion of the heavens,
> no longer a figure of speech but an act, even if all the life had
> been temporarily drained out of it.   (*Three Poems,* 50–1)

When one relaxes in one's quest for the unachievable goal of absolute understanding ("in an ambiance of relaxed understanding" [*Three Poems*, 51]), the pure language that hides in not-understanding becomes available again. The constellations are the creative configurations that symbolize pure language; just as they call up our imaginative projections to give them shape and significance, so pure language calls up the words that will form a new code of signification. The constellations are a kind of leaving out that requires our imaginative filling in, and thus "The New Spirit" does not resolve its own initial question but comes to a restatement of it in ontological terms as "the major question that revolves around you, your being here":

> And this is again affirmed in the stars: just their presence, mild
> and unquestioning, is proof that you have got to begin in the
> way of choosing some one of the forms of answering that
> question, since if they were not there the question would not
> exist to be answered, but only as a rhetorical question in the
> impassive grammar of cosmic unravelings of all kinds, to be
> proposed but never formulated.   (*Three Poems*, 51)

Realizing that the goal of a complete mimesis of life's way of happening is unattainable, *Three Poems* moves toward an acceptance of the fact that imagination and reality cannot be coextensive, that both putting in and leaving out are essential for understanding. As Stevens says, "He had to choose. But it was not a choice / Between excluding things." At the beginning of "The System," the late sixties seem to be evoked as a time when many people tried to live as though imagination and reality were consonant, as though history were at an end, love ubiquitous, and choice unnecessary:

> Hence certain younger spectators felt that all had already come to
> an end, that the progress toward infinity had crystallized in
> them, that they in fact were the other they had been awaiting,
> and that any look outward over the mild shoals of possibilities
> that lay strewn about as far as the eye could see was as gazing
> into a mirror reflecting the innermost depths of the soul.
>   (*Three Poems*, 60–1)

The failure of this vision mirrors the poet's failure to reach a perfect accord between reality and imagination in an absolute reproduction of experience: "We are trying with mortal hands to paint a landscape which would be a faithful reproduction of the exquisite and terrible scene that stretches around us" (*Three Poems*, 112). If art were to move so close to

life, it would lose its redemptive power, its ability to promote understanding, to frame questions for evaluation:

> Perhaps this was where we made our mistake. Perhaps no art,
> however gifted and well-intentioned, can supply what we were
> demanding of it: not only the figured representation of our days
> but the justification of them, the reckoning and its application,
> so close to the reality being lived that it vanishes suddenly in a
> thunderclap, with a loud cry.   (*Three Poems*, 113)

As a writer of translative prose Ashbery is left with the recognition
that he will remain one of the "necessarily inaccurate transcribers of the
life that is always on the point of coming into being." He has arrived at
and accepted the paradox that only within the undifferentiated aura of
not-understanding will he be able to know the "new spirit": "A vast
wetness as of sea and air combined, a single smooth, anonymous matrix
without surface or depth was the product of these new changes" (*Three
Poems*, 118). Within this aura the pure language hides, like the constellations in fog.

ASHBERY AND THE FRENCH PROSE POEM

There is another level on which John Ashbery, like Wallace Stevens, does
not have to choose "between, but of," and this is the level of the two
conflicting traditions in modern American poetry, the Emersonian and
the Symbolist. Both Williams and Creeley reside squarely within the
Emersonian tradition (though Creeley arrives there to a certain extent
through exorcising Valéry) in which form is discovered by the writer in
the act of composition and is a sign of the intimate relation between the
mind and nature. The Symbolist tradition, sprouting in Poe and then
transplanted and assuming gigantic proportions in French, to be re-
grafted onto English by Eliot, Stevens, and Crane (themselves dissenting
Emersonians) and adopted aggressively by New Criticism, sees form as
the achievement of an intended though mysterious effect to which every
element of the poem must contribute; the poem expresses a spirit wholly
apart from nature. The contemporary terms in which this opposition
between Emerson and Poe survives include pairs such as whole-
ness/completeness, objective/literary, concrete/abstract, speech/wri-
ting. Though in manifestos poets may claim to do so, no poet actually
embraces a single term in one of these antinomies to the exclusion of its
complement. In contemporary poetry, however, John Ashbery is remarkable for his ability to choose both halves of such opposing pairs. For
instance, his translative prose combines the Mallarméan quest for an
abstract, absent, pure language with the Emersonian discovery of form

and a panharmonicon of diction and syntax. Ashbery effects a union of
the elaborate artificiality of Symbolism, in which the imagination creates
a counter-reality in an autotelic form, and the processual poetry of the
Emersonian tradition aimed at the experience of the moment, trusting to
a wholeness gradually revealed in the act of writing. "Union" is not the
right term; rather, he plays these formal and philosophical tendencies off
one against the other, always deferring a resolution that would favor
either.

In order to emphasize both the American and the sui generis character
of the prose treated in this study, I have, on the whole, eschewed discussion of the relation of the texts under scrutiny to the prose poem and to
French writing in general. The prose poem existed for Williams and
Creeley as merely one of many indicators that generic mixture or even
nongeneric writing was desirable and possible; the form of the prose
poem and specific poems or poets were not directly influential. For
Ashbery the situation is more complex: He has read and also translated
much French writing, including, for example, Max Jacob's prose
poems,[31] and so his relation to French Symbolism, its offspring Surrealism, and the genre of the prose poem deserves further consideration.
Alfred Corn suggests a useful perspective in which to place the discussion of Ashbery's French side:

> Ashbery is something of an American Symbolist, and his poem
> "The Tomb of Stuart Merrill" is by way of *hommage* to a not too
> well known American poet of the fin-de-siècle who expatriated,
> wrote in French, and enlisted in the Symbolist movement. (Inci-
> dentally, if mention of the French tradition always comes up in any
> discussion of Ashbery, nonetheless his Americanism remains ob-
> vious and inescapable, as Wallace Stevens' does. Ashbery only oc-
> casionally reproduces the formal restraint, sensuousness, and lu-
> cidity of characteristically French art; more often his work exhibits
> the sincerity, distrust of artifice, and studied awkwardness we asso-
> ciate with achievement in the American grain.)[32]

To begin our enquiry into Ashbery's relation to French writing, let us
start at the heart of the issue, with the French prose poem. John Simon
has condensed his 700-page dissertation on the prose poem[33] into a succinct entry in the *Princeton Encyclopedia of Poetry and Poetics*. The meat of
Simon's definition is in the first paragraph:

> PROSE POEM (poem in prose). A composition able to have any
> or all features of the lyric, except that it is put on the page – though
> not conceived of – as prose. It differs from poetic prose in that it is
> short and compact, from free verse in that it has, usually, more

pronounced rhythm, sonorous effects, imagery, and density of expression. It may even contain inner rhyme and metrical runs. Its
length, generally, is from half a page (one or two paragraphs) to
three or four pages, i.e., that of the average lyrical poem. If it is any
longer, the tensions and impact are forfeited, and it becomes –
more or less poetic – prose. The term "prose poem" has been
applied irresponsibly to anything from the Bible to a novel by
Faulkner, but should be used only to designate a highly conscious
(sometimes even self-conscious) artform. (Enlarged ed., p. 664)

Simon endeavors to rectify the terminological tangle surrounding the
term "prose poem" and to confine the term to a consciously employed
lyric genre. His definition is particularly directed toward minimizing the
distance between the prose poem and the lyric, calling attention to the
devices of "pronounced rhythm, sonorous effects, imagery, and density
of expression" in the prose poem. The point where this neat definition
begins to unravel is in Simon's disclaimer that the prose poem is "put on
the page – though not conceived of – as prose." Is it prose or isn't it?
And what, one then wonders, distinguishes prose from poetry? Simon
begs the question that would appear to be at the center of a definition of a
hybrid genre such as the prose poem.

On the face of it he seems to insist that prose is merely writing that
occurs within justified margins. But he must have a more essential definition of prose in mind, or he would not claim that something written in
prose could be conceived of as not prose. The poet and critic David
Antin makes precisely this argument about justified margins in his distinction between prose and poetry:

I don't really think that the notion of prose exists on the same plane
as the notion of poetry. As far as I'm concerned there is the language art. That's poetry. All of it. There are then genres within it.
Like narration. And there's a subform of narration. Called fiction.
And a subform of that called, "the novel," a narrational form with
an enveloping commitment to a certain notion of "reality," constructed out of common-sense intuitions about character and objects, and social and psychological events, and probability. That's
not "prose." The idea of "prose" is only an additional prop for a
novel. "Prose" is the name for a kind of notational style. It's a way
of making language look responsible. You've got justified margins,
capital letters to begin graphemic strings which, when they are
concluded by periods, are called sentences, indented sentences that
mark off blocks of sentences that you call paragraphs. This notational apparatus is intended to add probity to that wildly irresponsi-
ble, occasionally illuminating and usually playful system called lan-

guage. Novels may be written in "prose"; but in the beginning no books were *written* in prose, they were *printed* in prose, because "prose" conveys an illusion of a common-sensical logical order.[34]

I agree with Antin that there is only one language art. Within this art, however, prose and poetry have operated historically to defamiliarize each other; the terms have been used as polemical tools, as Antin uses them here, on the side of either innovation or conservation. The values and even some of the characteristics assigned to each term have fluctuated over time.[35]

Where does this leave us, then, in our discussion of the prose poem? We see that Simon's definition skirts the basic generic issue raised by the prose poem and operates merely as an ex post facto description of the French prose poem and its imitators. As such, the definition continues Poe's aesthetic of the poem as a short, intense, lyrical moment; Simon claims that if the intended prose poem is too long, "the tensions and impact are forfeited, and it becomes – more or less poetic – prose" (note another evasion of the prose/poetry issue here through the equation: length = prose). This definition fits the prose poem into an oddly shaped but closed and contained package. Simon comments that "the prose poem as such is with us still, but its accomplishments having been absorbed by other genres, it has become the occasional 'aside' of writers whose essential utterance takes other forms" (665), and the more ambitious American poets who write prose are inclined to leave it there.

At the beginning of his career John Ashbery wrote at least two prose poems, "The Young Son," a surrealist prose poem included in his first book, *Some Trees* (1956), and "A Dream," a fairly straightforward recounting of a dream, published in Charles Henri Ford's "A Little Anthology of the Poem in Prose."[36] A brief quotation from "The Young Son" will suffice to display the standard combination of a matter-of-fact tone with a hyperbolic rhetorical flourish that one finds in surrealist prose poetry:

> The screen of supreme good fortune curved his absolute smile into a celestial scream. These things (the most arbitrary that could exist) wakened denials, thoughts of putrid reversals as he traced the green paths to and fro. Here and there a bird sang, a rose silenced her expression of him, and all the gaga flowers wondered.

While making use of many of the lyric devices Simon mentions, this kind of poet's prose seems to rely almost exclusively upon cleverness and surprise for its impact, an instance of artfulness at the service of nothing but itself. From the vantage point of *Three Poems* Ashbery says of these early prose poems and the French prose poem in general, "There's something very self-consciously poetic about French prose poetry which I wanted to avoid and which I guess I found disappointing in my earlier prose poems; it's very difficult to avoid a posture, a certain rhetorical tone" (COP, 126).

In confining the prose poem to a close relative of the lyric, Simon and many of its practitioners ignore the real discoveries a nongeneric prose can make by poeticizing (i.e., foregrounding and manipulating for poetic ends) elements traditionally assigned to prose. Taking over grammatical, rhetorical, narrative, and, as Antin points out, "notational" elements that normally occur in prose sentences (and by prose I mean the language of fact, argument, narration, or other similarly encoded forms in which syntax provides structure to the relative exclusion of meter or rhetorical figures), poet's prose, as we have seen, is able to increase the literary significance of these elements. An intuition of these possibilities, rather than an impulse to continue the tradition of the French prose poem, lies at the base of Ashbery's decision to write Three Poems in prose:

> I had written one or two prose poems many years ago and not
> found it a particularly interesting form and then it began to creep
> into a couple of poems in The Double Dream of Spring and then
> suddenly the idea of it occurred to me as something new in which
> the arbitrary divisions of poetry into lines would get abolished.
> One wouldn't have to have these interfering and scanning the pro-
> cesses of one's thought as one was writing; the poetic form would
> be dissolved, in solution, and therefore create a much more – I hate
> to say environmental because it's a bad word – but more of a
> surrounding thing like the way one's consciousness is surrounded
> by one's thoughts. And I was also very attracted by the possibility
> of using very prosy elements, conversation or journalese, what
> libraries classify as "non-fiction"; to extract what's frequently po-
> etic and moving in these forms of communication which are very
> often apparent to us and which haven't been investigated very
> much in poetry. (COP, 126)

As Ashbery relates it, his decision to write in prose was influenced by three factors: the freeing impulse of a prosody of syntax in sentences rather than a metrical prosody in lines; a dissolution of poetic form into something that sounds like the aura of not-understanding surrounding the text; the incorporation of "very prosy elements" into poetic settings that illuminate the modes of signification of these elements.

Whereas John Simon attempts to define the prose poem as a species of lyric, Michael Benedikt takes another angle of definition. In the introduction to The Prose Poem: An International Anthology (New York: Dell,

1976), Benedikt, following Robert Bly's notion of associative leaping (discussed in the introduction to the present study), defines the prose poem as a virtual ink blotter for the unconscious. The editor as well of *The Poetry of Surrealism: An Anthology* (Boston: Little Brown, 1974), Benedikt sees the progressive liberation of the unconscious championed by Surrealism as the paramount development in modern poetry, with the prose poem, written by many surrealists, as a major initiator of this trend. The inadequacy of defining the prose poem as merely a vehicle for the unconscious becomes patent whenever Benedikt tries to draw the implications of his position. For instance, he quotes the famous passage from Mallarmé's "Crise de vers" discussed in our introduction, which speaks of generic breakdown and the resultant formal innovations required of individual writers, and introduces it with this dubious reasoning: "Mallarmé called for an absolutely self-questioning, conscious art, it is true – but it is clear that this new consciousness in art was to be in response to the awareness on the part of the creator of his inner being or individual unconscious" (44–5). As Benedikt admits, the passage he has chosen from Mallarmé makes no mention whatsoever of the unconscious or even of inner being:

> What is remarkable is that, for the first time in the literary history of a people, in rivalry to the great general organs of past centuries where orthodoxy is exalted in accordance with a concealed keyboard, an individual possessing a talent for individual execution and hearing can make of himself an instrument as soon as he touches, strikes or blows into it with skill; can play that instrument and dedicate it, as with other methods, to Language . . . There is verse as soon as diction is emphatic, rhythm as soon as there is style. (45)

Mallarmé's description does not confine itself specifically to the prose poem; he speaks of a broad shift in modern poetry that could apply as easily to Walt Whitman as to John Ashbery. Does this modern poetry manifest the unconscious any more than poetry of another age? Psychologically speaking, that is a nonsensical question; unconscious forces are at work in any human creation. For Benedikt, the lack of traditional lineation indicates the presence of the unconscious, and thus the prose poem is the ultimate unconscious form: "This attention to the unconscious, and to its particular logic, unfettered by the relatively formalistic interruptions of the line break, remains the most immediately apparent property of the prose poem" (48). Obviously there is no logical connection between the degree of formal structure in a poem and the amount of unconscious material revealed. Many madmen, for instance, who supposedly speak directly from the unconscious, do so in obsessively formalized utterances (e.g., Christopher Smart's *Jubilate Agno*). The freedom that many of the poets we are discussing claim to find in poet's prose is a heuristic freedom to explore and understand many realms of being, not merely the freedom to unreflectively reproduce the unconscious. Benedikt's idea of the unconscious, as in classic Surrealism, seems to be a justification for arbitrary images, for playfulness, and for narcissistic solipsism.

Ashbery has maintained an interest in the French Surrealists, though more in fringe figures like Reverdy, Roussel, and Artaud than in the central Surrealists such as Breton, Éluard, and Aragon. The coupling of this acknowledged interest with the alleged difficulty of his writing has led readers to view Ashbery mistakenly as an American Surrealist, practicing an automatic writing that, as Benedikt would have it, directly expresses his unconscious. Ashbery flatly denies the assertion that he composes by automatic writing:

> I'm bored by the automatic writing of orthodox surrealism. There is more to one's mind than the unconscious. I have arranged things so that, as this stream is coming out, I make a number of rapid editorial changes. My poetry has an exploratory quality. I don't have it mapped out before I sit down to write.[37]

The exploratory quality, which is an aspect of creative not-understanding rather than of the unconscious per se, is Ashbery's goal, and it was the promise of exploration that drew him, he says, to French Surrealism in the first place:

> One had to look to France, and even there the freedom was as often as not an encouraging sentiment expressed in poetry ("*Il faut être absolument moderne, plonger au fond du gouffre*") than as [sic] a program actually carried out in search of new poetic forms. Even French Surrealist poetry can be cold and classical, and Breton's call for "*liberté totale*" stopped short of manipulating the grammar and syntax of the sacrosanct French language.[38]

This echoes Alfred Corn's characterization of French poetry as formally restrained and preeminently lucid. And Ashbery has pointed out the same qualities: "Only Rimbaud has managed to get beyond the *lucidity* of the French language, which doesn't allow you to do much 'in the shadows'."[39] In line with this lucidity, surrealist poetry usually presents clearly defined images that aim to startle by clashing with their context, often in very static verse forms or classically constructed sentences. Ashbery, on the other hand, is interested in *Three Poems* in "manipulating the grammar and syntax" in order to investigate language at a much deeper level. As opposed to the static quality of much surrealist writing, Ashbery, like Gertrude Stein, works to maintain a dynamic flow that startles as much by its relentless onward movement as by any individual locution or juxtaposition.

Beside the sophisticated explorations of language and experience conducted by Ashbery in *Three Poems*, the parabolic prose of an American Surrealist such as Russell Edson looks static and predictable. In doctrinaire surrealist prose poems the unconscious process is represented by a dreamlike inversion of normal reality.[40]

When the Ceiling Cries

A mother tosses her infant so that it hits the ceiling.

Father says, why are you doing that to the ceiling?

Do you want my baby to fly away to heaven? the ceiling is there so that the baby will come back to me, says mother.

Father says, you are hurting the ceiling, can't you hear it crying?

So mother and father climb a ladder and kiss the ceiling.

By inverting reality without providing a realistic frame, a surrealist prose poem copies the frameless inversion that often occurs in dreams. The conscious aspect of Edson's poem declares it a parable of the cruelty that results from a ceaseless testing of limits through a misplaced and mechanical attention; this quality in Edson's prose relates it to the farce. The shift of perspectives and loss of familiar grasp upon the world that one experiences in dreams inform Ashbery's poet's prose at many points, but the dream representation always appears as part of the general hermeneutic project of *Three Poems* rather than as a reproduction or justification of the unconscious:

At this point a drowsiness overtakes you as of total fatigue and indifference; in this unnatural, dreamy state the objects you have been contemplating take on a life of their own, in and for themselves. It seems to you that you are eavesdropping and can understand their private language. They are not talking about you at all, but are telling each other curious private stories about things you can only half comprehend, and other things that have a meaning only for themselves and are beyond any kind of understanding. And these in turn would know other sets of objects, limited to their own perceptions and at the limit of the scope of visibility of those that discuss them and dream about them.   (*Three Poems*, 84)

The surrealist prose work most frequently mentioned by Ashbery and others in connection with *Three Poems* is the novel *Hebdomeros* (1929), written in French by the Italian painter Giorgio de Chirico.[41] Aside from

Roussel's parenthetical sentences, this seems to be the only work of surrealist writing that Ashbery finds interesting for its innovative sentences:

> The hypnotic quality of *Hebdomeros* proceeds from Chirico's incredible prose style. His long run-on sentences, stitched together with semicolons, allow a cinematic freedom of narration: the setting and the cast of characters frequently change in mid-clause. In this fluid medium, trivial images or details can suddenly congeal and take on a greater specific gravity, much as a banal object in a Chirico painting – a rubber glove or an artichoke – can rivet our attention merely through being present. His language, like his painting, is invisible: a transparent but dense medium containing objects that are more real than reality.[42]

Ashbery is clearly intrigued by the way de Chirico shifts character or perspective within sentences and by the density achieved by long run-on sentences. In *Three Poems,* however, neither characters nor perspectives but modes of signification shift, for language itself becomes the protagonist. Ashbery's language is not by any means invisible or transparent; on the contrary, it is opaque and dense, calling attention to itself rather than to "trivial images or details."

That Ashbery has read attentively and translated with dedication a whole range of French writers is undeniable, and his sophisticated knowledge of French writing clearly adds to the technical and imaginative possibilities at his command. This accounts, to some extent, for his ability to include "the whole, / The Complicate, the amassing harmony" of Emersonian and Symbolist traditions in his poetry. When we try to locate specific formal influences exerted upon Ashbery's *Three Poems* by either the French prose poem or by Surrealism, we find that Ashbery maintains a dialectical relationship with French writing, negating many of its defining qualities and then synthesizing certain imaginative or formal possibilities (such as the sentence structures of Roussel and de Chirico) into his translative, postgeneric prose. The closest analogue to *Three Poems* in French might well be Edmond Jabès's remarkable three-volume work of poet's prose, *The Book of Questions* (1963–5).[43] Jabès, like Ashbery, sets a profound though enigmatic spiritual meditation against the background of an equally inexplicit love relationship; though his sentences are less complex than Ashbery's – less involved in the interplay of wholeness and completeness – Jabès too doubles back and forth across his aphoristic propositions, creating a highly charged and resolutely unresolved emotional and spiritual locus. As many Americans do when they return from Europe (literally or imaginatively), Ashbery has found a rekindled appreciation of America and American writing fostered by his immersion in Europe: "Since I returned [from France], I have gotten more involved in the American scene, the American land-scape, language, the funny way we live. We're constantly sort of making up our lives and our personalities as we go along in a way Europeans don't do. Luckily, I think, we improvise."[44]

Chapter 4

THE CRISIS AT PRESENT: TALK POEMS AND THE NEW POET'S PROSE

The poetic climate today seems to include as much criticism and philosophy as it does poetry. At present, one finds that ideas, those prime "don'ts" for imagists, radiate excitement and allure. American poets read with poetic appreciation and sometimes envy the prose of Roland Barthes and Jacques Derrida because it is so deeply aware of its engagement with language and with the process of composition yet simultaneously offers ideas and images of great force and currency. As we have seen, there is a strong tradition of poet's prose in America that makes easy and attractive the incorporation of such critically self-aware writing into American open-form poetry. Poets today who are writing a new poetry often do so alongside the writing or reading of criticism and are beginning to create a nongeneric poet's prose (or other types of nonlineated poetry) that continues but moves beyond the concerns we have explored thus far. Investigations by contemporary poets no longer concern the boundary between prose and poetry but rather the boundary between literature and factual or theoretical discourse – philosophy, criticism, linguistics, and so forth. In our reading of *Kora in Hell,* we noted the critical and polemical prose surrounding the improvisations; contemporary poets often integrate argumentative or analytical functions into their improvisations.

The orphic, bardic impulse in American poetry has always coexisted with a critical intelligence – Poe and Emerson are initial instances of this dichotomy – but only in the twentieth century, with writers like Stevens, Pound, Eliot, Zukofsky, and Olson, have these two strains been yoked together within a poetry. In the new poetry of David Antin, David Bromige, Ron Silliman, and Michael Davidson, the balance is tipped – sometimes more, sometimes less – in favor of the critical intelligence. Critical thinking does not merely buttress the mythopoeic imagination in these poets; rather, they are originally critical, practicing a vigilant self-awareness that calls forth language and subjects it to an examination of its mediatory function. For these poets the critical activity of deconstruction, of investigating a text as an endless play of subtexts, is a means of poetic creation. Such characterizations can be made as well of Creeley and Ashbery. The new poets – Antin with his "talk poems" and the writers of poet's prose such as Bromige, Silliman, and Davidson – or their equally interesting and demanding colleagues on the West and East Coasts – Michael Palmer, Barbara Einzig, Kathleen Fraser, Lyn Hejinian, Bob Perelman, Barrett Watten, Bernadette Mayer, and Clark Coolidge – work more intensively and exlusively in this domain.[1] Though they adopt some of the hermeneutic practices and phenomenological attention of Creeley and Ashbery, these poets focus more relentlessly upon the ability of language to predicate. All of these poets define poetry broadly as, in David Antin's words, "the language art"; the choice of prose or verse, which forms a highly conscious decision in the poetics of Williams, Creeley, and Ashbery, becomes incidental to the writers of the new poet's prose. They no longer care to defamiliarize poetry with prose for the purpose of generic innovation; in their heightened self-consciousness about language they employ forms as mere ways of moving, strategies at hand for the moment, rather than as claims about the correct mode of representation. For Antin the distinction between prose and verse becomes trivial when confronted from what he considers the more fundamental standpoint of talk. All of these poets require the act of representation to be self-aware and self-questioning: No medium or method may be assumed as a transparent vehicle of truth.

DAVID ANTIN'S TALK POEMS

David Antin is one of the more fascinating and original figures to emerge in the American arts in the second half of the twentieth century. Following an earlier poetry characterized by a striking series of Duchampian "moves" meant to erase the boundaries between poetry and philosophy, his invention of the "talk poem" challenges us to conceive of poetry, criticism, and philosophy as a single activity.[2] Antin performs a talk poem by standing up in front of an audience and improvising speech around a certain intellectual territory, combining critical questions about the nature of poetry or art with philosophical speculations about the way language influences our behavior and thought, and provoking or complementing these ideas by often humorous anecdotes about himself, his family, and friends. One might describe him as a brilliant cross between Socrates, Wittgenstein, and Lenny Bruce (the leftist Jewish comedian). Antin is a kind of Renaissance man, whose professional experience in engineering, linguistics, and art criticism affords him a range of reference far beyond that of most other poets; where many poets draw isolated ideas or metaphors from the exact sciences, the social sciences, or the other arts, David Antin maintains an uncanny professional grasp in nearly all of these areas. Revealing his commitment to ordinary language and to addressing a live audience, Antin translates sophisticated paradigms from various fields into nontechnical stories and examples that can be applied to the larger epistemological and ethical questions his improvisations consider.

Looking back to Emerson, we can think of Antin as a new advocate of the panharmonicon. One could well say of the talk poem,

> Here is all the orator will ask, for here is a convertible audience & here are no stiff conventions that prescribe a method, a style, a limited quotation of books, & an exact respect to certain books, persons, or opinions. No, here everything is admissible, philosophy, ethics, divinity, criticism, poetry, humor, fun, mimicry, anecdotes, jokes, ventriloquism . . . Here he may lay himself out utterly, large, enormous, prodigal, on the subject of the hour.[3]

Or, as Antin himself puts it,

```
            i wanted to talk about something      the situation
        that comes up when a poet comes to a place      to do
        something that is a poem      i mean what am i doing
          coming here to talk poetry?      that is if I thought
          that poetry was a sort of roman enterprise      if i
        thought that poetry was a roman enterprise i would
            assume that talking poetry was a reasonable and
        clearcut enterprise      i would get to the place and then
        use all the wonderful rhetorical charm that i could put
          behind me and offer you poetry      that is i would
          improve talking      you see      talking would be just
        talking      the way people talk      and poetry would be
          improved talk      it would be talk that ends kind of
            funny      it rhymes say      or it beats out a tune
        or it does what it does in some unusual and exotic way
          theres nothing wrong with that a lot of people do it
            its fun walking tightropes      its fun talking while
        drinking water      its fun talking while standing on your
            head      i propose not to consider poetry putting
        something on top of talk      i consider it      in this case
            coming with a kind of private occasion to a public
        place      i mean youre all here      and its a public place
            and im addressing a public situation      and im doing
        what poets have done for a long time      theyve talked
```

out of a private sense   sometimes from a private need
    but theyve talked about it in a rather peculiar
context   for anybody to eavesdrop   which is strange
    that a man would come out here to talk to you   not
knowing you   you not knowing him and you should
    care about anything he has to say   and its exotic
    theres something strange about it   except that if
we share some aspect of humanness   it may be perhaps
    less exotic   that is   people have been known to
walk into a bar   find someone they didnt know   and
    start a conversation with this person   tell them their
    life story   disappear and never see them again[4]

Antin brings a subject for meditation into the presence of a particular audience and then, as an orator, endeavors both to speak convincingly to the audience and to explore the territory his subject proposes. He introduces the Emersonian element of discovery directly into his performance. The titles of the talk poems collected in *Talking at the Boundaries* give a sense of the generalized questions he addresses: "what am i doing here?", "is this the right place?", "talking at the boundaries," "remembering recording representing," "the invention of fact," "the sociology of art," "a private occasion in a public place," "a more private place." Each of these topics is made particular by repeated references to the actual occasion and by Antin's skillful discourse upon a number of levels simultaneously. For instance, at one level all of these pieces interrogate ideas of poetry and art and the kinds of boundaries or limits we apply to artistic practice. Because Antin endeavors to produce a seamless discourse, the extraction of quotations is not easy; in the following passage, from "talking at the boundaries," he characterizes his work as

going to places   to improvise something   because as
a poet i was getting extremely tired of   what i considered
    an unnatural language act   going into a closet   so
to speak   sitting in front of a typewriter and nothing
is necessary   a closet is no place to address anybody
    or anything   and its so unnatural   sitting in
front of a typewriter   that you dont address anyone[5]

This passage and the other quoted above, both obviously torn from a particular context, give a good sense of Antin's playful, provocative, agile style of defamiliarizing the very activity of writing. Antin's texts represent the furthest possible incorporation of speech into writing. While aware that a reader experiences the published texts differently from a live performance (or a tape recording of it), Antin hopes, as he says, "that I have encoded in the text (because it is after all being carried in a text) the qualities of this oralness I am seeking."[6] The qualities of oralness account for the form (a concept that Antin rejects, construing it to mean strait jacket) of his pieces at the level of both the individual utterance and the piece as a whole. At the former level Antin translates his oral performance into a series of nonlineated, breath-unit utterances. One can imagine this as a further development of Olson's breath-unit line; both poets try to incorporate the mental and physical dynamism of their projective performances into their texts. At the level of the whole piece, the shape of Antin's text reflects his hermeneutic and phenomenological commitments:

> It *is* too long – for a literary text, which it isn't. And all oral work faces the same problem – that the way the mind works at formulating under these phenomenologically more natural conditions – of being up on your feet and talking – is more relaxed or casual, gradually feeling for doors in a wall say or the right turn off the commonplace road. Naturally it will also take occasional wrong ones, but to erase the false step will also erase the way of discovery. Which is what I am after. I want nothing less than a paradigm of the true working of the mind at some real thing. We have to get out of the hubris of Cartesianism or even Baconian empiricism. And the cost will at first seem very great, because it was the 17th century that named the terms of "respectable" thinking. One may even say they invented "the fact." What I'm offering is one step against this sanctified position as it is congealed into "style." Homer is too long too, and so is Beowulf. Too long for a text to be looked at – but not too long for the ear-mind. I hope and feel my own work is similarly justified.

As an oral poet Antin continues the generative use of parataxis we first noted in Williams. In addition to Homer and *Beowulf*, Antin's avowed antecedents include other American writers renowned for their use of speech elements like parataxis and the vernacular: "Implausible as it may seem I feel a strong identity with Twain and Kerouac and Whitman, without their lyricism maybe, and without the folksiness, but I never was plain folks, nor are my neighbors."[7] Though it does not take into account his Jewish wise-guy posture, the qualifier Antin adds to the end of this statement is important as an admonishment not to view his work as a nostalgic attempt to reinvoke the tribal values of ritual and mythology. Antin's primary activity, in fact, is demythologizing.[8] Because he wants to shake loose from some of the formal, social, and discursive restrictions imposed by Western technological culture, Antin has recourse to tribal or "primitive" ideas as a means of dethroning or suggesting alternatives to, our own particularly rigid ways of thinking. "So you see, what I'm interested in in these cultures is their intelligence – their inventiveness, their tact, and their good sense."[9] Unlike tribal poets Antin shows no intention of eschewing reading or writing. In fact his mind is so thoroughly textualized, so insistently aware of the problems of reference and mediation created by discourse in a text, that his very speech is a kind of spoken text. It is impossible to imagine anyone with the preoccupations and habits of mind Antin displays not arising from within a literate culture. He creates a theatrical persona for himself, a kind of Molière character who insists that he is engaged in conversation while actually speaking uninterruptibly in the somewhat artificial style of a text. Speech and writing remain intertwined for Antin, as they have been for other poets in the Emersonian tradition; Antin's contribution is to further radicalize the notion of speech and to use it as a bridge between the realms of imagination and fact.

His poetry and criticism are meant to be shocking and subversive. Antin defamiliarizes complex constructs by stating them in ordinary language, and he defamiliarizes habitual ways of thinking by undermining their validity. With this two-pronged inversion of ordinary expectations, Antin reveals the illusory nature of the things we cling to to show us reality – the notion of fact, the language of emotion, and the activities of remembering and representing. On the one hand he classifies these illusions as artificial metaphorical systems (as parts of a curious and elaborate mannerist art) that we pose between ourselves and the real. On the other hand he claims that true art must always be a fundamental exploration of reality. Though Antin would never approve of Hans-Georg Gadamer's nostalgic elevation of Greek tragedy to a paradigm of art (*Truth and Method* [New York: Continuum, 1975]), Gadamer's critical stance may provide a useful analogy to flesh out the extraordinary claims Antin makes in and for his talk poems. In both is found (1) a high valuation of the occasional and a concomitant deconstruction of the eternal, as well as the recognition that all understanding occurs phenomenologically and has a temporal grounding; (2) the dismissal of aestheticism (what Gadamer calls "aesthetic differentiation") and its scientific complement of the literal and the factual, as dead formalisms; (3) the recognition that all discourse, in its attempt to represent, is a kind of art; (4) the claim that method is not value-free but rather that the method chosen prejudices the truth one can achieve; (5) the elevation of play to a philosophically meaningful description of art and science.

If, as was stated in the introduction to this book, the breakdown of genres in literature and philosophy leaves the conscientious writer faced with the more fundamental (though seemingly superficial) medium of language, then David Antin has carried this recognition of generic breakdown and the mediation of language to a remarkably trenchant position. His "heroic accommodation" to the world and to the language around him is noticeably greater than that of the other writers we have studied, and yet his highly individual position and assumption of responsibility for trying to understand everything in his own way make for a resolutely lonely and powerful stance. Antin continues the adversarial thrust of the avant-garde poet and raises the stakes by situating his talk poems on the boundary between poetry, art, criticism, and philosophy.

DAVID BROMIGE, RON SILLIMAN, AND MICHAEL DAVIDSON

[Gertrude Stein] was the writer in English with the deepest interest in language, the only one with an interest in language as language. I know almost everybody will object to this, but I've never understood why anybody thought Joyce, Eliot, Pound, Stevens or Williams were innovators in language. Essentially all of their interest was concentrated at the level of rhetoric . . . But Stein of all of them had a philosophical commitment to the problematic double system of language – the self ordering system and the pointing system – and from the beginning of her serious work she had encountered the peculiar conflict between the two, even in her early stories.

Antin

Once again Gertrude Stein, the shadow heroine of this book, provides a point of transition between poets who write beyond verse. This testimonial by David Antin concerning Stein's interest in language offers a useful focus for a discussion of the new poet's prose.[10] Stein's example of a literary investigation of language itself, a writing that probes the connections and disjunctions inherent in the dual nature of language as a self-enclosed system and as a means for grasping the world, stands squarely behind the explorations of language by contemporary poets. The three poets to be touched upon briefly in these last pages – David Bromige, Ron Silliman, and Michael Davidson – adopt a variety of strategies in their prose to expose the way language works and to point out how pervasively our experience is linguistic.

David Bromige (b. 1933), though a follower of the projectivist poets Creeley, Duncan, Olson, and Levertov, is a demonstrably unique phenomenon. Born in England, migrating to Canada as a teenager, and settling in California at the age of twenty-eight, Bromige speaks with what he calls "an accent of one." His poetry likewise combines a vast range of influences into a quirky, thoughtful, wry, thorny discourse. As a mature poet Bromige has maintained an aloofness from peers and predecessors – an attitude that has delayed recognition of his talent – while at the same time offering himself unstintingly as mentor to younger poets such as Silliman, Davidson, Barbara Einzig, and Bob Perelman. A restless, inquisitive poet, Bromige has shifted his style a number of times; in 1972 he began to write short investigations of language on three-by-five-inch cards, calling them "Tight Corners":

The truck had nearly struck their car. He had screamed. She had asked him not to.

The man whose path is blocked by his own frontal bone will forever lose himself in the precious arbitrariness of a particular arrangement of words. Power to the People, Robert David Cohen. But I don't know how to cut sugar-cane.

I wanted to worship you. I wanted to send you on ahead. I wanted to send you on a head on a platter.

Having thinking as my inferior function, I fell under the sway of Jung's "Psychological Types."

Think of the truth. Think about poetry. Imagine a number. Double it. Add too. Halve what now you have. Surrender the figure you first thought of & your answer's won.

It all, he tells us, rests firmly on the edge of oblivion. Living on, we will not see his face again. I don't want to see what I shall never again see. That's why it all has to look permanent. I want to rest. He hasn't found rest, rest is a sentient occasion. He is permanent. I can alter his significance with every sentence.[11]

The subtitle of *Tight Corners,* the book of poet's prose and verse from which the above "tight corners" are taken, reads "being the brief and endless adventures of some pronouns in the sentences of 1972– 1973"; it places these linguistic conundrums in a perspective that we examined during the discussion of Ashbery's *Three Poems.* For Bromige, too, the pronouns "very often seem to be like variables in an equation," and I think he would agree with Ashbery that they "are somehow all aspects of a consciousness giving rise to the poem."[12] The humorous and sometimes terrifying recognition of oneself (and one's society) as a band of pronouns trapped in the realm of language continues to inform Bromige's prose and verse. In his next book, *My Poetry* (1980) Bromige employs prose to deconstruct his previous verse – a further unraveling of the orphic or bardic voice. Bromige applies a relentless self-consciousness to the end of denaturalizing any poetry and rendering its status as linguistic artifact absolutely evident. Events, whether actual or imagined (often with an emotional or humorous interest of their own), are not absent from the text, but no event is allowed the mystification of seeming to exist beyond its figuration in language. In the following piece, one of seven entitled "Six of One, Half-a-Dozen of the Other," Bromige constructs a situation not exactly plausible though not wholly apocryphal, as a spurious "biographical" commentary upon an earlier, published poem:

A Defect

The doctors doubted any cause for it
since birth or even conception

but he finds a way to suffer it,
Couldn't it have been something

I did? Long ago, some blow struck
for meaning.

Here is the commentary:

"A Defect" takes me back to the time I met Freud. The year was 1939, the day, a Sunday, & my father was taking me for a walk across Hampstead Heath. This cottage was where John Keats wrote "Ode to a Nightingale," this patch of gorse was where Eeyore lost his tail, this pub was where Jack Straw roused the rabble a scant 600 years before, this small hollow in the crotch of a tree, filled with rainwater, beside the dark duckpond, was Pooh's Cup. This was all too much, I had to run in widening spirals or pee my pants, so he gave me my head, my foot snagged in a gnarled tree-root & my knees skidded in the gravel. Someone like my grandfather was bending over me, though at first I hardly noticed him, for I'd glimpsed my own blood & was howling in panic. Taking out his hankie, he dipped it in Pooh's Cup, & then applied it to my wounds. When my father came up he thanked the old man, giving him a rather stiff grin. Facing my father he said, Not to worry. Then, patting my head, he added: Later, he vill remember zis differently.

My father led me away. Ruddy foreigners, he said, when we were out of earshot, Always shoving in where they're not wanted. Why don't they go back where they came from. When we got back home, my mother removed the makeshift bandage so she could put iodine on the sensitive places. This isn't one of yours, Harold, she said. No, it belongs to some old alien, he told her, You know, the kind with horns, they ought to be suppressed. Throw it away. But my mother was too fond of fine linen to worry about its origins. It was laundered, & after a

decent interval it surfaced in my father's breast pocket, folded so
that two neat points poked out. What he doesn't know won't
hurt him, my mother always said.

Many years later, I saw a picture of the old man in a book &
recognized him right off. Later yet, when I turned diabetic, I
read him, conjecturing my disorder must be psychosomatic in
origin. By a curious coincidence, my wife was in hospital, about
to have our only son, when I went into the same hospital
pregnant with disease. I was diagnosed by my father-in-law,
who said with a chuckle, If you must get a chronic condition,
this is the best you could have chosen. Now you'll have to mind
your P's & Q's. – I'd long had the habit of drinking in the pub
with the rabble until closing time & then running around town
in widening spirals looking for someone to rub iodine into my
wounds. It had gotten so I couldn't recall the next day how I
wound up where I found myself. Possibly the drinking it was
that had knocked out my Isles of Langerhan, lapping with
inaudible sound on their shores. I was Pooh, & every cup was
mine.

Now it was high time I grew up & husbanded my resources
& fathered what had been conceived in forethought & furthered
my career as an insurance adjustor. It was then I sat down &
wrote "A Defect." It took me several hours & when I came out
of the trance I realized that the baby was crying, my wife was
phoning my father-in-law, & the room was so full of smoke that
I couldn't see what was on fire. But, with the rhythms of the
poem still coursing through my limbs, I was able to stand up,
cross to the window & throw it open. The flames quickly
became visible.[13]

This deconstruction of the autobiographical "origin" of the poem is
itself a skillful poet's prose, interrogating the completeness of explanation through a largely paratactic association of images, often turning on
puns. Ultimately we recognize this attempt to explain the short lyric as
no more transparent than the poem itself. The commentary functions as
a kind of translation of the poem, examining modes of signification
historically embedded in its background. Like David Antin's talk poems,
these pieces of fanciful commentary keep our attention through their
resemblance to the accomplished patter of a stand-up comedian. And
also like Antin's texts, Bromige's poetry gains in appeal by the perfect
timing and intonation with which he delivers it orally. The comedy wins
listeners and readers into a poetry acutely aware of itself in crisis: Writing
a commentary upon one's earlier poetry is not an innocent act; it be-

speaks an immense anxiety about the future of one's writing. The dark
side of Bromige's enterprise is its cannibalism – a transgression whose
implication in all acts of criticism or translation Bromige brings to the
surface. *My Poetry* presents a poetry that teeters between the paralysis of
verse and the manic proliferation of critically self-aware prose.

From the many poets of my own generation who write in prose, I
have selected two, Ron Silliman (b.1946) and Michael Davidson
(b.1944), as excellent representatives of two further trends in contemporary poet's prose. The fact that each of these poets is an articulate and
prolific critic also underscores the present interpenetration of poetry and
criticism. Silliman's poetry evidences primarily theoretical and abstract
concerns, though its language ranges through all levels of diction and
reference. His most enduring influences appear to be the projectivist
poets, on the one hand, and the abstract poetics of Stein, Russian Formal-
ism, and Louis Zukofsky on the other. The experience of reading his
longer poet's prose, *Ketjak* (San Francisco: This, 1978) and *Tjanting*
(Berkeley: The Figures, 1981), is akin to the experience of modern music
("Ketjak" is the Balinese monkey chant from the *Ramayana*) or art, in
which the exfoliation of formal patterns – of repetition and variation
defined by complex operations – gives the aesthetic pleasure. Functioning like sound or visible pattern in the other arts, language comprises a
self-enclosed world, yet one inexhaustibly permeable by an outside reality. The poet casts nets of varying theoretical complexity into the world
of language, exhibiting his catch in a text that asks the reader to make his
or her own perceptual and ideological discoveries. *Tjanting* (a drawing
instrument for use in batik; an exact pun on "chanting") consists of
nineteen progressively expanding paragraphs (the last paragraph takes
seventy-five pages) that run to over two hundred pages. Here are the first
seven paragraphs:

> Not this.
> What then?
> I started over & over. Not this.
> Last week I wrote "the muscles in my palm so sore from
> halving the rump roast I cld barely grip the pen." What then?
> This morning my lip is blisterd.
> Of about to within which. Again & again I began. The gray
> light of day fills the yellow room in a way wch is somber. Not
> this. Hot grease had spilld on the stove top.
> Nor that either. Last week I wrote "the muscle at thumb's
> root so taut from carving beef I thought it wld cramp." Not so.
> What then? Wld I begin? This morning my lip is tender,
> disfigurd. I sat in an old chair out behind the anise. I cld have
> gone about this some other way.

Wld it be different with a different pen? Of about to within
which what. Poppies grew out of the pile of old broken–up
cement. I began again & again. These clouds are not apt to burn
off. The yellow room has a sober hue. Each sentence accounts
for its place. Not this. Old chairs in the back yard rotting from
winter. Grease on the stove top sizzled & spat. It's the same,
only different. Ammonia's odor hangs in the air. Not not this.

Sentences are presented and then they are repeated, contradicted, broken up, or reconstituted: "It's the same, only different." In the beginning
this prose sounds quite a bit like Beckett, but once Silliman gets going
he conjectures much more wildly and abstractly with language.[14] Here
is a group of sentences chosen from a random location:

O ambientes! Rendered proposition of wind delicate by hat.
Facing pages. Tufts of swift fog. Birds in the pet shop died in
the fire, but they saved the pups. Away, I recognized her year
blocks later. The limit of performance to audience ratio. Eros
bows. A mote of dust gets in under eye's lid. Sleep your
remember. Recently I rid myself of books I'll not read again. All
of a single cat condensed into a glance of religion. Is Mickey
Mouse black? (98)

Within this odd combination of the theoretical and the concrete, words
seem to be the generative element, rather than the sentence. A kind of
treatise on language as a mediating factor and on textuality as endless
differentiation, this text also maintains a tenacious specificity and factual
quality through concentrating on the tactile qualities of words. Wrap-
ping up the mystery of the text's simultaneous abstraction and referentiality into an aphorism, the poet Lyn Hejinian declares about *Tjanting*,
with evident delight, that "the reader recognizes every word."[15] In an
earlier credo of his own, Silliman expands this notion of language as the
world in which human beings exist:

What I want when I write is a total engagement with language. It is
this only which is possible in poetry which cannot be had elsewhere. The structure of language is one with that of mind, consciousness, all perception. What I confront when I write is that
which makes the human so.[16]

If there is an idealism in Silliman's relentlessly informal poetry, it lies in
this dream of a total engagement with language, which is something like
a desire to fully invoke the messianic pure language of Benjamin and
Mallarmé. The closer Silliman and others of the new poets of San Francisco and New York come to this total engagement, the more forbidding
and opaque the writing may seem to any but the most intrepid, active

reader. But when his sentences hover between the presentation of fact and the self-consciousness of mediation, Silliman offers a grand example of the crisis of verse.

Michael Davidson has no such desires for totality. When he calls his poet's prose in *The Mutabilities* (Berkeley: Sand Dollar Books, 1976) and *The Prose of Fact* (Berkeley: The Figures, 1981) a "prose of fact," he recognizes the term itself as "a point of conjecture around which I am constantly writing and thinking about things."[7] Davidson's prose is always engaged in a task, continually trying to get somewhere, but, like Ashbery's its completion is always forestalled. The interruptions are not merely obstacles (though as such they can be winningly clownish); they also drive the text deeper and deeper into the psychological and political implications constantly lurking in language. Adapting a title from one of Heidegger's books, we could say that Michael Davidson is "on the way to facts." In the following self-description, he explains the genesis of a writing that exists in the tension between language and fact:

> I have a kind of naive idea of what a fact is. To paraphrase Wittgen-
> stein, it's a point of departure for further investigation. I think it
> began with my interest with lists. At one point the idea of a list was
> a sort of ultimate autistic construct, because it would create the
> illusion of a random series that would relate immediately to my
> life. I would be able to go through my day and check off items on
> the list. They were words after all, but the syntax of the list was my
> activity. In that sense, it was a hermeneutic of reading a list. And
> then I began to realize that I wanted to tell stories; I wanted to
> describe events. And the problem, of course, occurred in the first
> few words: as I began to describe the event I was faced with my
> own language staring me back in the face. I simply couldn't de-
> scribe. I found myself involved in the forms of mediation that were
> constantly coming up in front of me.[18]

Davidson's prose combines a traditionally tuned poetic ear with a crit-ically sophisticated mind, resulting in the most artful (in both senses of the word) prose of those considered in this chapter. In his elegance he resembles, too, the Wittgensteinean Surrealism of Michael Palmer, who composes by foregrounding and compressing language, like raw coal, into diamonds. Davidson does not compress quite so forcefully; his prose has a conjectural motion akin to Creeley's, as in this untitled piece from *The Mutabilities*:

> "Sunshine today." But her letter brings news within which he
> reads the news. It is clear what is there to be said – even the
> inflection remembered. Something about having heard through
> the grapevine in closing so as to leave the case open.

One wishes for the old dichotomies at times: "Poor soul, the center of . . ." But then sun is a corrective for this endless reading between the lines.

The flesh is "there." There is no word for it and still it is intensive in the way of "expense of spirit" which reads as "expensive spirit." In this sense, like all else, compelling. Certainly everything has been paid for unless one creates a world of smaller and smaller guilts. Otherwise there is the sun for one walking in it, watching gulls eating out of an old woman's hand.[19]

The statement "sunshine today" refers to a time in writing, not an actual present; unlike *Presences,* this poem meditates upon the absence incarnated in writing. The thinking in the poem is highly philosophical, and the sentences interrogate, through overlapping frames, the way that language mediates our notions of reality. The sexual infidelity hinted at by both the letter writer ("having heard through the grapevine") and the speaker ("the flesh is 'there'") mirrors the mediative infidelity of language (through over- or mis-statement) to a wholly external reality: The speaker is implicated in both the sexual and the linguistic transgressions. By the end the absent sun, available only in a letter received by the speaker in another time and place, has become an imaginative reality, though whether the "one" who walks in it is the one who wrote or the one who read the letter remains ambiguous. It would seem that language has created the sun, just as the near rhyme with "guilts" may have created the "gulls." These shifts, ambiguities, and investigations are all aided by the self-conscious use of the grammar, syntax, usual rhetoric, and assumed intonation of the sentence.

In Davidson, as in Bromige, Ashbery, Duncan, Creeley, and Williams, the crisis in verse is felt as an existential crisis as well. Though Antin and Silliman take a cooler approach, for all of these writers the use of prose is a sign of engagement with the largest range of language in order to both understand and come into the world. Such a project is fraught, for modern American poets, with dangers from every direction: The only hope for success lies in confronting and even surrendering to the enemy by honoring scrupulously the claims of language and the world, and then in repeating and inventing it anew. As the latest testimony to the health of the objectivist and projectivist trends in American poetry, the talk poem and the new poet's prose appear to guarantee a lively future for poet's prose within the unfolding crisis in American verse.

EPILOGUE: 1990

The sole precedent I can find for the new sentence is Kora in Hell: Improvisations *and that one far-fetched.*

                                                                    Silliman

Although David Bromige, Ron Silliman, and Michael Davidson would all, for various reasons, have resisted the label of "Language poetry" when this book was first written, today the term has received critical acceptance, and the poets seem willing enough – or secure enough in their own work – to acknowledge major points of theoretical agreement.[20] As a group, the Language poets have been publishing now for two decades. The number of poets writing in this mode continues to expand; at a rough estimate, there are fifty to one hundred writers publishing a huge volume of poetry and commentary, in what represents the main line of continuity in the seventies and eighties of the objectivist strain in American poetry. The sheer amount and diversity of the writing, as well as its experimental quality, make a blanket evaluation impossible. Language poetry puts into question so many of our assumptions about poetry, language, and discourse, and it does this in such a large variety of forms, that it merits extended study both of individual poets and of the dominant issues it raises. David Antin, too, has not only continued to deliver talk poems and to publish them; he also has come to be perceived as a major innovator in the Performance movement, which has played a crucial role in defining postmodernism in the fields of art, music, dance, video, and theater. In approaching the Language poets and David Antin at this moment in time, I would like to do something other than update my readings of their texts or expand the number of poets considered. Instead, I would like to explore what we can learn about the situation of contemporary poetry through examining how these poets stand with respect to prose.

The most striking aspect of the contemporary scene is the extent to which poetry has become tied to the university. At its most obvious, this relationship is manifest in the vast number of recognized poets of every stripe who are employed by colleges and universities as teachers of writing or as critics. Although Jerome McGann, in an insightful article stressing the oppositional politics of Language writing, claims that the Language poets "are almost *all* situated – economically and institutionally – outside the academy," this simply is not true: Not only are some of the Language poets tenured professors, while others work more occasionally as adjuncts; their essays and anthologies are now beginning to appear from academic presses.[21] But just because poets are employed, or published, by universities does not mean that the black sheep have been welcomed wholeheartedly into the fold. Although members of philos-

ophy departments describe themselves as "philosophers," the only people
in English departments who call themselves "writers" are those hired to
teach creative writing; as professors, they have a tremendous uphill battle
to fight if they wish to be taken seriously by their colleagues or insti-
tutions. This reflects the general relationship at present between poetry
and criticism, in which the academic context seems nearly all-inclusive.
In explaining recently, to an incredulous philosopher, the relative prestige
of poets and critics, I found myself using the respective terms "minimal"
and "enormous." Robert von Hallberg has pointed out how recent this
state of affairs is, lamenting the passing of the poet-critic, whose influence
was felt by poets and scholars alike.[22] Virtually the last poet accorded
major attention by the academy was John Ashbery, whose impact was
registered a decade ago. It may be indicative of the academic hegemony
that Ashbery did not, as most other major poets have done, pave the
way for his acceptance through his own criticism or polemics; rather,
Harold Bloom, one of the few remaining major critics to make powerful
claims for the greatness of contemporary poets, brought the whole theoretical force of his "revisionary ratios" to bear, in order to situate Ashbery within the line of "strong" Romantic poets and to gain him a serious
hearing.

     To the ears of those who used to listen for it, the voice of poetry
seems curiously muffled, either because the poets themselves have accepted the diminished expectations placed upon them – developing what
Charles Altieri dubs "the scenic mode" of workshop poetry – or because
the many oppositional groups, like the Language poets, the ethnic poets,
and the feminist poets, have been squeezed to the farthest margins by
the conservative persuasion of the last two decades.[23] Language poetry
provides an interesting example of how poetry has become relatively
invisible today: From the point of view of the academy, one could say
either that the Language poets have removed themselves from serious
consideration by attacking established values from the leftist margin, or,
alternatively, one could say that they have camouflaged themselves so
carefully in a luxuriant underbrush of theory that their status as poets
remains almost completely hidden. This second charge is the more serious
one, for it correctly notes that Language poetry enters easily into critical
discourse as a species of theory. Jerome McGann, for instance, though
demonstrating its theoretical sophistication and sincerity, makes a cogent
case for Language poetry as the concerted effort by the Baby Boom
generation to write its political poetry; in doing so, however, he treats
the poetry as indistinguishable from theory. The relation of poetry and
theory seems to be the crucial issue now in understanding how poet's
prose has come to confront the expanding crisis of verse. The notion of
a theoretical poetry unsettles all of our expectations about poetry, raising

troubling questions about the status of the individual poem that are not unlike the questions about the status of the individual person raised by poststructuralism. From the perspective of a reader schooled in exegetical approaches to poems as discrete entities, the question arises: If the theory of this poetry occurs in the discursive prose (essays, introductions, notes, and commentaries) that has become the groundwork of Language poetry, then does not a poem become a mere demonstration of a theory, rather than an object of value in its own right?

One might imagine a meditation on the relation of poem to theory, by a sympathetic but skeptical reader, along the following lines: If a poem is a demonstration of a theory, then once one has read the theory and assented to it, or dissented from it, is there any need to read more than a few exemplary poems to "get" it? Although Language poetry is not unique in its polemical orientation (American poetry consistently has turned to polemic and theory in order to establish the grounds for its own production), in Language poetry polemic reaches its apotheosis: In the first place, without the framing of the polemic, most Language writing would strike the uninitiated as meaningless textual corruption (the result of mechanical malfunction by typographic or photographic equipment); but, more important for the informed reader, the poetry finally seems to exist for the sake of the polemic rather than vice versa. But look again – is there not something important that one can discover only by reading these poems? One does practice and refine a sensitivity to the mediatory function of language – how its material character contravenes any "message" or "expression" that it carries. But, having developed an awareness and understanding of the materiality of language through an encounter with several texts, both "theoretic" and "poetic," why would one return to read more? In the broadest sense, Language poetry proposes a way of life, a political praxis, in which the disruption of habitual patterns of linguistic control may result in the liberation of the committed reader from the whole matrix of social mechanisms defining late capitalism: Still, does it matter if we read one or another particular poet or particular poem? Even if we unconditionally abandon the notion of the author and dissolve all egotistical claims to uniqueness or individuality, the question refuses to be dislodged: Why go on writing or reading Language poetry?

While this meditation has raised many of the theoretical premises of Language poetry, it remains stuck in the dilemma of how to conceive of a "theoretical poem." Charles Bernstein denies the very distinction between poetry and theory by rewriting the famous projectivist dictum "Form is never more than an extension of content" as a credo for the Language poets: "Theory is never more than the extension of practice." Bernstein goes on to explain how the poet's approach to language and genre yields actively engaged theories. From the poet's point of view, all writing must be seen to inhabit the field of poetic/social composition:

> Critical forums for these writers – such as $L=A=N=G=U=A=G=E$ or *Hills / Talks* – have been investigations in a manner similar to the work of the "poetry," where writing and the meaning of its modes are actively engaged: no manifestos, no formulation of underlying principles, no "how to write" apart from the writing itself that at any moment has no claim except as another instance. So, implicitly, an interrogation of the meaning of any mode – of "poetry" or "theory" – and an acknowledgement that there is no escape from composition, no logic on which to base the work other than the sense developed ongoing in the actual activity itself.[24]

By referring to projectivist "composition by field" (continuing, in fact, to parody Olson's rhetoric), Bernstein wants to highlight as a central feature of Language writing the process of discovery, or what Olson calls "recognition." In "Projective Verse," Olson states that "from the moment he ventures into FIELD COMPOSITION – puts himself in the open – he can go by no track other than the one the poem under hand declares, for itself. Thus he has to behave, and be, instant by instant, aware of some several forces just now beginning to be examined." Whatever occurs in projectivist composition – and certainly, for Olson, that includes the constant propensity for theoretical statements – must remain responsible to that composition, rather than transcend it as a universal formulation of truth: "The objects which occur at every given moment of composition (of recognition, we can call it) are, can be, must be treated exactly as they do occur therein and not by any ideas or preconceptions from outside the poem, must be handled as a series of objects in field in such a way that a series of tensions (which they also are) are made to *hold*, and to hold exactly inside the content and the context of the poem which has forced itself, through the poet and them, into being."[25]

In Language poetry the field of composition, while still conceived in terms similar to Olson's, has expanded far beyond anything Olson could have imagined. In this new mode of composition, theoretical insights and understandings occur through the challenging acts of reading/writing (what Jed Rasula calls "wreading"[26]) that one learns to perform on specific texts and on the world. As the heirs to the modern poetic investigation of language, the Language poets discover endless opportunities for the comic unmasking of discourse's claim to transparency. Resisting the Age of Information, the Language poets act as an ever expanding army of saboteurs, turning up, in every ordinary language situation, to show us just how material – that is, poetic – it is. Rather than ask, Why read another Language poem? maybe one should ask, Why stop reading/ writing Language poetry? A theoretical poetry such as that written by the Language poets has designs on breaking down not just the distinctions between poetry and prose but those between reading and writing, criticism and creation, politics and life. The individual poem – when Language writing takes such a form – is a site in which the ongoing activity of theoretical poetry can occur, a site for theoretical recognitions about the language in which we live.

Hovering around the preceding discussion has been the felt need to consider the relation of a theoretical poetry to prose. Kittay and Godzich's theory, in *The Emergence of Prose*, of how prose became the dominant signifying practice in the modern age (which I discussed in the Introduction) offers a new purchase on the latest poet's prose, another perspective from which to reflect on its theoretical qualities. These two authors share with the Language poets, and with David Antin, a highly critical view of capitalism, particularly of its disruption of communal solidarity in nonliterate (or, as Antin would say, "nonliteral"[27]) societies. Into the debates about writing and orality that have formed a core of postmodern reflections upon culture, Kittay and Godzich have introduced an immensely important factor: prose. When one asks, for instance, whether the entry of writing into a traditional culture marks the disintegration of traditional authority, the answer cannot be categorical but must rely upon another question: Which kind of writing? Since the advent of writing, some traditions have not only been preserved in writing but preserved relatively intact. For most of the cultures that employ it, writing as scripture, for instance, has been just one of a number of symbolic presentations of a sacred tradition that is addressed to, and must be learned in, every aspect of life; the "interpretation" of a sacred text means a new recognition of how to proceed in life, either for an individual or for a group. As Kittay and Godzich demonstrate, the writing that precludes tradition – the secular, historical mode of writing – is prose. All previous writing had depended for its deixis, its grounding in an outside context, upon a living exemplar of the tradition. With the loss of the authority that had been invested in the person of the jongleur in late medieval France, a particular society began to turn away from the authority of collective tradition and toward the authority of the bureaucratic nation state, whose signifying practice is quintessentially prosaic:

> In a change of signifying practice, there is . . . a generalized shift among functions and holders of functions. We have seen certain jongleurian functions be assumed by discourses. There is therein

an abstracting-away of body. . . . Prose's ability to approach all existing communicative situations formally, to abstract them from
their mechanism without at the same time taking on the human
agents in the process, and finally to appropriate the mechanism for
itself under its own agency, is its most signal procedure, the very
basis of its strength. It truly marks the beginning of a process of
reification. Conseil [a prose allegorical character] shows that the
evolving modern state is the social formation in which such func-
tionaries have a constitutive part. They are the bearers, by virtue
of their narrow confines, of an increasingly faceless authority. Prose
is custom-made for the pros. (p. 74)

By learning to ground its deixis in the various discourses it contains,
prose transforms our relation to tradition; it presents itself as freestanding,
independent of the authorizing presence of any individual, and thus free
from the control of tradition. Although the matter of tradition remains
open and available to prose, the relation to that matter changes dramatically; the era of prose carries us all the way from the direct performance
of tradition to the rigid framing of tradition as mere archive. When,
through the invention of prose, the text and the individual responsible
for guarding and transmitting it lose their mutual accountability, texts
become free-floating and available for appropriation by whatever interests choose to employ them. If we think of modernity as the break from
a tradition guaranteed through the presence of its guardians, then maybe
the most apt description of modernity is "the age of prose." Prose frees
people from established relationships while constructing a new world of
power and authority within its self-supporting discourses. In conflict
with this form of liberation, poetry and religion have resisted prose,
recognizing that prose makes a sacred (or, perhaps we should say, a
material) language impossible: For a language to be sacred it must locate
its deixis outside the text, which prose does not allow; for a language to
be material, its words must take precedence over its significations, thus
countermanding prose's call for transparency.[28] As the basic signifying
practice of the modern world, prose has very effectively squeezed poetry
and religion into the margins, remaking the world in its own image. In
the world of prose, all kinds of discourse (though not all signifying
practices: oral performance, for example) can enter and signify, while
none maintains traditional authority; instead, prose grants authority to
its employers, the vast bureaucratic apparatus of the nation state – gov-
ernment and military bureaucracy, state-controlled education, the con-
tractually bound economic forces of capital and labor and consumption,
the communications and transportation media, and the professions. In
the face of this interlocking nexus of prosaic agencies, how can a poet

even imagine the conditions under which a nonprosaic discourse could find a place of power?

From Emerson to Williams, to Creeley and Ashbery, and on to the Language poets and David Antin, this book has charted the progressive attempt to come to terms with the overpowering determination of modern life by prose. In Emerson, as in other Romantic writers, a realization begins to dawn that poetry has lost its authority and that through the use of prose itself a poet might find ways both to acknowledge the power of prose and to subvert its authority from within.[29] By the early twentieth century, prose has so stripped poetry of the major part of its social function that a poet such as Williams must use prose to provide the backbone for his investigations into the role of language as a mediator between things and persons. Creeley and Ashbery have launched full-scale investigations of prose sentencing and prose signifying practice from the perspective of poetry. By presenting their work as poetry, they repeatedly force us to apply to the prose text our awareness of poetic signifying practices, thickening the prose world until it surrenders its transparency to poetic materiality. In a sense, this friction created by simultaneously holding two different signifying practices in mind dissolves with the Language poets. Because of their complete immersion in the prosaic world, they are capable of the most powerful and sustained critiques and subversions of that world. Language writing relentlessly deconstructs the signifying practice of prose, attacking it from the levels of semantics, grammar, referentiality, and narrative, defamiliarizing all of its practices in order to demonstrate, ultimately, *that it does not signify*. As an act of guerrilla warfare directed against the prosaic world, Language poetry can wreak tremendous devastation, undermining completely the instrumental capabilities of prose by revealing the poetic underpinnings of every language situation.

But what about David Antin? His talk poems adopt a position one could call "post-prose." While seeking very directly to return the deixis for his poetry to himself as a living presence, he includes within the newly oral signifying practice of the talk poem elements of prose textuality. His talks presuppose prose literacy, such as the ability to follow hypotactic syntax and to conceive of all sorts of prose demonstrations and prose narratives, but he attempts to break the stranglehold of prose as the dominant signifying practice – as the only way in which truth can be constructed and power delivered – by overcoming it through reinstating the conditions of orality. Appealing to our repressed desire for a powerful discourse that takes place in living conversation, in a face-to-face encounter of actual human beings with one another, where the prosaic rules of truth and power are relaxed, Antin invites us to reclaim authority from the faceless prosaic agencies and to find it in our attentive

interchanges with one another in particular occasions. Although the features of an oral-poetic signifying practice occur most directly in the actual
performance/composition of a talk poem – the body language, the whole
range of vocal musicality and accent, the display of a particular rhythm
of thought, the attunement of the discourse to its audience and circumstances – the point of employing such oral features remains when the
talk poem is translated into a text. By using print to make us imagine a
nonprosaic relation to truth and power, in which deixis is wrenched
away from the self-enclosed discursive logic of prose and returned to
individual people and groups as responsible to specific contexts, Antin,
too, attacks prose within its own lair.

In the Introduction, I spoke of one of the central tasks of poet's prose as
investigating the domain of truth. Over the centuries of prose domi-
nation, poetry has been channeled more and more narrowly toward the
lyric, in which the feelings of a self are reflected on and dramatized. While
the battle for truth has been waged by philosophers and scientists, who
have so mastered the use of prose that they provide our models of its
"rigorous" employment, poets have found themselves shunted aside into
a nostalgic corner reserved for greeting cards. In "Aristotle's Lyric: Re-
imagining the Rhetoric of Epideictic Song," Jeffrey Walker joins the
ranks of critics within a host of disciplines who have begun to insist
upon the rhetorical nature of their discourse; for Walker, this means
returning poetry to its early form of epideictic argument.[30] Of the three
kinds of rhetoric that Aristotle defines – deliberative (political debate),
judicial (legal argument), and epideictic (demonstrative) – the epideictic
is the only one that argues, by example, for specific *values* rather than
seeks to promote political or legal *decisions*. "Epideictic argument belongs . . . to the domain of theory, and it invites its listener/'spectator'
(or *theoros*, as Aristotle says) to an act of contemplation, evaluation, and
judgment" (p. 8). Here we have the notion of a theoretical poetry proposed once again, but from a different perspective, in which the long-
range career of poetry is taken into account. The archaic tradition of
epideictic poetry reached its final stage in poets like Pindar and Sappho,
who are rendered "archaic" to our sensibilities, Walker argues, by Aristotle. Attempting to save poetry through revising the Platonic critique,
Aristotle effects the splitting apart of poetry, rhetoric, and philosophy
and then defines for lyric poetry the role of representing a character (a
speaker) in a particular dramatic situation. This leaves us with "the essentially apostrophic lyric – the short poem neither narrative nor discursive in itself. . . , the 'lyrically' self-expressive outburst by a speaker
with his back turned to the reader/listener (and often with his face toward
some imaginary, absent presence)" (p. 13).

We can argue that this rhetorically restricted paradigm for lyric is, in principle, a paradigm for minor poetry. First of all, it is by definition subordinate to narrative (or to embodied narrative, in drama proper). . . . The real poetic act, then, and the intellectually substantive act, is the creation of the fable itself – so that epic, tragedy, and (eventually) prose fiction become definable as the necessary major venues for "serious" and challenging literary work. The lyric, by comparison, is at least potentially understandable as a sort of purple patch, an interlude, an elegant attitudinal display which derives its significance from the implied or given narrative-dramatic frame. . . . The displayed emotion of this interlude, moreover, is likely to be conventional – that is, what the context "should" produce, or would be expected to produce by the poet's audience. Otherwise, and insofar as the apostrophic poem does not (or cannot) adopt the argumentational means of explaining or justifying its mimetically displayed or enacted state of consciousness, the speaker's feelings run the risk of seeming to the reader/listener unreasonable, neurotic, or just plain unintelligible (however skillful and/or elegant the poet's rendering). (p. 14)

This is exactly the sort of critique of lyric poetry that David Antin mounts, claiming that by going into a closet and imagining itself as overheard by an audience lyric poetry has given up its situation within a community, and thus its ability to argue for public agreement about values. Moreover, Antin and Walker agree that the lyric poem's abstraction from communal enactment leads to a progressive alienation from the audience, due to the representation of ever more idiosyncratic and mannered states of consciousness. In contrast, Antin's talk poems fulfill the demands for an epideictic discourse by (1) being addressed to a specific occasion, (2) arguing for specific values by presenting particular exemplary stories or images, and (3) attempting to reach agreement with an audience about general issues of understanding and of action. Trying to determine exactly which values he espouses, however, becomes a more tricky matter: For although Antin joins Walker in seeking a poetry that addresses collective issues in public, Antin differs from the early Greek poets by not endorsing particular values, like heroism or patriotism or the worship of divinity, values that promote social bonding through identification with a character or performer; instead he promotes more subtle values, such as respect for the human abilities of other people and of oneself, which underlie any social intercourse and determine its tenor. Antin's concern with ordinary language and ordinary people is a way of accepting the heteroglossia and the heterodoxy of the world, rather than an argument for specific ways of thinking and acting. His second book

of talk poems, *Tuning*, centers on the endeavor to imagine a more satisfactory, socially based notion of understanding, which would respect
differences among people by replacing the metaphor of "under-standing"
with that of "tuning." In an elaborate description of tuning as the effort
of two people to adjust their strides so as to walk along together for a
while, he emphasizes simultaneously the ordinariness, the gracefulness,
and the inherent quality of difference in our acts of understanding:

> there is something cyclical and
> periodic in all our motions   even being still   and it is this
> repetition of many small nearly equivalent acts making up our
> characteristic motions   our ways of going and knowing that
> may explain how we can undertake this negotiation between
> one way of going and another   because if someone is walking
> near to me or next to me   i can watch his way of stepping
> or hers and choose to walk along with her changing my direction
> slightly to join her in her walking as she may also change her
> pathway slightly to prevent colliding[31]

We accomplish our understanding of one another by simultaneously
taking cognizance of ourselves and of the other. The most satisfying
moments of understanding occur when we reach an attunement so carefully modulated as to seem "musical." *Tuning* opens with a short anecdote (there are discrete anecdotes framing the beginning and end of
each talk poem), in which Antin describes the performance at a funeral
of a piece of music composed by Pauline Oliveros: "we were all to rise
and form a large single circle joining hands with our nearest neighbors
    to listen until we heard a tone we felt like tuning to   to try to
tune to it and when we were satisfied with our tuning we could fall silent
and listen   choose another tone and try to tune to it   and go on
like this listening and tuning and falling silent as long as we wished
    until we felt that we were through" (p. 1). From this description,
one can see that Oliveros has been influenced by Karlheinz Stockhausen's
remarkable *Stimmung* (the German word for "tuning" or "mood"), a
composition in which the members of a group of specially trained singers
tune harmonically to one another while chanting an interpenetrating
series of names of gods from around the world, producing a startling
array of ringing overtones, both harmonic and cultural. It is a short step
from the reverberating tones of Stockhausen's chant to Heidegger's discussion of *Stimmung* in *Being and Time*, where he speaks of our moods
as our basic attunement to being-in-the-world.[32] Like Heidegger, Antin
is concerned to keep the process of tuning focused upon worldly rather

than purely metaphysical considerations; in contrast to Heidegger, Antın attends carefully to other people, with whom he hopes to reach attunement: "i was holding hands with a carefully dressed young history professor and a smart looking dark haired woman from a travel agency in la jolla   i listened for a while and could make out several humming tones coming from various places about the room   i could hear the history professor clear his throat and start to hum a tone in the middle of the baritone register   i thought i would join him there and my partner on the left opened a lovely mezzo just above us" (pp. 1–2). As the people in the room yield themselves more and more fully to this simple, unformalized ritual, a striking instance of communal bonding occurs:

> at one point a high clear soprano tone
> floated out across the room and i saw the history
> professor start to cry   i squeezed his hand and
> tried to join a high tenor almost beyond my range
> the history professor nodded and joined us there
> our dark haired neighbor to the left opened a flute
> like tone a fifth above us   all around the room
> people were crying and smiling and singing in
> waves of sound that throbbed and swelled and ebbed
> and climbed and peaked and dropped away into a
> silence that lasted until pauline thanked everyone
> because the piece was over (p. 2)

In David Antin's talk poems the "prose" functions of philosopher, critic, and storyteller are incorporated into a poetic discourse aware of its linguistic, its figurative, and its argumentative qualities. In his own cool, seemingly uninflected tone, Antin combines the central American modes of oratory and meditation that we have seen as creatively intertwined in the best poet's prose. Although his oratory eschews impassioned pleas and his meditation remains unconcerned with the relation of a self to something transcendent, Antin fulfills the requirements of these two modes by opening a public space for consideration of values and by deliberating with great care upon the issue of identity as a linguistic and social construction. Insisting on similar criteria for the Language poets, Ron Silliman reminds us, in his preface to *In the American Tree*, that "much, perhaps too much, has been made of the critique of reference and normative syntax inherent in the work of many of the writers here, without acknowledging the degree to which this critique is itself situated within the larger question of what, in the last part of the twentieth century, it means to be human."[33] Joining the witty but dense exposures of the materiality of language in the theoretical poet's prose of the Language poets, Antin's theoretical poetry, too, opens up tremendous possibilities for future investigations of what it means to be human, indicating ways in which our various faculties of thinking, of poetic sensitivity to language and image, of narration, and of living in the daily world of other people can all be brought into accord in a single "language art." Wherever this language art occurs, whether in conversation, on television, movie, or computer screens, in performances and rituals, or in print media, we are beginning to see the poetics of these situations as an active apprehension of the ways language constitutes the very texture of our lives. By this awareness the prosaic world is dyed poetic.

NOTES

Abbreviations are used for works frequently cited. See the "List of Abbreviations," near the front of the book.

INTRODUCTION

1   Jeffrey Kittay and Wlad Godzich, *The Emergence of Prose: An Essay in Prosaics* (Minneapolis: Univ. of Minnesota Press, 1987), pp. 34–5.
2   "To Arsène Houssaye," in *Paris Spleen*, trans. Louise Varèse (New York: New Directions, 1970), pp. ix–x.
3   Trans. Michael Benedikt, in *The Prose Poem: An International Anthology*, ed. Michael Benedikt (New York: Dell, 1976), p. 45. I dispute Benedikt's reading of this key passage from Mallarmé during my discussion of Ashbery's relation to the prose poem, in Chapter 3 of this volume.

   For an excellent general discussion of the importance of language as an issue in modern poetry, see Gerald L. Bruns, *Modern Poetry and the Idea of Language* (New Haven: Yale Univ. Press, 1974). For Bruns, Mallarmé and Heidegger represent two major directions modern poets have taken in their investigations of language. Bruns revises and deepens his discussion of the relation of poetry to language in *Heidegger's Estrangements: Language, Truth, and Poetry in the Later Writings* (New Haven: Yale Univ. Press, 1989).
4   For a book-length treatment of the relation of the prose poem to politics, see Jonathan Monroe, *A Poverty of Objects: The Prose Poem and the Politics of Genre* (Ithaca, N.Y.: Cornell Univ. Press, 1987). Using theoretical insights supplied mainly by Mikhail Bakhtin and Fredric Jameson, Monroe considers an international cast of figures: Schlegel, Novalis, Baudelaire, Rimbaud, Max Jacob, Gertrude Stein, Ernst Bloch, Francis Ponge, Robert Bly, and Helga Novak.
5   *Children of the Mire: Modern Poetry from Romanticism to the Avant-garde*, trans. Rachel Phillips (Cambridge, Mass.: Harvard Univ. Press, 1974), p. 159.
6   In addition to the book by Monroe cited earlier, there are two other book-length studies of the prose poem: Suzanne Bernard, *Le poème en prose de Baudelaire jusqu'à nos jours* (Paris: Librairie Nizet, 1959), and John Simon,

The Prose Poem as a Genre in Nineteenth-Century European Literature (New York: Garland, 1987), a reprint of his 1959 Harvard dissertation. Mary Ann Caws has edited two volumes of essays, *About French Poetry from Dada to "Tel Quel": Text and Theory* (Detroit: Wayne State Univ. Press, 1974), and *The Prose Poem in France: Theory and Practice*, edited with Hermine Riffaterre (New York: Columbia Univ. Press, 1983); the former includes several essays on the French prose poem, and the latter is wholly devoted to it. In two original and ambitious books, the prose poem occupies an important place in more general arguments about avant-garde poetry: Richard Terdiman, *Discourse/Counter-Discourse: The Theory and Practice of Symbolic Resistance in Nineteenth-Century France* (Ithaca, N.Y.: Cornell Univ. Press, 1985), and Donald Wesling, *The New Poetries: Poetic Form since Coleridge and Wordsworth* (Lewisburg, Pa.: Bucknell Univ. Press, 1985). Although their arguments have mostly been subsumed into later discussions, two other articles are worthy of mention: Renée Riese Hubert, "Characteristics of an Undefinable Genre: The Surrealist Prose Poem," *Symposium*, 22(Spring 1968):25–34, and Clive Scott, "The Prose Poem and Free Verse," in Malcolm Bradbury and James McFarlane, eds., *Modernism: 1890–1930* (Harmondsworth: Penguin, 1976), pp. 349–68. The signal contribution of Marjorie Perloff, with whom I have engaged in fruitful dialogue about prose poetry and contemporary American poetry for a number of years, will be noted later.

7 "The Desert Music," *Pictures from Brueghel and Other Poems* (New York: New Directions, 1962), p. 120. For treatments in greater depth of the American poet's self-consciousness regarding the possibility of an American poetry, see Albert Gelpi, *The Tenth Muse: The Psyche of the American Poet* (Cambridge, Mass.: Harvard Univ. Press, 1975), pp. 1–11, and Joseph G. Kronick, *American Poetics of History: From Emerson to the Moderns* (Baton Rouge: Louisiana State Univ. Press, 1984).

8 Michael Bernstein, *The Tale of the Tribe: Ezra Pound and the Modern Verse Epic* (Princeton: Princeton Univ. Press, 1980): A strong revisionist argument for the view that the Pound tradition in the long poem is a serious attempt to write from a historical consciousness.

9 I use the masculine pronoun in this sentence because long poems by American women do not pretend to the sort of cultural centrality, in which the poet serves as the focal point of cohesion, that their male counterparts often claim.

10 *Mayan Letters*, ed. Robert Creeley (1953; rpt. London: Jonathan Cape, 1968), pp. 26–7.

11 Michel Foucault develops many nuances for the term "discipline" in *Discipline and Punish: The Birth of the Prison*, trans. Alan Sheridan (New York: Pantheon, 1977), and *Power/Knowledge: Selected Interviews and Other Writings, 1972–1977*, ed. and trans. Colin Gordon (New York: Pantheon, 1980). A summary definition of "discipline" might be "the power created through regulation."

12 For a satisfying book-length treatment of the importance to Williams of the concept of measure, see Stephen Cushman, *William Carlos Williams and the Meanings of Measure* (New Haven: Yale Univ. Press, 1985).

13 "The Prose Poem in America," *Parnassus*, 5, no. 1 (Fall/Winter 1976):325.

14   "... Poetically Man Dwells ... ," in *Poetry, Language, Thought*, trans. Albert
      Hofstadter (New York: Harper & Row, 1971), p. 216.

15   American poet's prose presumes an aesthetics something like the one set
      forth by Hans-Georg Gadamer in *Truth and Method* (New York: Continuum,
      1975). Gadamer deconstructs the post-Kantian separation of the subjective
      from the objective, of aesthetics from truth, of art from science, demon-
      strating how this schism mistakenly arose and what dire consequences have
      attended upon it. Gadamer wishes to reinvoke a philosophy in which ex-
      perience is shared (because hermeneutic), in which art and science make
      equal claims to truth, and in which all truth is located not in the "logical"
      application of a method but in the play of representation.

16   "An Interview: With Gerard Malanga," *Open between Us*, ed. Ralph J. Mills,
      Jr. (Ann Arbor: Univ. of Michigan Press, 1980), p. 114.

17   *The Poetics of Indeterminacy: Rimbaud to Cage* (Princeton: Princeton Univ.
      Press, 1981); *The Dance of the Intellect: Studies in the Poetry of the Pound
      Tradition* (Cambridge: Cambridge Univ. Press, 1985). Nearly all of Perloff's
      work of the eighties treats issues that are pertinent to the present study. In
      addition to these books, two articles in particular should be mentioned: "The
      Linear Fallacy," *Georgia Review* 35(1981):855–69, and "Lucent and Inescap-
      able Rhythms: Metrical 'Choice' and Historical Formation," in Robert Frank
      and Henry Sayre, eds., *The Line in Postmodern Poetry* (Urbana: Univ. of
      Illinois Press, 1988), pp. 13–40. The latter book, in turn, offers a number
      of articles that touch on or consider at length issues raised in the last chapter
      of the present study.

18   "Looking for Dragon Smoke," in *Leaping Poetry: An Idea with Poems and
      Translations* (Boston: Beacon Press, 1975), pp. 1, 4. Michael Benedikt praises
      Bly's essay, "which bids fair to become as central to our time as 'Tradition
      and the Individual Talent' was to Eliot's," because, he says, it introduces
      "imagery" into American poetry, thus making us ready for the prose poem
      (*Prose Poem*, pp. 41–2).

19   *Selected Letters of Ezra Pound*, ed. D. D. Paige (1950; rpt. New York: New
      Directions, 1971), p. 160 (silently corrected here to correspond with auto-
      graph copy). Mike Weaver, *William Carlos Williams: The American Background*
      (Cambridge: Cambridge Univ. Press, 1971), p. 42. For more extended ar-
      gument see the following two essays, which are important for discriminating
      the American and French sides of Williams: Sherman Paul, "A Sketchbook
      of the Artist in His Thirty-Fourth Year: William Carlos Williams' *Kora in
      Hell: Improvisations*," in *The Shaken Realist: Essays in Honor of Frederick J.
      Hoffman*, ed. Melvin J. Friedman and John B. Vickery (Baton Rouge: Lou-
      isiana State Univ. Press, 1970), pp. 21–44; and Marjorie Perloff, " 'Lines
      Converging and Crossing': The 'French' Decade of William Carlos Wil-
      liams," *Poetics of Indeterminacy*, pp. 109–54.
          Curiously, Gilbert Sorrentino has tied Rimbaud and Williams together as
      the informing spirits of his improvisations in *Splendide-Hôtel* (1973; rpt.
      Elmwood Park, Ill.: Dalkey Archive Press, 1984). See also Robert Creeley's
      "Afterword," pp. 62–4.

20   "Some Questions about Modernism," *Occident*, n.s. 8(Spring 1974):27.

21 In many ways, deconstruction is more properly conceived of as parallel to, rather than critical of, American poetic thinking. Rightly understood, deconstruction is a philosophy and (often) an aesthetic performance, not an easily adaptable critical method. To simplify tremendously, one could say that it proposes an attack on the center (unity, presence, speech, logos, phallus, etc.) in favor of the margins, a demystifying of the unified authority of tradition. As a revisionist enterprise, it evinces a reformative spirit akin to the reformative impulse responsible for the founding of America. Right from the outset, Americans left the center behind in Europe and have been trying to conjure a culture out of a condition of decenteredness ever since. So, while deconstruction as a philosophy can help to describe some of the philosophical situations, and even strategies, available to American writers, a criticism that seeks, as deconstructive critics often have, to uncover significant anomalies that undermine traditional assumptions of centeredness runs the risk of missing the point when applied to American writing. An indiscriminate deconstructive criticism can find itself in the awkward position of seeking to unmask a villain who never existed.

At the end of an article entitled "Politics as Opposed to What?" in W. J. T. Mitchell, ed., *The Politics of Interpretation* (Chicago: Univ. of Chicago Press, 1983), Stanley Cavell – one of the few writers today who seem genuinely able to listen to American literature in the philosophical terms it requires – makes this same point:

> If the sun is an old symbol of the metaphysics of presence, of a concentric centeredness of our orienting polarities (say between heaven and earth, and past and present, and culture and nature), an American is apt to be perplexed in being told that this metaphysics is to be undone, since he or she will conceive of his literature and his philosophy as having begun with the knowledge and the tasks of its passing. If deconstruction, as in de Man's recommendation of it, is to disillusion us, it is a noble promise and to be given welcome. Disillusion is what fits us for reality. . . . But then we must be assured that this promise is based on a true knowledge of what our illusions are. (pp. 201–2)

In other words, Americans and their writers may have many illusions about themselves, but the illusion that we are at the center – the assumption, in terms of the three polarities Cavell offers, that our culture is "natural," that tradition grounds the actions of the present, and that God speaks through our history – is just not available. Like (as?) deconstructive thinkers, American writers begin from a premise of belatedness, from an awareness of their marginal metaphysical status, from a sense that the tradition is broken and therefore cannot provide a definitive ground for literary production.

Even Jacques Derrida, in a memorial lecture for Paul de Man, *Memoires: For Paul de Man*, trans. Cecile Lindsay, Jonathan Culler, and Eduardo Cadava (New York: Columbia Univ. Press, 1986), finds himself tempted to "risk, with a smile, the following hypothesis: America *is* deconstruction (l'Amerique, mais c'est la deconstruction)." Then, recognizing that the whole burden of his philosophical program is bent upon undoing the power created

by reifying such proper names as "deconstruction" and "America," Derrida
amends his hypothesis: "Let us say instead: deconstruction and America are
two open sets which intersect partially according to an allegorico-metonymic
figure. In this fiction of truth, 'America' would be the title of a new novel
on the history of deconstruction and the deconstruction of history" (p. 18).

1. WILLIAM CARLOS WILLIAMS'S KORA IN HELL

1   The quotation that heads this section is from "A Novelette," *Imaginations*,
    p. 285. Besides this apt evaluation, the other published statements by Wil-
    liams concerning *Kora in Hell: Improvisations* occur in the following works:
    Spring and All (*Imaginations*, 115–17); *The Selected Letters of William Carlos
    Williams*, ed. John C. Thirlwall (New York: McDowell, Obolensky, 1958),
    nos. 32, 37, 171, pp. 46–7, 52–3, 266–7; *The Autobiography of William Carlos
    Williams* (New York: New Directions, 1951), pp. 158–62; *I Wanted to Write
    a Poem: The Autobiography of the Works of a Poet*, ed. Edith Heal (Boston:
    Beacon Press, 1958), pp. 26–31.
2   Geoffrey Movius gives the most careful discussion of the Williams-Pound-
    Eliot relation at this moment in " 'Two halves of . . . a fairly decent poet':
    William Carlos Williams and Ezra Pound, 1914–1920," *Visionary Company:
    A Magazine of the Twenties*, 1, no. 1 (Summer 1981):121–48. See also Douglas
    Messerli, "A World Detached: The Early Criticism of William Carlos Wil-
    liams," *Sagetrieb*, 3, no. 2 (Fall 1984):89–98.
3   *I Wanted to Write a Poem*, p. 27.
4   In "Kora in Opacity: Williams's *Improvisations*," *Journal of Modern Literature*,
    1(May 1971):463–76, Joseph Evans Slate offers convincing evidence for this
    dating.
5   "De Improvisatione," *Iowa Review*, 9, no. 3 (Summer 1978):66. Peter
    Schmidt, in his chapter "The Improvisations: Williams, Dada, and the The-
    ory of Automatic Writing," in *William Carlos Williams, the Arts, and Literary
    Tradition* (Baton Rouge: Louisiana State Univ. Press, 1988), pp. 90–135,
    refines our understanding of Williams's relation to Dada by paralleling Wil-
    liams's use of automatism to that of André Breton.
6   For a cogent meditation on the distinction between a beginning and an origin,
    see Edward Said's *Beginnings: Intention and Method* (New York: Basic Books,
    1975).
7   *The Singer of Tales* (Cambridge, Mass.: Harvard Univ. Press, 1960). In *Ways
    of the Hand: The Organization of Improvised Conduct* (Cambridge, Mass.:
    Harvard Univ. Press, 1978), David Sudnow provides an impressively thor-
    ough phenomenological description of "the acquisition of jazz hands" by a
    pianist. Sudnow recounts in great detail the paradoxically rigorous routine
    one undergoes in order to become capable of the free play of sustained
    improvisation.
8   *Concerning the Spiritual in Art*, trans. M. T. H. Sadler (1914; rpt. New York:
    Dover, 1977), p. 57. For a discussion of how Williams discovered this Kan-
    dinsky text and how he made use of these three modes of expression, see

Mike Weaver, *William Carlos Williams: The American Background* (Cambridge: Cambridge Univ. Press, 1971), pp. 37–42.

9   Harvey Feinberg applies the myth of Kora to a detailed reading of *Kora in Hell* in "The American Kora: Myth in the Art of William Carlos Williams," *Sagetrieb*, 5, no. 2 (Fall 1986):73–92. For a discussion of Pound's lifelong devotion to Persephone, see Guy Davenport, "Persephone's Ezra," *The Geography of the Imagination* (San Francisco: North Point Press, 1981), pp. 141–64. For bibliographies of the critical treatment of *Kora in Hell*, see Jack Hardie, " 'A Celebration of the Light': Selected Checklist of Writings about William Carlos Williams," *Journal of Modern Literature*, 1(May 1971):593–642, and Linda W. Wagner, *William Carlos Williams: A Reference Guide* (Boston: G. K. Hall, 1978). The volume *William Carlos Williams: Man and Poet*, ed. Carroll F. Terrell (Orono, Maine: National Poetry Foundation, 1983) contains Joseph Brogunier, "An Annotated Bibliography of Works about William Carlos Williams: 1974–1982," pp. 453–585. More recent books with valuable discussions of *Kora in Hell* include Schmidt, mentioned earlier; David Frail, *The Early Politics and Poetics of William Carlos Williams* (Ann Arbor: UMI Research Press, 1987), pp. 173–80; Bernard Duffey, *A Poetry of Presence: The Writing of William Carlos Williams* (Madison: Univ. of Wisconsin Press, 1986), pp. 49–60; and William Marling, *William Carlos Williams and the Painters, 1909–1923* (Athens, Ohio: Ohio Univ. Press, 1982), pp. 136–56. Roy Miki devotes a whole monograph, *The Prepoetics of William Carlos Williams: Kora in Hell* (Ann Arbor: UMI Research Press, 1983), to a careful exposition of Williams's text, arguing, as does the present study, that *Kora in Hell* provides the basis of Williams's mature poetics; aside from the value of his detailed, appreciative reading, Miki's most original contribution is his argument for the influence of *King Lear*, especially in the language of the Fool.

10 *Writing Degree Zero*, trans. Annette Lavers and Colin Smith (Boston: Beacon Press, 1970), p. 47.

11 *Autobiography*, p. 380.

12 Barthes, *Writing Degree Zero*, p. 50.

13 *Imaginations*, 67. These propositions, though they arise in *Kora in Hell*, are given their fullest airing in *Spring and All* (1923). J. Hillis Miller, in *Poets of Reality: Six Twentieth-Century Writers* (Cambridge, Mass.: Harvard Univ. Press, 1965), pp. 309–10, formulates clearly the divergence of Williams's theoretical stance in *Spring and All* from classical and romantic theories of art:

> The prose parts of the original edition of *Spring and All* . . . are his fullest expressions of a subtle theory of poetry which rejects both the mirror and the lamp, both the classical theory of art as imitation, and the romantic theory of art as transformation. In their place is proposed a new objectivist art in which a poem is "Not prophecy!/NOT prophecy!/but the thing itself!"

The next chapter of the present study contains a general discussion of the place of objectivist aesthetics in American poet's prose.

Kerry Driscoll, in *William Carlos Williams and the Maternal Muse* (Ann Arbor: UMI Research Press, 1987), argues the importance of Williams's mother as a muse and as a model of imaginative regeneration and of linguistic and formal attitudes. Driscoll concentrates upon *Yes, Mrs. Williams* as a key text but sees these issues of the maternal foreshadowed in *Kora in Hell* (see esp. pp. 96–108).

14   Discussions of Williams's relation to cubism appear in Schmidt; Henry Sayre, *The Visual Text of William Carlos Williams* (Urbana: Univ. of Illinois Press, 1983); Dickran Tashjian, *William Carlos Williams and the American Scene, 1920–1940* (Berkeley: Univ. of California Press, 1979), and Bram Dijkstra, *Cubism, Stieglitz, and the Early Poetry of William Carlos Williams: The Hieroglyphics of a New Speech* (Princeton: Princeton Univ. Press, 1969).

15   *A Recognizable Image: William Carlos Williams on Art and Artists*, ed. Bram Dijkstra (New York: New Directions, 1978). The reader will find Gertrude Stein to be a notable presence throughout this study of poet's prose. Stein is an important modernist innovator, a prolific investigator of language and discourse, and a direct inspiration to all of the writers considered in depth in this volume. To devote a separate chapter to her writing, however, would take us beyond the scope of this book. Stein's texts constitute something like the mirror image of poet's prose: She is primarily a prose writer who expands the possibilities for meaning in her sentences by adopting poetic devices like meter, rhyme, puns, and foregrounding; she is the inverse of the poets who use the prose sentence as a way to extend possibilities of meaning in their poetry. Only from the vantage point achieved by the nongeneric writers in the final chapter of this volume does that distinction cease to hold.

16   Ezra Pound made use of similar propellants to keep the paratactic syntax of *The Cantos* in motion. Canto I, for instance, begins with "and then" and ends with "so that." Despite his championing of the linguistic theories of Ernest Fenollosa, who saw the sentence as the basic unit of language, reflecting "natural process" (*The Chinese Written Character as a Medium for Poetry* [1920; rpt. San Francisco: City Lights, n.d.], p. 12), Pound cared little for the sentence as a unit in poetry. He used propellant conjunctions in *The Cantos* to keep the reader from stagnating among the juxtaposed images of his poetry.

For a study of how Williams's syntactic structures counteract normal syntactic logic, see Patrick Moore, "William Carlos Williams and the Modernist Attack on Logical Syntax," *ELH*, 53, no. 4 (1986):895–916.

17   *I Wanted to Write a Poem*, p. 29. See also Dijkstra, *Hieroglyphics*, pp. 67–76.

18   The quotation that heads this section is from *Imaginations*, 17.

19   Ron Silliman's defense of the prose produced by the Language poets, "The New Sentence," in *The New Sentence* (New York: Roof Books, 1987), pp. 63–93, provides the starting point and some of the rationale for this definition of the sentence. See also the subsequent essay in that volume, "Towards Prose," pp. 94–108, for further reflections on prose poetry.

20   Walt Whitman, "Slang in America," in *Prose Works 1892*, vol. 2 (*Collect and*

Other Prose), ed. Floyd Stovall (New York: New York Univ. Press, 1964), p. 572.

21 See, for example, the anonymous review of *Nature*, "Nature – A Prose Poem" (1838), in *Emerson's "Nature": Origin, Growth, Meaning*, 2d ed., ed. Morton M. Sealts, Jr., and Alfred R. Ferguson (Carbondale: Southern Illinois Univ. Press, 1979), pp. 90–7.

22 *The Journals and Miscellaneous Notebooks of Ralph Waldo Emerson*, vol. 7, *1838–1842*, ed. A. W. Plumstead and Harrison Hayford (Cambridge, Mass.: Harvard Univ. Press, 1969), p. 265. A slightly earlier journal entry may round out further the meaning of the term "panharmonicon":

> Why should we write dramas, & epics, & sonnets, & novels in two volumes? Why not write as variously as we dress & think? A lecture is a new literature, which leaves aside all tradition, time, place, circumstance, & addresses an assembly as mere human beings, – no more – It has never yet been done well. It is an organ of sublime power, a panharmonicon for variety of note. But only then is the orator successful when he is himself agitated & is as much a hearer as any of the assembly. In that office you may & shall (please God!) yet see the electricity part from the cloud & shine from one part of heaven to the other. (pp. 224–5)

(Notice how the requirement of listening, as a component of authentic saying, parallels Heidegger's formulation of the essence of poetry quoted in my introduction.)

23 F. O. Matthiessen, *American Renaissance: Art and Expression in the Age of Emerson and Whitman* (London: Oxford Univ. Press, 1941), pp. 64–5.

24 Walt Whitman, *An American Primer* (1904; rpt. San Francisco: City Lights, 1970), p. 6.

25 See George Steiner's critique of American culture, "The Archives of Eden," *Salmagundi*, 50–1(Fall 1980–Winter 1981):57–89.

26 *American Poets: From the Puritans to the Present* (Boston: Houghton Mifflin, 1968), p. xvii.

27 The quotation that heads this section is from "Notes from a Talk on Poetry," *Poetry*, 14, no. 4 (July 1919):213. For a meditation upon Williams's relation to Emerson, see Carl Rapp, "Emerson as Precursor," *William Carlos Williams and Romantic Idealism* (Hanover, N.H.: Univ. Press of New England, 1984), pp. 53–77. For a book-length reading of Williams and Whitman from the perspectives of one another, see Stephen Tapscott, *American Beauty: William Carlos Williams and the Modernist Whitman* (New York: Columbia Univ. Press, 1984).

28 Marianne Moore, "*Kora in Hell*, by William Carlos Williams" (1921), in *William Carlos Williams: A Collection of Critical Essays*, ed. J. Hillis Miller (Englewood Cliffs, N.J.: Prentice-Hall, 1966), p. 37. The sentence from Williams's prologue has been slightly emended by the reviewer.

29 *Egoist*, 3, no. 10 (October 1916):148–9, rpt. in *The Collected Poems of William Carlos Williams*, vol. 1, ed. A. Walton Litz and Christopher MacGowan (New York: New Directions, 1986), pp. 137–41.

30 Cataloged as A 195, "March." See the notes to "March" in *Collected Poems*, vol 1, pp. 493–5.

31 The strength of her late work, beginning with *Trilogy* (1944–6), derives in part from her growing ability to integrate into the dialectical movement of her poetry the mocking voice that previously was able to paralyze her with statements like "poets are useless" (*Trilogy* [New York: New Directions, 1973], p. 14).

Nietzsche sees to the heart of the issue at hand – and much beyond – in a note entitled "Prose and Poetry":

> It is noteworthy that the great masters of prose have almost always been poets, too – if not publicly than at least secretly, in the "closet." Good prose is written only face to face with poetry. For it is an uninterrupted, well-mannered war with poetry: all of its attractions depend on the way in which poetry is continually avoided and contradicted. Everything abstract wants to be read as a prank against poetry and as with a mocking voice; everything dry and cool is meant to drive the lovely goddess into lovely despair. Often there are *rapprochements*, reconciliations for a moment – and then a sudden leap back and laughter. Often the curtain is raised and harsh light let in just as the goddess is enjoying her dusks and muted colors. . . . Thus there are thousands of delights in this war, including the defeats of which the unpoetic souls, the so-called prose-men, do not know a thing; hence they write and speak only *bad* prose. *War is the father of all good things;* war is also the father of good prose.
>
> Four very strange and truly poetic human beings in this century have attained mastery in prose, for which this century was not made otherwise – for lack of poetry, as I have suggested. . . . I regard only Giacomo Leopardi, Prosper Mérimée, Ralph Waldo Emerson, and Walter Savage Landor, the author of *Imaginary Conversations*, as worthy of being called masters of prose. (*GS*, 145–6)

32 *Selected Letters*, no. 32, pp. 46–7.

33 Robert von Hallberg has explored this issue with reference to Olson in *Charles Olson: The Scholar's Art* (Cambridge, Mass.: Harvard Univ. Press, 1978), pp. 96–9. Robert Pinsky argues for "prose virtues" in poetry in his chapter "The Discursive Aspect of Poetry," in *The Situation of Poetry: Contemporary Poetry and its Traditions* (Princeton: Princeton Univ. Press, 1976).

34 This discussion of the difference between prose and verse poetry ignores, for the time being, the case of free verse. The reasons for doing so will become clear as I proceed to consider two poems by Williams in free verse. The rhythm of one of these poems ("The Late Singer") is governed substantially by meter, while the rhythm of the other ("The Great Figure") is governed by syntax. Thus free verse does not designate a unilateral phenomenon that can be placed exclusively in either of the two categories I am developing.

35 *Collected Poems*, vol. 1, p. 137.

36 This poem (*Collected Poems*, vol. 1, p. 174) has been discussed in several

places, usually in conjunction with the Charles Demuth painting it inspired. See, for example, Tashjian, *Williams and the American Scene*, pp. 71–2.

37 J. Hillis Miller, in his introduction to the collection already cited, speaks of Williams's isolation of individual words in these terms: "Words are nodes of linguistic power. This power is their potentiality for combining with other words to form grammatical structures" (p. 12).

38 Reprinted in Benedikt's *Prose Poem*, pp. 480–1.

39 Translation by Benedikt of "Windows" in *Prose Poem*, p. 64.

2. *ROBERT CREELEY'S* PRESENCES: A TEXT FOR MARISOL

1   The review is reprinted in QG, pp. 20–2. Mary Novik, in *Robert Creeley: An Inventory, 1945–1970* (Kent, Ohio: Kent State Univ. Press, 1973), p. 124, establishes the date of composition as April 1, 1952.

2   "Walking," in *Excursions* (Boston: Houghton Mifflin, 1899), pp. 251–304.

3   See Frye's *Anatomy of Criticism: Four Essays* (Princeton: Princeton Univ. Press, 1957), pp. 308–14.

4   Creeley has long been a devoted reader of Stein. See, for example, his essay on *The Mother of Us All*, entitled "Here" (*WTRP*, 91–5), or his statement in $L=A=N=G=U=A=G=E$, 2, no. 1 (March 1979): n.p., replying to a request for a list of "five non-poetry books . . . read in the last few years that had significant influence on your writing or thinking": "Then – almost as personal memorial, now that he's sadly dead – Donald Sutherland, *Gertrude Stein: A Biography of Her Works*. Still for me the most provocative book on her particular genius, with equal range as to forms and specific cultural patterns in writing, e.g., Spanish/American take on Surrealism." (Sutherland's discussion of the affinities between Spanish and American senses of Surrealism, which he links through the physicality of the landscape in both countries [cf. Charles Olson's preoccupation with Space], occurs in his chapter on *Tender Buttons*, "Insides and Outsides." "Inside Out" is the title of a lecture of Creeley's that bears importantly on *Presences*.)

Gertrude Stein is present by proxy in the epigraph to *Presences*, taken from Donald Sutherland: "Classicism is based on presence. It does not consider that it has come or that it will go away; it merely proposes to be there where it is." Sutherland sees Stein as alternating between classicism and romanticism; Creeley does the same in *Presences*: Presence is classical, process is romantic.

In *On, Romanticism* (New York: New York Univ. Press, 1971), Sutherland attempts to build a whole literary typology based upon notions of classicism, romanticism, and, as a combination, the baroque, which he sees as three eternal types. Sutherland's greatest attraction for Creeley (in addition to his excellent analysis of Stein) is probably his essentialist, numerical (1,2,3) bent. Creeley loves to work within the simple and arbitrary limits of such a system (see his ordering of *Presences*, for instance, discussed later in this chapter), where absolute boundaries allow him a paradoxical (existential) freedom for movement within them. Gertrude Stein, whose *Making of Americans* is an attempt to delineate all possible character types, is also a noted essentialist.

5 This quotation from Creeley, the next quotation from Marisol, and the subsequent quotation from Creeley are all taken from a letter written by Creeley on October 23, 1976, to Marjorie Kinsey of the University of Notre Dame. I am grateful to Professor Kinsey for her permission to quote from this letter. *Presences* has been reprinted in *The Collected Prose of Robert Creeley* (Berkeley: Univ. of California Press, 1987) but still without Marisol's contribution.

6 *Marisol*, text by José Ramon Medina, photographs by Jack Mitchell (Caracas: Ediciones Armitano, 1968), pp. 102–6. William Sylvester meditates on the correspondences between *Presences* and Marisol's sculpture in "Is That a Real Statue or Did Marisol Just Make It Up?: Affinities with Creeley's *Presences*," in Carroll F. Terrell, ed., *Robert Creeley: The Poet's Workshop* (Orono, Maine: National Poetry Foundation, 1984), pp. 275–87. For a full bibliography of works on Robert Creeley, see Willard Fox, *Robert Creeley, Edward Dorn, and Robert Duncan: A Reference Guide* (Boston: G. K. Hall, 1989), pp. 9–170. A useful selection of criticism covering the whole range of Creeley's career to date appears in John Wilson, ed., *Robert Creeley's Life and Work: A Sense of Increment* (Ann Arbor: Univ. of Michigan Press, 1987).

7 Creeley's source is Joseph Campbell, *The Hero with a Thousand Faces* (New York: Pantheon, 1949), pp. 84–5.

8 Altieri wrote a ground-breaking, and probably the most referred to, essay on Creeley, "The Unsure Egoist: Robert Creeley and the Theme of Nothingness," *Contemporary Literature*, 13, no. 2 (Spring 1972):162–85. The essay is reprinted, substantially intact, in Altieri's *Enlarging the Temple: New Directions in American Poetry during the 1960s* (Lewisburg: Pa.: Bucknell Univ. Press, 1979), pp. 172–93. Altieri has expanded his tremendously useful essay on conjecture to form a chapter, "Robert Creeley's Poetics of Conjecture: The Pains and Pleasures of Staging a Self at War with Its Own Lyric Desires," in his *Self and Sensibility in Contemporary American Poetry* (Cambridge: Cambridge Univ. Press, 1984), pp. 103–31. On pp. 129–30, he contrasts Creeley's conjectural abilities with Ashbery's, arguing that Ashbery is richer in his constructions of identity within social worlds. The quotation from Creeley appears in *APR*, 5.

9 Novick, *Creeley*, p. 124.

10 *Charles Olson and Robert Creeley: The Complete Correspondence*, 8 vols., ed. George F. Butterick (Santa Barbara: Black Sparrow Press, 1980–7). See also Olson's letters to Cid Corman, *Letters for Origin: 1950–1956*, ed. Albert Glover (New York: Grossman, 1970), and the selections from his letters to Creeley in *Mayan Letters* (1953), reprinted in *The Selected Writings of Charles Olson*, ed. Robert Creeley (New York: New Directions, 1966), pp. 68–130.

11 Novick, *Creeley*, p. 80. In the essay "Projective Verse," in *Human Universe*, pp. 51–61, Charles Olson makes the following major points about projective verse or "composition by field": (1) "The poem itself must, at all points, be a high energy-construct and, at all points, an energy-discharge"; (2) "From the moment [the poet] ventures into FIELD COMPOSITION – puts himself in the open – he can go by no track other than the one the poem under hand declares"; (3) "FORM IS NEVER MORE THAN AN EXTENSION OF CONTENT" –

attributed to Robert Creeley; and (4) "ONE PERCEPTION MUST IMMEDIATELY
AND DIRECTLY LEAD TO A FURTHER PERCEPTION" – attributed to Edward Dahl-
berg. Olson also suggests that the typewriter may be used to "score" breathing and other rhythmic qualities of verse more exactly than traditional
meters.

12 "Introduction to Robert Creeley," originally printed in *New Directions*,
    13(1951), and reprinted in Olson's *Human Universe and Other Essays* (1965;
    rpt. New York: Grove Press, 1967), pp. 127–8. Novik (*Creeley*, p. 136)
    states that this introduction and Creeley's "Notes for a New Prose" (*QG*,
    11–17) were both products of the Creeley–Olson correspondence of 1950,
    which is also responsible for the second part of Olson's "Projective Verse"
    (*Human Universe*, pp. 59–61).

13 *Human Universe*, p. 128.

14 The several senses Creeley unites in the term form a kind of microcosm of
    his particular mélange of qualities associated with both modernism and
    postmodernism. Creeley frustrates critics who wish to locate him exclusively
    within either the modernist terrain of centered self-consciousness or the
    postmodern terrain of decentered indeterminacy. Marjorie Perloff, for in-
    stance, at the end of her fine article on Creeley's novel *The Island*, entitled
    "Four Times Five: Robert Creeley's *The Island*" (*b2*, 491–507), rightly dif-
    ferentiates this novel from the postmodern fiction of "Beckett or Coover
    or Butor or Barthelme" on the grounds of its eschewal of indeterminacy (a
    point that cannot be made about *Presences*). She argues that "Creeley's pro-
    jectivism is a transitional stance, half way between what we usually call
    'high modernism' and post-modernism" (*b2*, 504).

15 *For Love*, p. 97, rpt. in *The Collected Poems of Robert Creeley: 1945–1975*
    (Berkeley: Univ. of California Press, 1982), p. 195.

16 *The Gold Diggers and Other Stories* (New York: Scribners, 1965), pp. 31–2.

17 "Projective Verse," in *Human Universe*, p. 55.

18 In an early review (1962) of *For Love*, Cid Corman quotes the following
    statement from Yeats to explain the intensity of Creeley's line:

> We make out of the quarrel with others, rhetoric, but of the quarrel with
> ourselves, poetry. . . . We sing amid our uncertainty; and, smitten even in
> the presence of the most high beauty by the knowledge of our solitude,
> our rhythm shudders.

At Their Word (Santa Barbara, Calif.: Black Sparrow Press, 1978), p. 78.
Robert Duncan, in *Robert Duncan: An Interview by George Bowering and Robert
Hogg, April 19, 1969* (Toronto: Coach House Press, 1971), n.p., offers a
more psychological interpretation of the quality of Creeley's line:

> Yes, but the figure of Creeley stumbling after the muse, it's a fool stum-
> bling after the White Goddess; the White Goddess is not the figure of a
> man with no wife at all. It's the wife that undoes you and that leaves you
> stumbling and actually crippled, isn't it, finally? There is a subdued cas-
> tration in which your heel is injured, so you're a stumbler, and Creeley's

practised stumbling is an embodiment of a castration and impotency which is the experience we have in his poems.

19   Actually, as Creeley informed me in a conversation on February 28, 1982, the statement occurs in Blake's *French Revolution* (l. 189). Creeley heard the phrase from Slater Brown, took it to mean something like "energy delights in its form," and only much later searched out its provenance in a concordance. Because of the pre-Socratic tenor of Creeley's thought and the importance of fire as a primary element that mutates into the other elements in Heraclitus ("All things are an equal exchange for fire and fire for all things, as goods are for gold and gold for goods" – G. S. Kirk and J. E. Raven, *The Presocratic Philosophers* [Cambridge: Cambridge Univ. Press, 1971], p. 199), it would seem that Creeley conflates the Heraclitean sense with Blake's declaration that "energy is eternal delight."

20   The first publication of the written text of *Presences* (minus pictures of Marisol's sculpture) in *Io*, 14(Summer 1972):183–226, includes the date of composition for most of the units, written in their present order from December 1, 1971, to April 12, 1972 (the postscript was written April 11). These dates and Creeley's statements in *APR*, 5–6, indicate that each unit was completed in a single day.

21   This character also appears in one unit of *Presences* (III.2, *Mabel*, 88–91). In "Hearing 'Here': Robert Creeley's Poetics of Duration," in *Robert Creeley: The Poet's Workshop*, pp. 87–95, Charles Bernstein discusses *WTRP* and the texts in *Mabel* as precursors of the new poet's prose practiced by the Language poets.

22   The epigraph to this section is from *GS*, 116.

23   Recounted in *Ecce Homo*, trans. Walter Kaufmann (New York: Random House, 1969), p. 295.

24   Cynthia Dubin Edelberg, *Robert Creeley's Poetry: A Critical Introduction* (Albuquerque: Univ. of New Mexico Press, 1978), p. 16.

25   Cornelia P. Draves and Mary Jane Fortunato, "Craft Interview with Robert Creeley," *COP*, 213.

26   Ibid.

27   Linda W. Wagner provides some useful notes on the relationship of Wittgenstein to Creeley's recent writing in "Creeley's Late Poems: Contexts" (*b2*, 301–8).

28   *Tractatus Logico-Philosophicus*, trans. D. F. Pears and B. F. McGuinness (London: Routledge & Kegan Paul, 1974), p. 74.

29   David Antin makes the half-playful suggestion that "the only modernist prose writer is Wittgenstein," in "Some Questions about Modernism," *Occident*, n.s. 8(Spring 1974):6–38.

30   *Philosophical Grammar*, ed. Rush Rhees, trans. Anthony Kenny (Berkeley: Univ. of California Press, 1974), pp. 59–60.

31   Ibid., p. 63.

32   Ibid., p. 87.

33   *Poetry, Language, Thought*, trans. Albert Hofstadter (New York: Harper & Row, 1971), pp. 215–16.

34 *Children of the Mire: Modern Poetry from Romanticism to the Avant-Garde*, trans. Rachel Phillips (Cambridge, Mass.: Harvard Univ. Press, 1974), p. 160.

35 *Human Universe*, p. 128.

36 This argument is addressed, in part, to a nagging question in the criticism of recent poetry: If contemporary theory valorizes writing and absence and contemporary American poetry valorizes speech and presence, then how do we reconcile intuited analogies between the two endeavors? For complementary treatments of this issue, see Michael Davidson, "Exiled in the Word: Orality, Writing and Deconstruction," *New Wilderness Letter*, 2, no. 8 (Spring 1980):43–7, and Donald Wesling, "Difficulties of the Bardic: Literature and the Human Voice," *Critical Inquiry*, 8, no. 1 (Autumn 1981):69–81. See also n. 21 of the Introduction to this volume.

37 The epigraphs are from *WTRP*, 49 (Creeley) and *Human Universe*, p. 127 (Olson).

38 *WTRP*, 51. Olson develops this Herodotean sense of history in *The Special View of History*, ed. Ann Charters (Berkeley: Oyez, 1970). See p. 20 for the definition of 'istorin. In the essay "A Foot Is to Kick with" (*QG*, 193–4), Creeley praises Olson's discussion of the grammatical middle voice, that is, the self-reflexive.

39 Marisol, quoted by Leon Shulman in the catalog *Marisol* (Worcester, Mass: Worcester Art Museum, 1971), n.p.

40 See Nathaniel Mackey's handling of the solipsism issue (*"The Gold Diggers,"* *b2*, 486, 487 n. 12).

41 *Lorca / Blackburn: Federico García Lorca, Chosen and Translated by Paul Blackburn* (San Francisco: Momo's Press, 1979), n.p. Creeley misspells *inmenso* and deletes accents in his quotations from the poem.

42 *For Love*, p. 38.

43 Altieri, in "The Unsure Egoist," gives an illuminating discussion of how Creeley "attempts to wrench the formulas of 'idle talk' into authentic speech" (p. 170). I would differ with Altieri, however, in his characterization of authentic speech as more "essential" than "the merely phenomenal images provided by language." Phenomenal appearances in language – presences – are precisely what Creeley's authentic speech seeks to support.

44 "The Presence of the Present: Morality and the Problem of Value in Robert Creeley's Recent Prose," *b2*, 556.

45 *Literary Essays of Ezra Pound*, ed. T. S. Eliot (New York: New Directions, 1968), p. 9. Note how Pound continues Whitman's championing of a poetry based upon speech, which "breaks out of the little laws to enter truly the higher ones."

46 "On Measure – Statement for Cid Corman," *Selected Essays of William Carlos Williams* (1954; rpt. New York: New Directions, 1969), p. 340. Stephen Cushman, in *William Carlos Williams and the Meanings of Measure* (New Haven: Yale Univ. Press, 1985), studies the concept of measure throughout Williams's poetry and criticism, clarifying his employment of it both as a formal scheme and as a central trope. In "A Visit with Dr. Williams," *Sagetrieb*, 3, no. 2 (Fall 1984), 27–36, Creeley testifies to the influence of Williams upon his early development as a poet.

47 Mike Weaver, *William Carlos Williams: The American Background* (Cambridge: Cambridge Univ. Press, 1971), pp. 48, 53–4.

48 Robert von Hallberg, *Charles Olson: The Scholar's Art* (Cambridge, Mass.: Harvard Univ. Press, 1978), offers an illuminating discussion of philosophical and literary Objectivism as they relate to Charles Olson, in the chapter "A Common World: Olson, Whitehead, and the Objectivists" (pp. 82–125).

49 "Sincerity and Objectification," *Poetry*, 37, no. 5 (February 1931):273–4.

50 The epigraph is from "A Sense of Measure," in *WTRP*, 15.

51 *Additional Prose: A Bibliography on America, Proprioception & Other Notes & Essays*, ed. George F. Butterick (Bolinas, Calif.: Four Seasons Foundation, 1974), pp. 17–19.

52 Merleau-Ponty took as one of his major philosophical tasks the restoration of the body to its rightful position of primacy in epistemology. See, for example, "A Prospectus of His Work," in *The Primacy of Perception and Other Essays*, ed. James M. Edie (Evanston: Northwestern Univ. Press, 1964), in which he gives an outline of work completed, in progress, and projected. In this essay one finds the following description of the measuring activities of the body:

> We grasp external space through our bodily situation. A "corporeal or postural schema" gives us at every moment a global, practical, and implicit notion of the relation between our body and things, of our hold on them. A system of possible movements, or "motor projects," radiates from us to our environment. Our body is not in space like things; it inhabits or haunts space. . . . For us the body is much more than an instrument or a means; it is our expression in the world, the visible form of our intentions. Even our most secret affective movements, those most deeply tied to the humoral infrastructure, help to shape our perception of things. (p. 5)

53 Creeley related in conversation (February 28, 1982) a further literal aspect of this unit. When he accompanied William Katz on a visit to Marisol, she actually tossed a doll into a chair; Creeley was intrigued and somewhat horrified to learn from Katz that the doll's face contained a photo-transfer (thus the "blurred eyes") of Marisol's former lover. Creeley was also "dazzled" to find a large block of ice in the freezer containing a copy of the *Paris Review*: "The glass was very large. The ice cubes were huge blocks of solidified water" (*Mabel*, 64).

54 *Roland Barthes*, trans. Richard Howard (New York: Hill & Wang, 1977), pp. 48–9.

55 See von Hallberg, *Charles Olson*, pp. 98–9, for a discussion of Olson's Whiteheadean use of abstraction and generalization. Creeley, on the other hand, is not given to programmatic pronouncements such as Olson's "translation" of Heraclitus (in "The Kingfishers"), "What does not change / is the will to change." Olson's commitment is to process in the act of composition; Creeley's extends beyond process to include the recognition and evocation of presence, though always through the mediation of language.

56 Sherman Paul, in "A Letter on Rosenthal's 'Problems of Robert Creeley,' " *boundary 2*, 3 (Spring 1975):750–1, speaks incisively of Creeley's nakedness:

Though Creeley's poems are often spare and small and his insistences always personal, there is, in view of his standing in the "primary situations" of his experience, nothing that merits the usual limiting characterizations of his work: minimal, domestic. He understood early what Olson told Cid Corman, that the poet starts with nothing, with only his personal details, with what he actually knows, and he was ready to accept "nakedness," the shedding of preconceptions by which one finds himself, in Emerson's words, in an original relation to the universe. Nakedness has antecedents in American literature just as projectivist verse has: it simply states the condition of the intrinsic form proposed by Emerson and the free verse practiced by Whitman – and reminds us of the body, and the physical aspect of this poetry. Creeley takes the term from Olson, who, in *Maximus*, provides, among others, the following instance:

> He left him naked,
> the man said, and
> nakedness
> is what one means
>
> that all start up
> to the eye and soul
> as though it had never
> happened before

And Creeley says, in explanation, that " 'Nakedness' is to stand manifestly in one's own condition, in that necessary *freshness*, however exposed, because all things are particular and reality itself is the specific content of an instant's possibility."

57 "The Structure of Rime," Pts. 1–2, in *The Opening of the Field* (New York: Grove Press, 1960), pp. 12–13.
58 "Notes on the Structure of Rime," *Maps*, 6(1974):44–45.
59 "The Museum," *Ground Work: Before the War* (New York: New Directions, 1984), pp. 59–61.

3. JOHN ASHBERY'S THREE POEMS

1 "The Impossible," *Poetry*, 90(July 1957):250–4. The quotation that heads this section is from this review, p. 251.
2 Quoted by David Shapiro in his *John Ashbery: An Introduction to the Poetry* (New York: Columbia Univ. Press, 1979), p. 29. Shapiro has conducted many private interviews with Ashbery that he has not committed to print. The footnotes to the interviews give only dates, and the reader has no direct access to the material by which to ascertain the context of quoted statements. Though the first full-length study of Ashbery, Shapiro's analysis is rather unhelpful in that it constitutes a passionate defense of the poet by a disciple and consists mainly of attributions of affinity between Ashbery and other writers, painters, and composers. One statement by Shapiro does concur

with the direction I have chosen: "Ashbery is a poet concerned with the ecstasy of not understanding" (p. 66).

3   To the reader anxious for some heuristic device, however provisional, to carry into an encounter with the text, I offer a set of descriptive titles as a summary of the book. Each description accounts for one or more sections of the text (with page numbers in parentheses), and no description ends in midsection. These titles are arbitrary, not exhaustive, minimally interpretive; I hope they afford a useful means of location in the text.

"The New Spirit"
1. Putting it all down versus leaving all out (3).
2. The question of truth (3).
3. Other major themes announced: dreaming, confusion, midlife crisis, happiness, time (4–6).
4. The nature of *Three Poems* is a question, which turns out (51) to be the question of "your being here" (6–7).
5. The issue of identity (7–8).
6. Selectivity – narrowing down, climbing a mountain that then opens into a valley of arbitrariness (8–9).
7. Is communication merely a dream? Is this good or bad? The issue of not understanding (9–13).
8. The attempt to "put everything in" results in confusion between subject and object (13–16).
9. We got the magic we asked for, and it turned into realism (16–17).
10. The change has obliterated distinctions between true and false ways, but we could only have taken the way we took (17–19).
11. The "you" (the lover or psyche) is taken apart, and then "a new you takes shape" (19–23).
12. Becoming accustomed to living in change ("you are the change") (23–5).
13. As "progressive thinkers and builders of the art of love" we imprison ourselves in "growth without change" (25–8).
14. The new spirit arrives and breaks down the walls, instituting change (28–9).
15. First entrance of the Archer (Sagittarius), who seems to represent direct intuition of the true way (see 42, 51) and the correct relation between thought and action (29–31).
16. Looking into the past "in the interests of getting at the truth" (32–4).
17. Taking the first few steps forward on a constructive path (34–6).
18. A syzygy, imaged as a "fixed flame" (36–7).
19. Indifference follows the syzygy (38–9).
20. "The way that leads to understanding" blocks completion of the process of change (39–41).
21. How one views time and the course of life "when one is in one's late thirties" (41–3).
22. A surprising spectacle: a "Thirty Years' War of the human will." "The

one of whom this is written" takes this "universal emotional crisis on his own shoulders" and sinks beneath its weight (43–7).

23. The mass of others becomes "a mountain of statistics" that resolves into a totality ruled by "the enthusiasm of the whole." This mass of humanity "lay stupified in dreams of toil and drudgery" as it struggled to build the Tower of Babel. Meanwhile the constellations rain down their influence from afar, prompting you to continue asking the "major question" with which "The New Spirit" began: "your being here." You have still "to begin in the way of choosing" that was proposed initially as the choice between putting it all in (the Tower of Babel) or leaving it all out (the constellations – elided points joined by the imagination) (47–51).

"The System"

1. The system, which relates the imagination to reality for both the poet and society, was breaking down, and one stood viewing life from the outside (53–4).

2. There was a time when truth was "all life," and it included "a kind of fiction that developed parallel to the classic truths of daily life" (55–6).

3. Humorous description of that time (the late sixties) as one in which love was uncharacteristically dominant. "Younger spectators" thought this dominance of love signaled "the logical last step of history," an end to change. But this condition became a "mockery" and necessitated "an end to the 'end' theory" (56–64).

4. A meditation on the cyclical motion of time (65–7).

5. Discussion of the methodology of understanding. "Three methods: reason, sense, or a knowing combination of both." The first is chosen (67–9).

6. "Twin notions of growth": "the 'career' notion" and "the life-as-ritual concept" (69–71).

7. "Two kinds of happiness . . . : the frontal and the latent." Two ways to experience the "grace" of the "new spirit." The latent way is chosen, proves perilous, and we come to realize finally that "this second kind of happiness is merely a fleshed-out, realized version of that ideal first kind." A reconciliation of inside and outside results, inducing drowsiness. Dreaming begins and evokes the truth: "Whatever was, is, and must be." "When will you realize that your dreams have eternal life?" This experience of truth in dreams propels you swiftly forward (71–86).

8. Philosophy and the rational approach break down in the face of the convoluted "business of day-to-day living." We realize that the "summit" we've reached excludes the "mass" of life "below" (87–9).

9. Entering the hermeneutic circle (90–1).

10. As the confused seeker, you arrive at the point where everyone awaits what you will say. You repeat to yourself, "Whatever was, is, and

must be," though you see it in a new, more inclusive way. Everyone
is still waiting to hear you speak. "Suddenly you realize that . . . you
must have said *it* a long way back without knowing it." This "buried
word" has given us access to the meaning of the "outward things" of
the world (91–6).

11. You review the steps you've taken in considering the system. You
    pause before answering the question (96–9).

12. The reply (99).

13. Your past is redeemed (99–100).

14. Reconciliation of the one and the many (100–2).

15. Meditation on time as a movie (102–3).

16. Return to the question of putting in and leaving out (103–5).

17. Recognizing that this whole journey has taken place within the self.
    The past is abandoned; the future offers a "wide way," both "pragmatic
    and kinetic" (105–6).

"The Recital"

1. "There is no new problem." Every day begins in promise and ends in
   disillusion (107–8).

2. When we left childhood and became adults, we left an old unhappy
   world for a new, happy one (108–9).

3. As adults we tried to put everything in but found we had to be selective:
   It is impossible to name everything we do (109–10).

4. The problem of choice and selectivity is unavoidable and insoluble,
   but one must attempt understanding (110–11).

5. We try to avoid illusions and give a "faithful reproduction" of reality
   (111–13).

6. When our art approached life so closely, it disappeared "in the confla-
   gration of the moment our real and imaginary lives coincided." Though
   a disaster for us, this illuminated the world with a new spirit (113–14).

7. We are both inside and outside and can never return to a primordial
   unity. (115).

8. The indeterminate nature of the present and the continuing necessity
   for choosing a way of action (115–16).

9. Somehow, and ineffably, the new spirit has been integrated into life
   (116–18).

4   The quotation that heads this section is from Ashbery's "Second Presentation
    of Elizabeth Bishop," *World Literature Today*, 51, no. 1 (Winter 1977):10.
    The phrase "perfectly useless concentration" is Bishop's.

5   May 23, 1976, pp. 18–33.

6   The poem appears in *The Tennis Court Oath* (Middletown, Conn: Wesleyan
    Univ. Press, 1962), pp. 64–85. Bloom's comment is in his "John Ashbery:
    The Charity of the Hard Moments," in *American Poetry since 1960: Some
    Critical Perspectives*, ed. Robert B. Shaw (Cheshire: Carcanet Press, 1973),
    p. 85; Kostelanetz's comment is in "How to Be a Difficult Poet," p. 33.

7   The essay is most readily available in *ILL*, pp. 69–82. Building on Benja-
    min's ideas, the next step in the elaboration of a theory of translation was

taken by George Steiner in *After Babel: Aspects of Language and Translation* (New York: Oxford Univ. Press, 1975). Steiner recognizes a "hermeneutic motion" to translation, which occurs in four stages: trust, aggression, embodiment, and restitution. Steiner's description of this hermeneutic motion makes it clear that translation can be seen as a paradigm for all acts of communication or understanding. See Steiner for bibliographical information on translation theory. Since Steiner's book, John Felstiner has done meticulous and illuminating studies of the interface of translation and criticism in *Translating Neruda: The Way to Macchu Picchu* (Stanford: Stanford Univ. Press, 1980) and in similar studies of Paul Celan (published as separate articles but forthcoming as a book). On the border of translation and philosophy, Jacques Derrida has performed many meditations upon translation as a primary condition of language. Two examples, from the same moment in his career, are *The Post Card: From Socrates to Freud and Beyond*, trans. Alan Bass (Chicago: Univ. of Chicago Press, 1987) and "LIVING ON . BORDER LINES," in Harold Bloom et al., *Deconstruction and Criticism* (New York: Continuum, 1979), pp. 75–176.

8   Kostelanetz, "Difficult Poet," p. 30.

9   Janet Bloom and Robert Losada, "Craft Interview with John Ashbery," in *COP*, 117–18. Compare this statement to Ezra Pound's judgment of Williams's improvisations: "The thing that saves your work is *opacity*, and don't you forget it." *The Selected Letters of Ezra Pound*, ed. D. D. Paige (1950; rpt. New York: New Directions, 1971), p. 124.

10   *CON*, 87.

11   Kostelanetz, "Difficult Poet," p. 33.

12   *CON*, 95–6. Ashbery's attachment to music for compositional purposes goes beyond the metaphorical; music also forms a medium in which his composition can occur:

> The thing about music is that it's always going on and reaching a conclusion and it helps me to be surrounded by this moving climate that it produces – moving I mean in the sense of going on. . . . While writing one of the three prose poems which is in my book that's coming out [*Three Poems*] I got listening to Brahms' first sextet and it seemed to be the only piece of music that would work for this particular poem but it's hard to say anything very meaningful as to why. Poetry is mostly hunches. . . . I played Elliott Carter's Concerto for Orchestra a lot while I was writing "The New Spirit." Mostly however I would say my tastes run to nineteenth-century music for purposes of poetry. (*COP*, 114)

13   Bloomington: Indiana Univ. Press, 1968. Counterfeiting, or direct quotation, has replaced the exaggeration of parody, Kenner says, in the Xerox age:

> We are deep, these days, in the counterfeit, and have long since had to forego easy criteria for what is "real." (And a counterfeit banknote is real.) We have sunk so deep into dubiety that our finest satire is discoverable in technical publications, where writers simply describe how things

are exactly. (And the most harrowing book of our principal comic writer is entitled *How It Is*; almost his next deed was Buster Keaton's last film script.) (p. 20)

14 Bloom dates the poems as follows: "Though 'The New Spirit,' first of the *Three Poems*, was begun in November 1969, most of it was written in January to April, 1970. In a kind of cyclic repetition, the second prose poem 'The System' was composed from January to March 1971, with the much shorter 'The Recital' added as a coda in April" *(American Poetry since 1960*, p. 103).

Keith Cohen, in "Ashbery's Dismantling of Bourgeois Discourse," in *Beyond Amazement: New Essays on John Ashbery*, ed. David Lehman (Ithaca, N.Y.: Cornell Univ. Press, 1980), sees *Three Poems* as "a frontal attack on the fundamental props of bourgeois discourse – continuity, utility, and closure – at the same time rejecting out of hand any notion of the homogeneous, integrated subject" (148). This makes Ashbery sound like a predecessor of the Language poets – which is certainly true for many of them, although some (as I mention in the Preface to the Second Edition, this volume) doubt his sincerity. David Lehman, "The Shield of a Greeting: The Function of Irony in John Ashbery's Poetry," in *Beyond Amazement*, links *Three Poems* with *The Tennis Court Oath*, which the Language poets have, like Kostelanetz, often designated as their favorite Ashbery book: "[*Three Poems*] appears to be an equal and opposite response to the fragmented 'pulverized' utterances of *The Tennis Court Oath*, a volume as revolutionary as its title suggests" (p. 110). Among the many Language poets who comment upon *The Tennis Court Oath*, Bruce Andrews, in a ten-page meditation on Ashbery's text, "Misrepresentation (A Text for *The Tennis Court Oath* of John Ashbery)," in *In the American Tree*, ed. Ron Silliman (Orono, Maine: National Poetry Foundation, 1986), makes a very similar point to Lehman's:

> "of course the lathe around
> he stars with privilege jerks"

It concerns the undercutting of the image, the visual picture – by juxtaposing the conceivable referents in unexpected ways and also by fragmenting the syntax, that gridiron of outwardness. "The reason ejected" by these 2 sentences – via the constitution of the image and via syntax, both of which are variously shattered. In fact, we could say that only here and in *Three Poems* does the disjunct formal structure fully *double*, or reiterate, the implicit lessons embodied in the discourse: about the fragility of relationships, doubts, breakage, tenuousness more generally, foreclosed dreams & the mortgages of dreamwork, lonesomeness. Not just an ornamentally rhetorical way of talking *about* these issues; here we find them displayed and played out and encoded in the very construction. This is *codic doubling* with a lovely vengeance. (p. 523)

15 *The Doors of Perception* (London: Chatto & Windus, 1954). In "Deconstructing Apocalyptic Rhetoric: Ashbery, Derrida, Blanchot," *Criticism*, 27, no.
4 (Fall 1985):387–400, Herman Rapaport compares *Three Poems* to writing
by Derrida (particularly *Glas*), Blanchot, and Levinas, in order to show how
the pervasive sense of the apocalyptic is domesticated in Ashbery's poetry.
Richard Jackson, *The Dismantling of Time in Contemporary Poetry* (Tuscaloosa:
Univ. of Alabama Press, 1988), pp. 156–63, also gives a sensitive Derridean
reading of *Three Poems*. David Shapiro, in his *John Ashbery*, was the first to
suggest significant parallels between Ashbery and Derrida.

16 "On Raymond Roussel," in *How I Wrote Certain of My Books*, by Raymond
Roussel (New York: Sun, 1977), pp. 53–4. This text also contains a translation of the third canto of Roussel's poem by Kenneth Koch.

17 "Ezra Pound: An Interview," *Paris Review*, 7, no. 4 (1962):26.

18 Kostelanetz, "Difficult Poet," p. 33. S. H. Miller, "Psychic Geometry: John
Ashbery's Prose Poems," *American Poetry*, 3, no. 1 (Fall 1985):24–42, sees
Three Poems as an "analytical prose poem" that represents a whole range of
mental processes, without attempting to reach any definitive statements
about the objects of those processes.

19 *COP*, 112. This attitude toward the relation between reader and writer
coincides with Roland Barthes's definition of *le scriptible* ("the writable,"
translated in the following quotation as "the writerly") as an evaluative
category:

> Our evaluation can be linked only to a practice, and this practice is that
> of writing. . . . Which texts would I consent to write (to re-write), to
> desire, to put forth as a force in this world of mine? What evaluation finds
> is precisely this value: what can be written (rewritten) today: the *writerly*.
> Why is the writerly our value? Because the goal of literary work (of
> literature as work) is to make the reader no longer a consumer, but a
> producer of the text. Our literature is characterized by the pitiless divorce
> which the literary institution maintains between the producer of the text
> and its user. . . . This reader is thereby plunged into a kind of idleness –
> he is intransitive; he is, in short, *serious*: instead of functioning himself,
> instead of gaining access to the magic of the signifier, to the pleasure of
> writing, he is left with no more than the poor freedom either to accept
> or reject the text: reading is nothing more than a *referendum*. Opposite the
> writerly text, then, is its countervalue, its negative, reactive value: what
> can be read, but not written: the *readerly* [*le lisible*]. We call any readerly
> text a classic text. (*S/Z*, trans. Richard Miller [New York: Hill & Wang,
> 1974], p. 4)

20 Modern Language Association convention, San Francisco, December 29,
1979.

21 Bonnie Costello, in "John Ashbery and the Idea of the Reader," *Contemporary
Literature*, 23, no. 4 (1982):493–514, discusses the sense of community created
in Ashbery's poetry, in which the reader and writer are joined through the
desire for meaning. Costello shows how Ashbery inscribes the reader directly
into his texts, much as Whitman does in "Crossing Brooklyn Ferry." For

further discussion of Ashbery's public quality, see Donald Crase, "The Prophetic Ashbery," in *Beyond Amazement*, pp. 30–65.

22 The quotation is from Wallace Stevens, "Notes toward a Supreme Fiction," *The Collected Poems of Wallace Stevens* (New York: Knopf, 1954), p. 403.

23 See Bloom's section "*Apophrades:* or the Return of the Dead" in *The Anxiety of Influence: A Theory of Poetry* (New York: Oxford Univ. Press, 1973), pp. 139–55.

24 Shapiro indicates that Ashbery wrote the blurb on the back cover of *Three Poems* in which these statements appear (*John Ashbery*, p. 157). David Kermani, in *John Ashbery: An Annotated Bibliography* (New York: Garland, 1976), p. 14, states that "jacket copy for all of JA's subsequent books [i.e., after *The Tennis Court Oath*, when a statement of his was printed against his will] has had his prior approval. He often supplies the publisher with a text which is then either used verbatim (unsigned) or adapted for various purposes."

25 Bloom gives a psychological interpretation of Ashbery's unemphatic tone: "This refusal to vary his intensities is one of Ashbery's defense mechanisms against his anxiety of influences. I can think of no poet in English, earlier or now at work, who insists upon so subtly unemphatic a pervasive tone. As a revisionary ratio, this tone intends to distance Ashbery from Whitman and Stevens" (*American Poetry*, p. 90). In Bloom's system, the anxiety of influences causes a poet to disguise his or her relation to predecessors through such "revisionary ratios."

26 Trans. M. D. Herter Norton, rev. ed. (New York: Norton, 1954), pp. 64–5. Shapiro also notes Ashbery's use of a Rilkean active passivity (*John Ashbery*, p. 144). See also pp. 133 and 141 for other mentions of Rilke.

27 *Duino Elegies and The Sonnets to Orpheus*, trans. A. Poulin, Jr. (Boston: Houghton Mifflin, 1977), pp. 65, 63. Marjorie Perloff, in " 'Transparent Selves': The Poetry of John Ashbery and Frank O'Hara," *Yearbook of English Studies: American Literature Special Number*, 8(1978):171–96, states that O'Hara and Ashbery "derived from continental writers, especially from Rilke, the notion that the poet is, in O'Hara's words, 'needed by things' " (175).

28 *American Poetry*, p. 85.

29 *Rivers and Mountains* (1966; rpt. New York: Ecco Press, 1977), pp. 38–41.

30 Ibid., pp. 38–9.

31 In *Art and Literature: An International Review*, 3(Autumn–Winter 1964):227–39; rpt. in Max Jacob, *The Dice Cup: Selected Prose Poems*, ed. Michael Brownstein (New York: Sun, 1979).

32 "A Magma of Interiors," *Parnassus*, 4, no. 1 (Fall / Winter 1975):117. Stuart Merrill wrote prose poems and translated a whole book of them by many major and minor French writers (excluding Rimbaud), entitled *Pastels in Prose* (New York: Harper, 1890). William Dean Howells's introduction to the book, "The Prose Poem," is unintentionally instructive as to why Merrill's translations did not influence Williams or other American modernists in search of formal innovation:

It is a form which other languages must naturalize; and we can only hope that criticism will carefully guard the process, and see that it is not vulgarized or coarsened in it. The very life of the form is its aerial delicacy, its soul is that perfume of thought, of emotion, which these masters here have never suffered to become an argument. Its wonderful refinement, which is almost fragility, is happily expressed in the notion of "Pastels;" and more than once, forgetting that modern invention has found a way of fixing the chalks, I have felt, in going over these little pieces, that the slightest rudeness of touch might shake the bloom, the color, from them. (viii)

33 See the Introduction to this volume, n. 6.
34 "Some Questions about Modernism," *Occident*, n.s. 8(Spring 1974):27.
35 I owe this view of the historical interactions of prose and poetry to Donald Wesling, who discusses it in greater depth in his chapter "Narrative of Grammar in the Prose Poem," in *The New Poetries: Poetic Form since Wordsworth and Coleridge* (Lewisburg, Pa.: Bucknell Univ. Press, 1985).
36 "The Young Son," in *Some Trees*, Yale Series of Younger Poets, no. 52 (New Haven: Yale Univ. Press, 1956), p. 42; "A Dream," in "A Little Anthology of the Poem in Prose," *New Directions*, 14(1953):358–9.
37 Kostelanetz, "Difficult Poet," p. 30.
38 Introduction to *The Collected Poems of Frank O'Hara*, ed. Donald M. Allen (New York: Knopf, 1972), p. viii.
39 Sue Gangel, "An Interview with John Ashbery," *San Francisco Review of Books*, 3, no. 7 (November 1977):9. The interview has been reprinted in J. D. Bellamy, *American Poetry Observed: Poets on their Work* (Urbana: Univ. of Illinois Press, 1984), pp. 9–20.
40 Edson's poem appears in Benedikt, *Prose Poem*, p. 528.
41 Trans. Margaret Crosland (London: Peter Owen, 1964). See Shapiro, *John Ashbery*, p. 29, and Neva Gibson Lyons, "The Poetry of John Ashbery" (Diss., Univ. of Oklahoma, 1977), pp. 140–1.

To give the flavor of de Chirico's prose, here is a paragraph translated by Ashbery:

In this atmosphere from which all true, actual noise is carefully banished the thoughts of the philosophers ripen; they pass onto paper and then form volumes of printed writing. And thus they travel abroad through the world; they cross Oceans, infiltrate all the races, become the bedside book of the rich man who suffers and the poor man who hates and then revolts and revolutions arise as the storm arises in the sultry sky of a summer afternoon. Gangs of fierce and resolute men led by a kind of Colossus with the beard of an ancient god grab timbers from construction sites and thrust them like catapults against the doors of the grand hotels, the luxurious palaces, the sumptuous residences where millionaires have amassed their riches and the most precious works of art, for they never believed in the danger and always listened to the reassuring speeches, read the soothing articles which began with the eternal refrain: *Our people are far too sensible*, etc., etc. ("On Silence," *Big Sky*, 9 [1975]: n.p.)

42 "The Decline of the Verbs," *Book Week*, 4, no. 15 (December 18, 1966):5.

43 All seven volumes of *The Book of Questions* have now been translated by Rosemarie Waldrop and published by Wesleyan University Press: *The Book of Questions* (1976); *The Book of Yukel* and *Return of the Book* (1977); *The Book of Questions: Yaël, Elya, Aély* (1983), and *El, or the Last Book* (1984).

44 Gangel, "Interview," p. 9.

4. TALK POEMS AND THE NEW POET'S PROSE

1 The reader may find poet's prose by these poets in a number of their books; I will list one book per writer: Michael Palmer, *Notes for Echo Lake* (San Francisco: North Point Press, 1981); Barbara Einzig, *Life Moves Outside* (Providence: Burning Deck, 1987); Kathleen Fraser, *Notes Preceding Trust* (San Francisco: Lapis, 1987); Lyn Hejinian, *My Life* (Los Angeles: Sun & Moon, 1988); Bob Perelman, *7 Works* (Berkeley: The Figures, 1978); Barrett Watten, *1–10* (San Francisco: This Press, 1980); Bernadette Mayer, *Studying Hunger* (New York: Adventures in Poetry / Big Sky, 1975); *Clark Coolidge, Mine: The One That Enters the Stories* (Berkeley: The Figures, 1982).

2 Antin's major books are *Definitions* (New York: Caterpillar Press, 1967); *Code of Flag Behavior* (Los Angeles: Black Sparrow Press, 1968); *Meditations* (Los Angeles: Black Sparrow Press, 1971); *Talking* (New York: Kulchur Foundation, 1972); *Talking at the Boundaries* (New York: New Directions, 1976); and *Tuning* (New York: New Directions, 1984).

3 *The Journals and Miscellaneous Notebooks of Ralph Waldo Emerson*, vol. 7, *1838–1842*, ed. A. W. Plumstead and Harrison Hayford (Cambridge, Mass.: Harvard Univ. Press, 1969), p. 265.

4 *Talking at the Boundaries*, p. 212.

5 Ibid., p. 56.

6 "The Oral Impulse in Contemporary American Poetry," ed. William Spanos and Robert Kroetsch, *boundary 2*, 3 (Spring 1975):600. The next quotation is taken from the same page. This special issue of *boundary 2* focuses upon Antin and Jerome Rothenberg. The two are also paired in *Vort*, 3, no. 1 (1975), which contains a valuable interview with and some preliminary criticism of Antin.

7 "Oral Impulse," p. 606.

8 Through his friendship with Jerome Rothenberg and his interest in anthropology and linguistics, Antin has been associated with the journals *Alcheringa* and *New Wilderness Letter*. Antin maintains a certain distance from Rothenberg's "ethnopoetry" and the primitivism of other poets like Gary Snyder. One senses his underlying commitment to demythologizing in his tongue-in-cheek definition of myth:

> a myth is the name of a terrible lie told by a smelly
> little brown person to a man in a white suit with a
> pair of binoculars   now you may not want to believe
>   that   because there were other men in white suits
> with field glasses   who followed the first ones   and

sometimes they were also the first ones   who heard
these lies and said "these arent lies   theyre secret
truths"   because at the back of every lie theres a
truth   and it belongs to a "primitive" culture to
have a truth thats not like your truth   and they gave
these lies all kinds of values   generally allegorical
meanings   by which i mean they constructed an ingenious
mechanism for   converting these colorful   nearly
incomprehensible and idiosyncratic lies into a series of
easily comprehensible and generally accepted platitudes
as a matter of fact   in its earliest uses this
notion of   primitive   was applied to the greeks
to the history of the "gentile nations"
(*Talking at the Boundaries*, p. 158)

On the other hand, Sherman Paul creates a convincing context for view-
ing Antin by placing him alongside Rothenberg and Snyder; see Paul's *In
Search of the Primitive: Rereading David Antin, Jerome Rothenberg, and Gary
Snyder* (Baton Rouge: Louisiana State Univ. Press, 1986).

9   "Oral Impulse," p. 644.
10   The quotation is from Antin's "Some Questions about Modernism," *Oc-
     cident*, n.s. 8(Spring 1974):13. This seminal essay of Antin's continues his
     equally incisive "Modernism and Postmodernism: Approaching the Present
     in American Poetry," *boundary 2*, 1 (1972):98–133. A third essay, "Is There
     a Postmodernism?" appeared in *Bucknell Review*, 25, no. 2 (1980):127–35.
11   *Tight Corners & What's around Them* (Los Angeles: Black Sparrow Press,
     1974), pp. 54, 33–4, 58.
12   Janet Bloom and Robert Losada, "Craft Interview with John Ashbery," in
     COP, 123.
13   *My Poetry* (Berkeley: The Figures, 1980), pp. 38–9.
14   For a discussion of the relation between Beckett and the Language poets,
     see Marjorie Perloff, "Between Verse and Prose: Beckett and the New
     Poetry," in *Dance of the Intellect*, pp. 135–54.
15   Back-cover blurb, *Tjanting*.
16   In "Poetry / Poetics: A Symposium in Practice and Theory," *Occident*, n.s.
     8(Spring 1974):184.
17   "The Prose of Fact," *Hills*, 6–7(Spring 1980):166. This issue reprints a num-
     ber of important lectures by poets in San Francisco. Of special interest are
     the talks by Davidson, Bromige, Silliman, Watten, and Perelman. Further
     talks appeared in Bob Perelman, ed., *Writing/Talks* (Carbondale: Southern
     Illinois Univ. Press, 1985).
18   Davidson, "Prose of Fact," p. 166.
19   *The Mutabilities (& The Foul Papers)* (Berkeley: Sand Dollar Books, 1976),
     p. 49.
20   The quotation that heads this section is from Silliman's essay "The New
     Sentence," in *The New Sentence* (New York: Roof Books, 1987), p. 63.
     Silliman brings us full circle by opening his essay on the latest poet's prose

with a parody of the initial sentence in Williams's prologue to *Kora in Hell:* "The sole precedent I can find for the broken style of my prologue is *Longinus on the Sublime* and that one far-fetched" (*Imaginations*, 6).

21   "Contemporary Poetry, Alternate Routes," *Critical Inquiry*, 13(Spring 1987):627. The article is reprinted in McGann's *Social Values and Poetic Acts: The Historical Judgment of the Literary Work* (Cambridge, Mass.: Harvard Univ. Press, 1988), pp. 197–220.

22   "American Poet-Critics since 1945," in Sacvan Bercovitch, ed., *Reconstructing American Literary History*, Harvard English Studies, no. 13 (Cambridge, Mass.: Harvard Univ. Press, 1986), pp. 280–99.

23   In *Self and Sensibility in Contemporary American Poetry* (Cambridge: Cambridge Univ. Press, 1984), Altieri defines a dominant mode in contemporary poetry and then sees stronger poets as writing in reaction to this "scenic mode." Herbert Leibowitz introduced the fifteenth-anniversary issue of *Parnassus*, the journal of poetry reviewing, with the following reflections: "If Plato were to return today, he would not have to bother banishing poets from his ideal republic: They have become as harmless as retired pensioners puttering in their gardens." He goes on to say, "In this unsettled period, poets and critics are either singing the fin de siècle blues or sniping at one another for failure of nerve. A sense of being marginal underlies these ideological frictions" (*Parnassus*, 15, no. 1 [1989]:5). In order to assess the state of poetry in America, Leibowitz "decided to scout the United States for poets on the fringe. The canon is not fixed in granite, so if the center lacked energy, we reasoned, perhaps we could find men and women whose work had been neglected or consigned to the periphery" (p. 7). Of the sixteen articles in this issue, five discuss work by Language poets (one of these concerns poet's prose), a sixth considers Gertrude Stein, and a seventh touches on David Antin in relation to ethnopoetics.

24   *In the American Tree*, p. 488.

25   *Selected Writings*, pp. 16, 20.

26   In one of his uses of the term "wreading," Rasula ties it to projectivism through Olson's handling of archeological texts: "Olson's own project in *The Maximus Poems* is to reactivate such particles of archaic texts in a genreless context, a locality which engages wreaderly energies in their full proprioceptive stamina and denies the restrictions generic frames imply for the reader." "The Compost Library," *Sagetrieb*, 1(Fall 1982):191.

27   See "the sociology of art," in *Talking at the Boundaries*, pp. 157–208.

28   For a theory of poetry as the resistance to the call for transparency, see Gerald L. Bruns, *Heidegger's Estrangements: Language, Truth, and Poetry in the Later Writings* (New Haven: Yale Univ. Press, 1989), in which he explicates Heidegger's late writings on poetry and language as a way of establishing the materiality – the fundamental opacity, or "thickness" (*Dichten*), of poetry and of all language, rightly understood. I am indebted to Professor Bruns for discussions of this and other aspects of this epilogue.

29   Cognate examples would be Baudelaire's *Paris Spleen* and Nietzsche's *Zarathustra*.

30 "Aristotle's Lyric: Re-imagining the Rhetoric of Epideictic Song," *College English*, 51, no. 1 (1989):5–28.
31 *Tuning* (New York: New Directions, 1984), p. 169.
32 See section 29, "Being There as State-of-Mind," in *Being and Time*, trans. John Macquarrie and Edward Robinson (New York: Harper & Row, 1962), pp. 172–9.
33 *In the American Tree*, p. xix.

INDEX

Cambridge Studies in American Literature and Culture

Editor

Albert Gelpi, Stanford University